A YEAR IN THE GREENHOUSE

The Green Capitalists
(with Tom Burke)

The Green Consumer Guide
(with Julia Hailes)

The Green Consumer's Supermarket Shopping Guide
(with Julia Hailes)

The Young Green Consumer Guide
(with Julia Hailes and Douglas Hill)

A Year in the Greenhouse

JOHN ELKINGTON

LONDON
VICTOR GOLLANCZ LTD
1990

Dedicated to Jim Lovelock
and, closer to home, to
Elaine, Julia (Hailes) and Liz (Knights)

First published in Great Britain 1990
by Victor Gollancz Ltd,
14 Henrietta Street, London WC2E 8QJ

British Library Cataloguing in Publication Data
Elkington, John
   A year in the greenhouse.
   1. Environment. Conservation
   I. Title
   333.72
   ISBN 0-575-04821-2

Typeset at The Spartan Press,
Lymington, Hants
and printed in Great Britain by
St Edmundsbury Press Ltd, Bury St Edmunds, Suffolk

Contents

List of abbreviations

ACE	Association for the Conservation of Energy
BAMA	British Aerosol Manufacturers' Association
BPF	British Plastics Federation
BT	British Telecom
BTCV	British Trust for Conservation Volunteers
CBI	Confederation of British Industry
CEED	Centre for Economic and Environmental Development
CEGB	Central Electricity Generating Board
CIA	Chemical Industries Association
CITES	Convention on International Trade in Endangered Species
CLEAR	Campaign for Lead Free Air
CPRE	Council for the Protection of Rural England
DoE	Department of the Environment
DTI	Department of Trade and Industry
EDAP	Environment & Development Advisory Panel
EEB	European Environmental Bureau
ENDS	Environmental Data Services
ESI	Electricity Supply Industry
FoE	Friends of the Earth
ICCE	International Centre for Conservation Education
IIED	International Institute for Environment and Development
ITDG	Intermediate Technology Development Group
IUCN	International Union for Conservation of Nature & Natural Resources
MAFF	Ministry of Agriculture, Fisheries and Food
MIGIT	Merlin International Green Investment Trust
NCC	Nature Conservancy Council
NERC	Natural Environment Research Council
NFU	National Farmers' Union
OECD	Organisation for Economic Co-operation and Development
OPEC	Organisation of Petroleum Exporting Countries
PMA	Property Market Analysis
RSA	Royal Society of Arts
RSNC	Royal Society for Nature Conservation
SDIA	Soap & Detergent Industry Association
UNEP	United Nations Environment Programme
UNESCO	United Nations Educational, Scientific and Cultural Organisation
WEN	Women's Environmental Network
WRI	World Resources Institute
WWF	World Wide Fund for Nature

INTRODUCTION

In the closing weeks of 1988, with the pressure of events on the environmental front building day by day, I decided to record some of the incidents and experiences of the time which might help to explain what it was like to be an environmentalist on the threshold of the last decade of the 20th century.

1988 proved to be the year that a number of world leaders woke up to the environmental challenge. In Britain, Mrs Thatcher had begun to execute her own astounding U-turn in October. Just a few years earlier she had described environmentalists as 'the enemy within'. Now she spoke of environmental protection as one of the great challenges of the late 20th century. In the United States, too, the Presidential election saw both George Bush and Mike Dukakis manoeuvring for environmental advantage, with Bush in particular claiming he would be remembered as the 'environmental President'. And in the East, where astounding events were about to unfold, Mikhail Gorbachev added the Soviet Union's voice to the Green debate for the first time.

But waking people up to the dangers ahead is only the first stage on a long, hard road. No attempt to protect our local, regional or global environments can ultimately succeed unless we are all willing to adjust our lifestyles. We must drive less, recycle more, procreate less, indeed do a thousand things differently in our everyday lives.

Environmentalism has achieved greater public awareness and a priority position on the political agenda. The real challenge now is to shift from the analysis and publicising of the very real problems to the development of practical solutions. As the landmark Brundtland Commission report, *Our Common Future*, put it, we must achieve 'sustainable development' — in order to meet the needs of the present without compromising the future.

1988 had seen green thinking beginning to break through in many different areas. By the end of the year, for example, my colleagues and I found we had a No. 1 bestseller on our hands. *The Green Consumer Guide* sold nearly 150,000 copies between its launch on 12 September and Christmas Day. To our surprise, it also began to sell to foreign publishers. By early 1989, foreign editions were planned in ten countries. As a result, we increasingly found our own operations 'going global'.

Paradoxically, too, the success of *The Green Consumer Guide*, which we had thought might frighten off some of the industrial companies we had been working hard to green through the 1980s, actually helped open up new opportunities. Our telephone lines positively burned. Doors we had been pushing against for years suddenly swung open — and then doors well beyond them. As a result, like everyone else involved in the 'green wave' that was sweeping around the world, we found ourselves pushed to the limit — and sometimes beyond it.

The very word 'green', meanwhile, was taking on a different meaning. Greens seek many things, but above all they aim to ensure that environmental sustainability becomes the world's top priority. As in any broad church, there are endless shadings, even diametrically opposed views in the movement. There are deep Greens, dark Greens, pale Greens, light Greens, Blue-Greens, Red-Greens, media Greens, grassroots Greens and, although some dark Greens persist in seeing it as a contradiction in terms, growing numbers of Greens in business.

No one has yet handed down graven stone tablets of Commandments telling us how we can move towards sustainability. But one thing is now clear: solutions can be found for even our most pressing environmental problems. To develop these solutions, environmentalists must increasingly work not only in the worlds of the media, politics and Government, but also with like-minded business people, including planners, economists, technologists, designers, engineers and investors. This diary is a record of some early attempts to do so.

Inevitably, *A Year in the Greenhouse* represents a personal and somewhat idiosyncratic trawl through some of the events of one — albeit quite extraordinary — year. Other environmentalists, other Greens, will have viewed the same events through different lenses. The diary is often kaleidoscopic, bringing into view a constantly shifting field of fragments, including hundreds of blips scooped from the media outpourings of our 'blip culture'. But, viewed from the right angle, many of them turn out to be important pieces in the jigsaw of our future, providing a strong sense of the shape of things to come in the 1990s and beyond.

THE WEEK BEFORE

Friday 23 December

In today's world, a shotgun blast can sometimes be heard around the world.

The newspapers carry the story of the assassination of Franciso ('Chico') Mendes Filho, the 44-year-old rubber tapper who won international acclaim as the 'Gandhi of Amazonia' during his non-violent campaign to protect Brazil's rainforests. Mendes, who was President of the Xapuri Rural Workers' Union, had been assigned three police guards following repeated death threats. He was killed on 22 December by at least one point blank shotgun blast outside his wooden home in Xapuri, near Brazil's border with Bolivia.

The issue for which he died is far from remote. The future of the world's rainforests has the potential to affect us all. For the Brazilians, the $64 trillion question is whether the Amazonian rainforests should be burned to the ground, for short-term gains, or be left standing and exploited in a sustainable way by people like the rubber tappers and brazil nut collectors.

Under the leadership of Mendes, the rubber tappers had achieved a number of major successes against the multinational ranching companies which had been burning down huge areas of the country's rubber and brazil nut reserves, known as *seringals*. Things had seemed to be going surprisingly well for Mendes. Not only had he won a major UN environmental prize in 1987, but the International Tropical Timber Organisation had voted to spend £2.5 million on a sustainable development research project which Mendes had campaigned for. The research project would show that it is possible to make more money from forest timber, rubber and fruits than from cattle ranching on cleared land.

My immediate reaction to the news, as a European environmentalist, is to wonder why I am fiddling around trying to change the shopping habits of European consumers when people like Mendes are dying in the environmental frontline. But, whatever each of us does and wherever we do it, it's all ultimately part of the same task. Indeed, earlier in the year, Mendes said that he would have been dead long before but for the interest shown by foreign environmental groups in the *seringueiros*' cause.

If my own experience during 1988 was anything to go by, environmentalists are increasingly linking up in a web of rapidly evolving national and international networks. It's almost as if the Earth is growing a complete new nervous system for sensing environmental damage — and developing a series of social and political reflexes to limit (and, hopefully, ultimately, prevent) much of that damage.

Sunday 25 December

Back at my parents' home in the Cotswolds, it's a bit like running off the rails into undulating sand dunes. The wheels spin for a while and then torpor sets in. No more dreaming up ideas about what the Green Consumer can do to ensure a Green Christmas, a theme which Julia and I have had to repeatedly expand upon for interviewers in the past few weeks.

Julia Hailes and I have worked together since late 1986, when she arrived out of the blue at the Earthlife Foundation, where I was a Trustee. Earthlife did some extraordinarily important pioneering work, particularly in relation to the conservation of the best-known Cameroonian rainforest, Korup. But ultimately the foundation ran into financial problems and Julia, Tom Burke and I launched SustainAbility Ltd to carry forward one project — *Green Pages*.

For almost two years, Julia and I have operated SustainAbility out of my family's home in south-west London. Her background in advertising and film production has proved invaluable. But, more importantly, she has provided much of the motive energy that has kept SustainAbility going through some pretty tough times. Now, in the wake of the extraordinary success of our latest book, *The Green Consumer Guide*, we are under pressures of a very different sort.

Tuesday 27 December

Occasionally we tear ourselves away from the log fire to walk out into the surrounding countryside. We visit Folly Farm, a wildfowl centre near Cheltenham which is built around a series of artificial ponds and lakes that spill down the valley below the old farmhouse. From jungle fowl to black swans, Folly Farm proves to be a riot of strange colours and forms. The winter sun is bright as we arrive, but a strange sausage-shaped cloud thrusts in across the hills within a quarter of an hour, bringing a front of chill air with it.

'Don't feed the horse' says a notice on one stable. We look inside to see a single fat black rabbit, staring suspiciously back as it munches a brussel sprout. Gaia and Hania (my 11- and 9-year-old daughters) love the farm, but in some ways it's a bit like visiting museums: too many rarities in too small a space. The brain threatens to curdle.

Otherwise, we confine ourselves to walks around our own village. It provides constant reminders of the intense development pressures now affecting much of the country, pressures compounded by the neglect of sites earmarked for development. Largely based on farming when we first arrived in 1959, it seemed to change very little during the 1960s and 1970s, but is now undergoing a rapid transformation. None of us like the results. Barns and farm buildings are being converted into homes, while orchards are felled and paddocks are first left to grow vast banks of nettles and then built over.

One evening, we walk up to the church. It stands isolated from the rest of the village, on the other side of a small valley and stream. (After the Black Death, people believed that crossing water would provide a barrier against further infection.) Built in the 12th century, the church stands on a slight hill and we are struck as we walk up the path by the extent to which the lights of nearby Bourton-on-the-Water have sprawled over the floor of the valley in recent years. The town has certainly grown considerably, following its 'discovery' as a tourism and retirement centre during the 1960s. But part of the explanation may be that much of the woodland which used to mask that glittering carpet of light was made up of elms, which have since succumbed to the ravages of Dutch elm disease.

Wednesday 28 December
Back to Barnes. It is interesting, in the light of developments during 1988, that in a Gallup Poll in today's *Daily Telegraph* Prince Charles emerged as the favourite Royal, and an overwhelming 86% of those interviewed felt that the Royal Family in general should speak out more forcefully on environmental issues.

1988 was the year that Prince Charles caused a storm with his TV programme attacking much of what passes for modern architecture. And there were signs that he was planning something on the environmental front, too. During the year I had been one of a small group of environmentalists invited first to dinner at Kensington Palace and then, in November, to lunch at Highgrove House in Gloucestershire. The idea behind the dinner was that the Prince should meet some environmentalists of his own generation. At the lunch it became clear that he was planning to follow up his architectural film with another on the environment.

Thursday 29 December
The day begins with great excitement. The girls' stick insect eggs are beginning to hatch. Gaia has always wanted a collection of pets to rival Gerald Durrell's in *My Family and Other Animals*, a tall order in a

London semi-detached. Apart from the odd fox walking along the garden walls, the best we had previously been able to manage was a combination of everyone else's cats, a tortoise inherited from a dead neighbour and a couple of ill-tempered golden loach.

And then, inevitably, the real world begins to intrude. Although Julia and Fiona (Byrne) are still on holiday, some people are clearly back at their desks and the phones start to ring. Most of the calls come from journalists wanting to put together 'end-of-the-year' articles or programmes. And there is also a call from Torben Hansen, a Danish environmental consultant I met in Copenhagen during 1988. He is considering a campaign to get the Danish textiles industry — currently under enormous pressure from Asian imports — to look at the possibility of going up-market, emphasising long-life, environment-friendly clothes.

However hard they try to come up with green fashions, though, the Danes are unlikely to rival the environment-friendliness of the Indian stick insect's wardrobe. She climbs out of her skin six times over a period of five months, and then immediately eats the shed skin.

In the evening, we drive across to Richmond Park, leave the car at the Sheen Gate and, pulling on wellington boots, stomp into the gathering dusk. The grass sparkles with mist-glazed spider webs. Passing between the oaks and chestnut trees, we stir the leaf litter and the smells of winter. In the distance, we hear the cries of waterfowl, crows cawing, owls hooting and low-flying 747s rumbling in towards Heathrow.

Gaia wonders why we don't find deer skulls or shed antlers, to add to her skull collection. Before I can answer I spot the torn body of a rook at the foot of an oak and sharp-eyed Hania finds the head. The process of decay is sufficiently advanced to allow Gaia to take the bird back for bleaching. But I end up carrying it. The inside edge of the beak is hideously sharp.

As we make our way up to the Ballet School on the hill, a Land-Rover passes and spills a long stream of food out on to the grass. Deer of several species, and many sizes, converge from the four horizons. As each animal faces in towards the food, a double line forms, head to grazing head. It looks like a living zip, with the slow-moving vehicle seeming to fasten the two antlered lines together.

Friday 30 December

In 1989, it will be 'in' to be Green, according to a breathless article in today's *Daily Mail*. 'It's the only colour to be.'

Mrs Thatcher clearly has some way to go before she fully grasps what this means, however. The Government says it will cut the budget of the Department of Energy's Energy Efficiency Office in half. She knows about the Greenhouse Effect, with carbon dioxide produced by burning fossil fuels leading to a global warming and climatic changes, and she also told a meeting of businessmen earlier in the month that 'energy efficiency is crucial' in tackling the problem.

Andrew Warren, who runs the Association for the Conservation of Energy (ACE), describes the announcement as 'a body blow against the battle to stop global warming via the Greenhouse Effect'. Already this year the Government has cut grant aid for loft insulation, energy surveys for industry and TV advertising on energy saving in the home.

Should Mrs Thatcher be given the 12 Environmental Stars or 12 Environmental Thorns? They are announced in a press release from the European Environmental Bureau (EEB), received this morning.

The EEB, representing European environmental organisations, has honoured Norway's Prime Minister, Gro Harlem Brundtland, with 12 stars — an echo of the 12 stars in the European Community's flag. The Brundtland Report, titled *Our Common Future* and produced by the World Commission on Environment and Development which she chaired, rammed sustainable development on to the international political agenda.

The booby prize, in the form of 12 thorns, went to Jacques Calvet, Managing Director of Peugeot-Talbot-Citroën. He lobbied the French Government to oppose tighter exhaust emission standards for European cars. His company also refused to put the clean version of the Peugeot 205 available in Switzerland and Austria and fitted with a catalytic converter, on to the market in the 12 EEC countries.

Saturday 31 December
The day's post, several clumps of letters and packages held together by straining rubber bands, includes copies of *National Geographic* and *Time* magazine. Sporting its first all-round hologram cover, *National Geographic* asks: 'Can we save this fragile Earth?'

Viewed from the right angle, the cover shows a crystal earth shattering as it is hit by a bullet. The magazine's editor, Wilbur E Garrett, notes that human destruction of the planet is currently moving slower than a bullet, but that the effects threaten to be just as shattering.

Among those quoted is Gus Speth, President of the World Resources Institute, our main US partner in recent years. 'People everywhere are offended by pollution,' Gus told a recent National Geographic Society symposium. 'They sense intuitively that we have pressed beyond limits we should not have exceeded. They want to clean up the world, make it a better place, be good trustees of the Earth for future generations.'

Time, meanwhile, features the 'Endangered Earth' as Planet of the Year on its front cover. The image is 'Wrapped Globe, 1988' by Christo, the artist who spends a lot of his time wrapping up bridges, valleys and even whole islands. When it came to wrapping the planet, though, he chose (understandably) to wrap a 16-inch globe in polyethylene and rag rope.

The magazine's editors had decided that the growing concern about the planet's future had become the year's most important story. Instead of simply publishing harrowing pictures of burning rainforests and hazardous waste problems, their approach is likely to be the hallmark of the 1990s. 'The new journalistic challenge,' said Managing Editor Henry Miller, is 'to help find solutions.'

The *Daily Telegraph* runs its 'Red alert in the Green year' story. Half a dozen leading figures in the world of environmental affairs had been asked about their hopes and fears for 1989. Jonathon Porritt, Director of Friends of the Earth, describes the political changes of 1988 as 'immensely important' and also highlights the 'growing consumer awareness of environmental issues; a real development from the days of brown rice, sandals and so on'.

Jonathon, whose background includes Eton and the Ecology Party, subsequently renamed the Green Party, is emerging as one of the key figures in the Green movement.

My contribution is as follows: 'British industry is waking up to the importance of green consumerism. In 1989 I hope that we'll see some substantial moves forward, in particular by the supermarket chains to meet their customers' demands. This means information will be particularly important; when ordinary consumers are given the facts they can make informed choices.'

New Year celebrated with friends, to the sounds of the Sixties.

JANUARY

Sunday 1 January
Finally get around to putting up a blind in the new bathroom. It's exactly
11 months since building work started on the house, with a new floor
materialising over our heads — and feet periodically coming through the
ceiling. The rebuilding was meant to have been finished in a few months,
but thundered on right through the period when we were writing *The
Guide* and pulling together Green Consumer Week.

People got used to interviewing us through the thud of hammers and
squeal of drills, the computer screens dulled under a fine coating of plaster
dust. If we can cope in such conditions, someone said, there should be no
stopping us when we get into proper offices! I comfort myself by recalling
that even Apple Computer, now a Fortune 500 company, started out in a
bedroom and garage at Steve Jobs' parents' home in California.

Spend much of the afternoon digging out one of our two compost
heaps with the children. Each contains four or five cubic metres of
beautifully composted soil. We gave up putting fresh waste on them
about a year ago, though, because of a plague of rats. The local cats
spent much of the summer of 1987 sitting motionless on the heaps, or
running back and forth with young rats dangling from their mouths.
Some of them ended up in unlikely places: neighbours climbing into bed
encountered a dead rat between their sheets, presumably deposited there
by one of their cats.

Running a compost heap eventually drums home the plastics problem.
Even apple tree branches break down in the heaps, but plastic garden ties
or tags come out unmarked. It's good to hear that the Tidy Britain Group
has helped persuade the International Maritime Organisation to make it
illegal to dump plastics, dunnage (pallets and packaging materials) and
other rubbish that will float at sea, although the restriction only applies to
areas within 25 miles of the nearest coast.

Trevor Dixon, who heads the Group's marine litter research programme, has spent the last 15 years surveying litter on Britain's beaches,
and estimates that 70% of the rubbish comes from ships. And about half
of the materials that end up littering our coastline are plastics. The
weakness of the new regulations is underscored by the fact that some of
the plastic objects found on Britain's beaches come from as far afield as
Canada.

15

Monday 2 January

Work like a demon in the garden for most of the day. Echoes, in digging out the second compost, of the Baka pygmies digging out a Giant Pangolin in the second of Phil Agland's 'People of the Rainforest' trilogy on Channel 4 last night. I first met Phil when we were Trustees of the Earthlife Foundation.

The films are brilliant. The overriding image last night was of the forest as a patchwork of poisons, evolved to protect plants and trees against predators. The Baka have learned to use many of these chemicals as medicines. Their forest pharmacy provides them with antibacterials, antifungals and many other useful chemicals. Baka healers also use fire: because of the building work, Lisa Silcock's extraordinary photograph of a healer using the heat of a fire to heal a child during a *nganga*, or Fire Dance, is still waiting to be hung a year since she gave it to us for Christmas 1987.

Something to live up to: the *Daily Telegraph* today runs a 'Who will shine in '89' feature, spotlighting 40 people. 'You may not know them now, but you soon will,' it predicts. Robin Grove-White and I appear in the Environment category.

Tuesday 3 January

Back (more or less) to normal routine. Cutting the newspapers from 08.15. Julia arrives at 08.30, Fiona at 09.00, and we chat over toast and coffee.

At 10.30, Julia and I drive across to St Katharine's Dock, near the Tower of London, for the press launch of *Creightons Naturally*. This is an 80ft maxi ocean racing yacht, entered by John Chittenden and Tony Allen for the 1989/90 Whitbread Round the World Race. The yacht is sponsored by Creighton Laboratories, who make toiletries, soaps and fragrances based on natural ingredients. For 13 years, Creightons have based their business on the scrupulous avoidance of product testing methods involving cruelty to animals. They supply products to The Body Shop and other retailers, but are branching out with a full range of toiletries sold under their own name.

Creightons Naturally, painted a brilliant yellow, with yellow and blue flags whipping from her rigging, is a splash of Van Gogh sunshine in an otherwise wintry scene. As gulls dip and squabble across the water, we walk around the vessel, hands deep in pockets.

Actress Jane Asher launches both the yacht and the new Creightons Natural Fund for World Conservation. 'Conservation is the most important cause of all,' she says. One charity in which both the Fund and the boat's crew are already interested is International Dolphin Watch. Dolphins, as Jane Asher puts it, 'sum up the mystery of so much that we don't understand'. Sadly, the IDW Dolphin Survey Project has run into financial difficulties, at a time when concern about the plight of dolphins has never been greater. They have been disappearing from the coasts of Britain, for example, and there has been great concern about the dolphin kills caused by tuna-fishing fleets, particularly in the Pacific.

The *Creightons Naturally* crew will maintain a dolphin log as they carry out their two transatlantic shakedown voyages, as well as on the Whitbread Round the World Race.

Wednesday 4 January
Quite a day. The *Director* magazine publishes an editorial and three-page feature on green consumerism. 'I am not aware of 1989 being as yet dedicated to any particular subject,' says editor George Bickerstaffe, 'but it seems highly likely that one of the most pressing issues that will confront business men and women during the next 12 months is one with which some may feel uncomfortable — "the environment".' Green consumerism, he concludes is the 'most dramatic' example of the pressures building on industry.

After discussing the *Guardian*'s invitation to write a monthly column with Tim Radford, who has commissioned most of my articles for the paper's 'Futures' section over the years, I fax across to Alan Rusbridger a proposal that I do a fortnightly Green Consumer column. We try to price it reasonably because I want to do the column. Alan calls back almost immediately to accept. The first piece has to be in by next Tuesday.

In the evening, Janet Barber of WWF comes to supper. From, 18.30 to after 23.00 we talk through what WWF ought to be doing to ensure that they respond appropriately to industry's environmental awakening. She has a striking ability to sum people up with a few well chosen words and gestures. Inevitably, as organisations like WWF grow steadily larger, their internal politics become a factor that outsiders have no option but to take seriously — and WWF has often struck us as particularly tricky to deal with in this respect.

But they have got to be a major actor in this area — and not just in terms of raising money. WWF are excited that they got the NatWest Bank to pledge £3 million over three years a few weeks back, but environmentalists should be aware that there are new opportunities to do more than help such companies apply a green gloss to their activities. We have much more leverage on such companies than we used to.

The pace of change is going to make it essential that environmentalists think strategically, working out where they want to be in five or ten years and then identifying the stepping stones they will need to get from here to there.

Thursday 5 January

Dick Johnson, Procter & Gamble's Director for Marketing Services, calls to say that they want us to work for them on a regular basis. This will be the first time that we have accepted a retainer from a major company.

Over the last couple of years, Lever and Monsanto have both suggested retainers, but I felt that there was a real danger that we might come across a company that would attempt to muffle us through a retainer agreement. Now that we have *The Green Consumer Guide* behind us, however, our position is very much stronger. Another factor in the decision is that this time we have to make a choice between those arch-rivals, Procter & Gamble and Lever. And our reading of the current situation is that P&G are likely to want to move faster than Lever in the environmental area.

A key issue of the moment revolves around the environmental impact of disposable nappies. There has been concern, particularly in Scandinavia, that the chlorine bleach used to whiten paper could expose babies to toxic dioxins. P&G announced yesterday, to defuse a competing announcement by Peaudouce, that it will switch to a new, more environment-friendly Swedish pulp from February for its *Pampers* product. P&G note that they have picked this particular pulp because of its 'environmental excellence'.

Jan Bongaerts of the Wissenschaftszentrum in Berlin arrived. Jan, Julia and I talk about the proposal we have submitted to the European Commission. Although the competition is likely to be intense, the project is an important one — involving working up a Europe-wide Green Label scheme for environment-friendlier products. We have long seen this as an essential step if the confidence of Green Consumers is not to be eroded by spurious claims from manufacturers and retailers.

It turns out to be a day for proposals. I complete another for the Nature Conservancy Council, who want to look at the potential for industrial guidelines on nature conservation. Since we developed the guidelines for the onshore oil and gas industry in 1986, we seem to be well placed.

Our main problem at the moment is time. Julia forced me to sit down at the computer today and tap in all the days of work that I am already committed to do in 1989. The average seems to be well over 25 days a month through the end of the year! All my instincts are to chase work, whereas these days the work is chasing us. The only way in which we are going to make any sense of this is to focus more, push up our prices and try to find additional people to help us.

Watch the first in a series of six BBC2 films on the North Sea. I had never realised that different European countries called the North Sea different names, for example the German Sea or the West Sea. Norwegian Prime Minister Gro Harlem Brundtland stresses that ecology and economy are two sides of the same coin, while the programme begins and ends with Prince Charles' speech to the North Sea Conference, in which he said that we were in danger of testing the North Sea to destruction.

The children shuddered at the inevitable images of dying seals, but actress Susannah York's presentation was very effective. Andy Booth of Greenpeace came across well, too, talking of two 'black holes' the size of Wales which have opened up — because of pollution — in the phytoplankton of the North Sea.

Friday 6 January
Glorious, spring-like day. The papers report on the green nappy announcements by Peaudouce and P&G. Julia and I drive down to WWF's HQ in Godalming. We are slightly early, so take a walk along the muddy side of the canal.

The meeting is an important one for us. We feel that WWF badly underestimated the likely impact of the Green Consumer, leading to a somewhat half-hearted WWF response in the build-up to Green Consumer Week last September. Now there potentially is a conflict of interest if we start raising large sums direct from industry, cutting into WWF's own fund-raising potential. They feel that where smaller groups might extract £10,000 from a company for conservation, they will get £100,000, or even £1 million. With the £3 million, three-year NatWest agreement under their belts, it is hard to disagree, but we point out that £10,000 in a small organisation's hand is worth more to them than £100,000 in WWF's! The key question we are asking is to what extent we can work alongside WWF in future?

Janet Barber's Conservation Review Group has already helped finance Green Consumer Week (£7,000), funded our environmental auditing project to the tune of £10,000 and is considering two further applications for projects on the Green Consumer in Europe and on the Green Tourist.

During the meeting, the tensions between the various parts of WWF are very clear, but the outline of a more coherent approach to the potential of the Green Consumer begins to emerge. We are asked to produce a short paper on ways in which the WWF/SustainAbility partnership could be developed.

Tonight is Twelfth Night. We have been invited by the parents of one of Hania's friends to a night of Scottish dancing at St Mary at Lambeth church, cheek-by-jowl with Lambeth Palace. A delightful evening with all ages, from nine to 90, bagpipes and an extraordinary, timeless feeling. As the kilts and sporrans fly, people's faces glow with pure pleasure.

Saturday 7 January
We visit the David Hockney retrospective at the Tate Gallery. Find his paintings strangely unsatisfying. It is easy to imagine a future world in which each continent is carpeted, ocean-to-ocean, with toothpaste-fresh swimming pools. The smell of wildflowers replaced by the tang of chlorine, the sinister hissing of lawn sprays draining the groundwater and drowning out the birdsong.

Liked his photocollages, including *Brooklyn Bridge*, very much. But it struck me as at least symptomatic that the subject of one of the most striking of these — *Pearblossom Hwy II* — is a highway slicing between desert cacti and lined with drifts of Castrol GTX cans, beer bottles and all the other debris that our restless world now leaves in its wake.

Sunday 8 January
The Peaudouce *Ultra Plus* green nappy campaign hits the Sunday papers. Both *The Sunday Times* and the *Observer* carry full-page ads headlined: Introducing the Friendliest Nappy on Earth. The ad shows a baby peering over — and sucking at the surface of — a massive globe. 'Now there's a nappy to help the world your baby will grow up in,' reads the copy. 'A nappy that's environmentally-friendly — and marks the start of a new era. For nature's sake, Peaudouce have now made a nappy that doesn't contain chlorine-bleached fluff pulp.'

I have argued for several years that one key to capturing the public's attention would be to capture and green industry's advertising budgets. Cleverly, the copywriter describes the new nappy as 'a natural, creamy colour'. Only a few months ago he or she would have been praising the brilliant, virgin whiteness of the chlorine bleached variety. But recruiting the advertising agencies to the environmental cause is going to be tricky; whatever the concerns of individual agency people, the agencies themselves are pursuing different goals.

The Sunday Times also carries a story which underscores the potential importance of our impending *Green Holiday Guide*. A traveller who went to see the flesh-eating Komodo dragons of Indonesia travelled in a group which had to buy a live goat to feed to the giant lizards. The guides slit the goat's throat and hurled it into the ravine which is the lizards' lair. The Komodo dragons, meant to tear out to rend the unfortunate beast, proved so satiated by the goats hurled down by successive parties that they simply couldn't be bothered to come out.

So the guides climbed down and pulled the giant lizards out by the tail to where the goats were bleeding in the sunshine. 'The fat dragons had a nibble, were photographed, and then crawled back to their shade. It was all so sad,' the traveller reported.

Monday 9 January

'Orchids and sods.' That's one answer you might have got a year or so ago if you had asked Tesco executives to say what came to mind when you mentioned the word 'environment'. Try the same word association game today and the first answer you will get is: 'the Green Consumer.'

Today's announcements by Tesco will shake the supermarket sector to its foundations. Four years to the day after it launched its revolutionary Healthy Eating Campaign, Tesco is launching the most exciting environmental initiative yet undertaken by a British supermarket. But the pace of events in this field is now so intense that even Tesco will have to look to its laurels if it is to hold the No. 1 slot in the green supermarket stakes.

At the launch, held in its new Colney Hatch superstore north of London, the £5bn-a-year retail group recalled what happened recently when it decided to pioneer a more modest form of earth-moving. Shortly after being given permission to build a new Solihull superstore, Tesco learned that part of site was an ecologically valuable meadow. To protect several species of wild orchids, the company linked up with local conservationists to move the entire meadow, in six inch deep turfs, to a new home. The price-tag: £40,000.

The financial stakes are dramatically higher now as the commercial ground begins to move under the entire supermarket sector. The health food and anti-additive campaigns alerted all the supermarkets to the extraordinary pace at which such trends can now develop. The potential for the Green Consumer to get on the supermarket fast track is clear. 'People understand the issues even more than they did the healthy eating issues,' explained Dr Richard Pugh, Tesco's Director of Technical Services and the man responsible for the company's new green strategy.

Once viewed as 'the enemy', supermarkets are still viewed as a key part of the problem by many environmentalists, noted Green Alliance Director Tom Burke. 'They remain the most obvious symbol of conspicuous consumption.' But Tesco's initiative provides convincing evidence that supermarkets could also become part of the solution. Their potential impact on consumer opinion is suggested by the fact that Tesco has given away 20 million leaflets on healthier eating since 1985. Next stop, on recycled paper of course, the environment?

I first came across Tom when he was Executive Director of FoE in the late 1970s. During 1986, he helped me put together *The Green Capitalists* and then, in the early days of SustainAbility, helped Julia and I write *Green Pages*. The relationship between us is strained at the moment, because of differences in opinion about the future direction of SustainAbility.

Tuesday 10 January

Took Mike Flux, Group Environment Adviser at ICI, out to lunch. Discussed environmental auditing and green consumerism. It's clear that there are a number of organisations which would like to muscle in on both areas.

A commodity broker called to say he has been trying to get supermarkets and confectionery manufacturers to label brazil nuts — and confectionery made with brazil nuts — as 'rainforest-friendly', where they come from the sort of 'extraction reserves' that Chico Mendes had been trying to establish and protect. Although there is clearly potential for this idea to be abused, I would wager that Mendes himself would have been intrigued by this scheme.

In Brazil, Senhor Darli Alves da Silva has been captured. He is the fugitive landowner who Chico Mendes named as one of the men who intended to kill him a few days before his murder. The arrest followed one of the most extensive manhunts ever mounted in Amazonia, where it is said that a large-calibre revolver is worth more than the penal code or the Constitution.

Yet another working day that ended well after 23.00 — with Julia staying on to supper, before returning to her word-processor.

Wednesday 11 January

I struggled to finish a paper on environmental auditing for the UN Environment Programme's (UNEP) Industry & Environment Office in Paris.

The Times carries an editorial today on the Tesco launch and John Hunt of the *Financial Times* rings to say he wants an article from me on green retailing for their March environment survey.

In the evening, Penny Ephson of Wide Open and her assistant Kirsten come round to discuss the Ideal Home Green Kitchen exhibition. The history: Lord Rothermere offered FoE a free stand; FoE asked us what they could do on it; Julia suggested a Green Kitchen. It is now getting to the stage where we will have to commit a fair amount of money, possibly over £5,000 to start with, to get the thing moving. Ultimately the cost will be over £45,000, but, although the time is precariously tight, we hope to raise that in sponsorship. Penny is half Ghanaian and full of energy. Julia is showing signs of flagging, not surprisingly. She informed me this evening, around 23.30, that I was not to try to turn her into a workaholic!

Thursday 12 January

Fax UNEP audits paper to Jacqueline Aloisi de Larderelle in Paris. It's pouring with rain as I walk to the bus-stop for the trip up to Brand New's offices in Princes Gardens, off Holland Park Avenue. I tend to take the bus to High Street Kensington and then walk north through the Park. Often there is no one about, except for the odd man-servant walking a string of lap-dogs and a benchful of truants in fashionable clothes.

The Brand New meeting goes well. It is extraordinary how well we work with Dorothy Mackenzie, the company's Managing Director. We originally met when, as a friend of Tom Burke's, she did some work for Earthlife on a proposed new magazine, provisionally entitled *Green*. Although we may be going through a honeymoon phase, there is a good deal of synergy between the two organisations.

Back to Barnes, to work on the copy for the Green Kitchen exhibition. I like Penny's headline for the stand: The Kitchen that Cooks without Roasting the Planet. Gollancz ring to say that the Canadians have made an offer for *The Green Consumer Guide*.

Friday 13 January
Julia has an early meeting with Chris Baines, who is finalising a major TV series, 'The Big E', to be shown in late spring. Fiona comes in sporting a haircut that looks as though it was done with a Flymo.

A lot in the papers at the moment about the Greenpeace campaign against the construction of a French Antarctic airstrip. This has involved violent confrontation with construction workers over the preservation of nearby colonies of breeding penguins. Pete Wilkinson, who I came across when he was a Director of Greenpeace UK, has led the campaign. Today they call off the campaign, in favour of a negotiated settlement. The French say Greenpeace can carry out a scientific study in the area. Pete is reported as saying that it was the first time that France had recognised Greenpeace as a legitimate organisation, rather than as 'a bunch of terrorists', since the sinking of the *Rainbow Warrior* in Auckland harbour.

While Julia continues working on the questionnaire, I represent us at a party at Gollancz, where Alex Huggins has just won a key award for national publishing publicity for her *Green Consumer Guide* promotion last year. Liz Knights had travelled up to North London the previous day to try and find organic champagne, but found the store shut when she got there. We make do with non-organic! Have a long talk with Livia Gollancz about the pressure of tourism on Sikkim, where she recently went on a trekking holiday. She wants to go back before the region is destroyed. My instincts are completely contrary: to shy well clear of areas under pressure.

In the evening, we watch a programme on Miriam Rothschild, whose diverse interests range across fleas, wildflowers and conservation. An extraordinary woman. Attention particularly taken by the idea that poisonous insects tend to smell the same, because they secrete a chemical which enhances learning in the animals they sting.

Saturday 14 January
Gaia and I talk over breakfast about brainwashing. We compare the style of the Stalin show-trials and the Korean War with the possibility of more sophisticated approaches, based on the 'learning chemicals' Miriam Rothschild talked about. The conversation drifts on to the question of which is the most effective style of environmental campaigning: Greenpeace's approach, of sending in the Zodiac inflatable boats, or ours, of trying to work with the environmental 'fifth column' in industry. Agree that both are essential to long-term success. Greenpeace, and similar groups, help create the middle ground in which people like us have chosen to operate.

Also a fair amount of coverage of the rainforest logging ban in Thailand where I should have been working next month for the US Agency for International Development. Pressure of work here has made it impossible to go, although I loved the last stint I did in Bangkok during late 1986. *The Independent* today notes that South-East Asia's forests are disappearing so fast that there will be none left in 30 years. In (Joseph) Conrad's day there were a million square miles of virgin forest: barely a quarter of that area remains. In 1986 it was clear that the Royal Thai Forestry Department was trying hard, although the chances of slowing, let alone reversing, the process looked impossibly remote.

The news that Thailand is imposing a logging ban is very welcome. The ban was prompted by the widespread floods last November, aggravated by deforestation, which left hundreds of Thais drowned. But the article by Terry McCarthy notes that all that will happen is that the logging pressures will simply be transferred to countries that are even more desperate for foreign currency, such as Burma, Laos and Cambodia.

Monday 16 January
Start the day feeling shattered. Off early for breakfast meeting with Paul Wachtel, Head of Creative Services, WWF International, at the Hyde Park Hotel. They are looking for help in screening companies. They are also planning to launch a biological diversity campaign in March and we talk about possible links with genetic engineering and biotechnology companies, like NPI and SeaPharm.

Then on to Victoria Plaza, for a meeting with Liz Culbard and David Wright of EuroTunnel, who are responsible for the environmental aspects of the Channel Tunnel project. Tessa Tennant of the Merlin

Ecology Fund joins in and asks some very useful questions, particularly about the possible spread of rabies through the Chunnel.

Tessa, Merlin's Head of Research and previously with the Green Alliance for many years, is emerging as one of the leading lights of the new green investment movement. As a member of Merlin's advisory panel, I have had an opportunity to work alongside her — and see her as one of the new breed of Greens, working deep in the heart of the system to promote environmental change. The challenge of greening the City is perhaps one of the most arduous — and important — we face.

One interesting story in the *Financial Times* covers a conference in Dresden, which has brought together East and West Germany to focus on a common enemy — the destruction of the environment. The Eastern bloc countries are beginning to own up to their problems. The Polish Academy of Sciences, for example, reports that 12 million Poles now live in 'ecological emergency areas'.

Tuesday 17 January
Off to the British Plastics Federation, to talk to BPF, the European Vinyls Corporation and Norway's Norsk Hydro about the prospects for plastics recycling materials like PET and PVC. They agree to produce a brief on ways in which supermarkets could help promote greater recycling of plastic.

After lunch, on to International Business Communications. Cab driver full of the recent crash of a British Midland jet on the M1 in Leicestershire, with the evidence suggesting that the cockpit controls were wired up the wrong way. A worrying possibility at a time when many safety and environmental systems are increasingly relying on computerisation. Will human error be replaced by computer error (or human/computer error) as a major cause of disasters?

Thursday 19 January
Panic call from Brand New to say that P&G have arrived in Holland Park for a meeting I thought we had reorganised for this afternoon. Hurled on suit and Elaine drove me through early morning fog to Princes Place. Interestingly, P&G had been to see the Women's Environmental Network (WEN), who are shortly to launch a consumer campaign against paper tissue products that either contain dioxin or contribute to dioxin levels in the environment. Our relationship with WEN has been uneasy, thanks to clashing politics and personalities.

We heard today that the *Mail on Sunday* will raffle our Green Kitchen just before the Ideal Home Exhibition opens, which should help pull in a good deal of publicity in March, and help with sponsors. Actress Greta

Scacchi has also agreed to write the foreword to our brochure. A productive day, but nursing a vicious sore throat as I try to clear my desk before leaving for Oslo at 06.45 tomorrow morning.

Friday 20 January

As the plane banks in towards Oslo, across a silver sea and a darker scattering of some of the country's 50,000 islands, the eye unconsciously scans the landscape for dead lakes and dying trees.

Like Sweden, Norway has long accused Britain of making a massive contribution to acid rain damage in Scandinavia. Hundreds of lakes are now dead in the southern part of the country and there is concrete evidence — in the form of a nationwide survey by the Norwegian Forest Research Institute—that the process of forest dieback is now as serious in Norway as it is in West Germany.

Tenk Globalt, Handle Lokalt. They may look like the result of a typesetter accidentally leaning on his keyboard, but these four words are in fact the Norwegian version of a phrase now guaranteed an entry whenever environmentalists finally get around to greening the Ten Commandments. In plain English, the message runs: Think globally, act locally.

No one doubts the ability of Mrs Brundtland to think globally. Ever since she chaired the World Commission on Environment and Development, the world has seen Norway as the test case for the Commission's prescriptions for a more sustainable future. If Norway fails to achieve sustainable development, even with Mrs Brundtland at the helm, you can effectively write off the rest of the world. Norway is already looking at the implications of the World Commission's report for its own policies, but this is election year in the 'Land of the Midnight Sun' and environmental issues are racing up the political agenda. Now a growing number of Norwegians are beginning to question Mrs Brundtland's willingness to ensure action on their local environment.

She was not among the more-than-capacity audience at the Green conference, organised by the Sosialistik Venstreparti, but the message for her Government came through loud and clear. Actions speak louder than words. Get on with cleaning up Norway's own environment!

Before arriving at the conference, where I was to speak after Lloyd Timberlake of Earthscan, I had meetings with Tove Storsveen of *Dagens Naeringsliv* (the Norwegian equivalent of the *Financial Times*, who will publish *The Green Capitalists*) and Kjersti Bale of H Aschehoug & Co (who may be interested in *The Guide*). Had lunch with Tove and a number of other people at the *D/S Louise*, a restaurant built like a ship and full of propellers, ships' lights and gulls upside down on cases attached to the ceiling!

I steered clear of the crispy fried cods' tongues, settling for delicious cod stew instead. Outside, the gulls swooped through ships' rigging and a U-boat slid through the choppy, chill waters beneath the battlements of Akershus Fortress, where the Germans executed members of the Norwegian Resistance during World War II.

The Norwegians are extraordinarily friendly. Apart from the Bergen talk, two more invitations to come over during 1989, with expenses paid. Don't know where the time will come from.

A great deal of new construction, so the paths, stairs and floors in the *Dagens Naeringsliv* building crunch with gravel. Riveters and other ship-building equipment line the walls of the converted shipyard buildings. Most distances seem walkable in Oslo, even with a bag full of books over my shoulder. Slightly post-hippy feeling to the people I am with. 'Don't walk on the grass. Smoke it,' says a message, in English, on a condom machine.

The publishing people couldn't believe that I was going to a Green conference wearing a pin-stripe suit. But I started off my speech with a joke about the suit — and it all went rather well.

Lloyd Timberlake was tremendous, as usual. An American living in London, Lloyd has one of the most attractive, drawling American accents I have ever heard. He was with the Reuters news agency before moving to Earthscan and the International Institute for Environment and Development (IIED). There he wrote a series of books, including the award-winning *Africa in Crisis*, before helping the Brundtland Commission put its ideas down on paper in *Our Common Future*.

Sunday 22 January
Decided to fly home a day early. As the plane took off from Oslo, I saw a house burning fiercely to the east, its wooden skeleton etched against the roaring orange flames.

Johnson Wax have offered £17,000 towards the Green Kitchen project. AEG look set to come in with £20,000 and a man from Italy's Montedison apparently came around on Friday and was interested to know whether we could help resurrect the company's battered environmental image.

I write the second *Guardian* article, concentrating on batteries and brazil nuts.

Monday 23 January
By train to Cambridge, to see Gordon Sellers of US consultants Arthur D Little. He recalls crawling through the sewers of the Grand Hotel in Paris, during an environmental audit of 40–50 hotels ADL carried out for

a major American hotel chain. An interesting illustration of the way our lives depend on systems which most of us never give a second thought to — or at least until they go wrong.

Back to Barnes by 17.00. Julia works until 23.00 on questionnaires and I finish off WWF proposal on SustainAbility's proposed Green Consumer research programme.

Tuesday 24 January

Early meeting with Lever, who manufacture products like *Persil* and *Domestos*, in Kingston. The discussion involves Dr Keith Watkin, the Technical Director, and Fred Lewis, External Relations Adviser.

I start by telling them about the P&G contract, which doesn't seem to throw them. It turns out that Lever have woken up to the fact that they have not been giving the environment sufficient weight — and have now appointed a 'fast-track' manager to overhaul the company's environmental performance in the UK. Part of the problem is that Lever sites like Port Sunlight and Warrington are well over 100 years old.

In the evening, I have dinner with Peter Bright and Mike Briggs, respectively public affairs people with Shell International and Shell International Chemicals. Then on with them to WWF's Royal premiere, with HRH Princess Alexandra, of 'Gorillas in the Mist'.

The film is built around the struggle of American Dian Fossey to save the mountain gorillas of Rwanda from poachers — and extinction. Only about 120 mountain gorillas are left in the wild in Rwanda and Fossey's efforts built the foundations on which the conservation programme of the Parc National des Volcans is now based.

The upbeat message at the end of the film is probably right for the audience. But, as Sigourney Weaver, who plays Fossey, told *The Independent*: 'It's a little misleading. The main question is whether the Rwandans will be able to keep the park going. Certainly I hope the film directs attention to what we're doing to the planet. It's all tied together; if we can succeed in letting animals live in dignity, if we can treat them as equals, we can begin to treat each other as equals too.'

Wednesday 25 January

Frantic day. In the papers, we see that Philips are about to introduce a new green battery, so I fax through a change to next Saturday's column to the *Guardian*. Julia and Fiona are assembling the hundreds of Green Supermarket Questionnaire packs, due to be posted out tomorrow.

I work on our speeches for the press launch of our Green Consumer

Marketing service tomorrow. In the evening, Ivan Hattingh of WWF and Richard Keefe of North–South Productions come to discuss the possibility of a Green Consumer video. We agree to push ahead with it.

Thursday 26 January
Walk to the station around 08.30. The low winter sun throws shadows on the mist which lies in great vapour pillows between the trees. The things one can now do on the move: a City gent shaves himself on the platform. Once in town, walk across Trafalgar Square to 11 Carlton House Terrace, where the Foreign Press Association is housed. The Green Consumer Marketing press conference is being held in an upstairs room with an extremely ornate plaster ceiling. The sun streams in.

The press turnout is not up to expectations, although the journalists who do come are very interested and the questioning goes on for a considerable time. My voice is still somewhat cracked after the Oslo trip. The man from *The Times* arrives after the discussion has ended — and is initially somewhat cynical, although he seems to come around.

David Gough speaks for PA Technology and is clearly waking up to some of the areas in which SustainAbility and PA might co-operate. One possibility is the development of biopesticides, based on viruses or microbes, rather than on synthetic chemicals.

Julia and I then take a taxi across to *Today*'s offices in Vauxhall Bridge Road. We discuss the planned Green Consumer survey of supermarkets which Julia and David Jones, the paper's Environment editor, are to undertake tomorrow. David's previously worked for the *News of the World* and the *Sun*, but he is clearly interested in green issues — and says that 1989 looks like a headline year for environmentalists.

Later, while we wait for a car to take us back to Barnes, I flick through a copy of *Today*, and come across an interesting news item. Yesterday, drivers swamped a garage offering free conversion of cars to unleaded petrol. Police had to be called as a half-mile queue of more than 100 cars formed. One driver queued for two hours, only to find his car had already been converted.

Once back in Barnes, we sign hundreds of letters and then continue packing up the Supermarket Questionnaire. It really is an enormous task — Fiona has been working on it all day, with help from my wife Elaine. The PR people call from Germany to say that they are trying to assemble a discussion panel for when I go over to launch *The Green Capitalists* — and the US deal for *The Green Consumer Guide* has been accepted by Viking/Penguin.

Friday 27 January

As far as I can see, none of the nationals mention Green Consumer Marketing today, although Saatchi's ring in the afternoon and mention that they have seen an article in an early edition of *The Times*.

But the papers do talk about a global warming meeting held by the Intergovernmental Panel on Climate Change (IPCC), set up last November by the World Meteorological Office and UNEP. GREAT SEA WALLS TO STAND GUARD AGAINST WORLD-WIDE FLOODS trumpets the headline in *The Times*. 'The Great Wall of China will soon be superseded as the largest man-made object on Earth,' Pearce Wright predicts. 'The 1,500-mile structure, the only sign of human activity on the ground that can be seen from the moon, might be usurped by the "Great Sea Walls" of the twenty-first century.'

The IPCC experts are due to publish a report in the summer of 1990, calling for international agreements to cut the carbon dioxide outputs from the burning of coal, oil and natural gas.

And the latest issue of the US Environmental Protection Agency's Journal, which came through this morning, contains a call from Denis Hayes for an international successor to America's Earth Day, which he helped co-ordinate in 1970. Sounds a great idea. We met when he was Director of the Solar Energy Research Institute, in Golden, Colorado, while I was criss-crossing the States as a Churchill Fellow, researching *Sun Traps*. He was sacked by the incoming Reagan Administration a week after we had had lunch. Solar power really wasn't Ronald Reagan's bag.

Earth Day 1990, Hayes suggested, should be held on 22 April, the 20th anniversary of the first Earth Day — when an estimated 25 million young Americans took part. Environmentalists shut down 5th Avenue in New York. Some broke into company offices and poured sewage on the carpets; others broke polluting cars apart with sledge-hammers. Earth Day was headline news. More positively, schools throughout the country held environmental teach-ins.

Liz Knights, our editor at Gollancz, calls to suggest a children's version of *The Guide*, as though we didn't have enough to do! We think it's a great idea, indeed Gaia has been suggesting it for a while. I contact Ivan Hattingh at WWF to see whether he would be interested in collaborating. He is.

Saturday 28 January

It's beginning to work. *The Times* reports that Tesco is at the epicentre of a battle to save 27 mature beech trees in Stroud. The trees are threatened by road improvements planned as part of a new Tesco store.

Will Tesco — and stores like it — try harder to minimise such environmental damage to protect their newly acquired green images? That's part of our strategy.

The second *Guardian* column appears and *The Independent* reports that *The Guide* is No. 2 in its latest list of 'Books in Demand'. God knows how they compile these lists — we are still at No. 8 in *The Sunday Times* general paperbacks bestseller list.

Among the first batch of letters in response to the first *Guardian* column, there is one on the question of why *The Guide* was not printed on recycled paper? 'Why could (John Elkington) not print his book on recycled paper? Was it because his publishers could not find a supplier, or was it (perish the thought) that they wanted to keep the cover price down and reap mega-green profits?' The letter concludes: 'Convince me otherwise Mr Elkington, but it would appear that you and Ms Hailes are wanting to have your wholefood carrot cake and eat it!'

The answer is that Gollancz found that recycled paper would be 40% more expensive — and, yes, the strategy was to keep the price down to break out of the 'green ghetto'. There were also problems with getting guarantees to resupply if the book sold rapidly. Next time, though, we plan to use recycled paper, provided we can find a reliable supplier. [We did.]

Meanwhile, in Antarctica, Greenpeace's ship *Gondwana* continues to play a cat-and-mouse game with the Japanese whaling fleet. Japanese sailors have been turning fire hoses on the Greenpeace inflatables as they tried to interrupt the killing of Minke whales. When the *Nisshin Maru* resumed whaling, the inflatables interposed themselves between the whales and the harpooners.

Greenpeace insists that Japan's 'scientific whaling' — with a kill of 300 whales planned — is simply commercial whaling under another name. The shadowing operation has been a considerable success, reports the *Guardian*'s correspondent aboard the Greenpeace ship. 'All the available evidence since our arrival is that the mouse has got the cat cornered,' said Pete Wilkinson of Greenpeace.

At home, the Government has commissioned Professor David Pearce to look at new natural resource accounting methods which could help define which forms of development are 'sustainable'. Announcing the new study, Environment Minister Lord Caithness said: 'We need to find ways of assessing the rate at which natural resources are being used and develop tools for ensuring that it is taken into account in investment appraisal.'

Tuesday 31 January
The *Marketing Week* conference at the London Marriott Hotel just off Grosvenor Square attracts a capacity audience. The organiser, Steve

Warshal, ticks me off at the door for not wearing my 'trademark' bow-tie. But *The Green Consumer Guide* gets an extraordinary series of pats on the back from Dorothy MacKenzie, Virginia Bottomley (who stresses that she gave it to all her friends and relatives for Christmas), the Corporate Affairs Director at Safeway and others.

The only jarring note was struck by the Cadbury's Marketing Manager who, time and again, stressed that his company's Wildlife Bar promotion with WWF was not stimulated by Green Consumer pressures. Clearly Cadbury's didn't mount the promotion because Green Consumers left them no choice, but they certainly hoped that the linking of the product with wildlife conservation would help them sell sweets to environment-conscious consumers.

As expected, John Hume, Director of Personnel and Public Affairs at Johnson Wax calls for a Green Forum, to bring together industry and environmental interests. At the end of our presentation, a series of companies come up to ask for help in preparing environmental audits.

. The day is chaired by Stuart Bull, Chief Executive of KHBB, the advertising agency. He hands me a copy of a KHBB report, *1990: The Dawn of Us-ism*. In it he describes *The Green Capitalists* as 'mould-breaking' — and in an update section of the latest version of the report *The Guide* and Green Consumer Week are highlighted as key steps in the process of greening Britain.

Interestingly, a spokeswoman from Marks & Spencer challenged us, asking: 'Don't you feel guilty about triggering this unwholesome competition between the supermarkets?' The answer, I replied from the panel, is that we are delighted that the supermarkets feel they have to compete in terms of their environmental performance.

FEBRUARY

Wednesday 1 February
On Monday, Sainsbury's announced plans to introduce a range of organic produce. Today, the news broke that Marks & Spencer are to follow suit shortly. Although organic produce is very unlikely to take up much shelf-space in most supermarkets for some time to come, these announcements have a considerable symbolic value — and will send a clear message to the agrochemicals industry.

Had a meeting with Marco Loprieno, who is co-ordinating the greening of Montedison, the Italian chemical company. They have appalling pollution problems and a reputation which has led to at least one major plant being closed following community pressure. They want help in developing an environmental strategy. We agree to fax a proposal next week.

Thursday 2 February
Julia's green survey of supermarkets is spread across the two centre pages of *Today* and we are also given a high profile in the latest issue of *Marketing Week*.

Walk across Westminster Bridge with Peter Bright of Shell International to launch of Groundwork's Brightsite Awards at the Institution of Civil Engineers' Conference Centre. Prince Charles gives the awards and ex-Minister and Groundwork chairman Christopher Chataway and Virginia Bottomley are among the panel members. 'No business has a secure future unless it is environmentally acceptable,' says Bob Reid, Chairman of Shell UK.

It's a completely different scene these days. Instead of my having to pursue companies, they are beginning to pursue us. As a result, it is even more important that we know where *we* want to go. Shortly after I get back to Barnes, AEG confirm that they are going to contribute £20,000 towards the costs of the Green Kitchen stand. With Johnson Wax's £17,000 and £5,000 from Varta, coupled with the £15,000 underwritten by Lord Rothermere, we now have the money to ensure that the project goes ahead. The initial artwork for the brochure comes through — and it's great.

Friday 3 February
The first Questionnaire comes back, in the form of an extremely friendly fax, from the Astley Dye & Chemical Company of Bolton, which

apparently has a 'cruelty-free' policy. Very clear that they see green issues as a method for achieving what the marketeers call 'product differentiation'. Also contacted today by a PR agency representing Ranks Hovis McDougall (RHM), reacting to the Questionnaire. It looks as though its campaigning impact could be considerable.

A key problem, however, will be to rein in the over-enthusiasm of the marketing profession. The quicker the enthusiasm builds, the faster it is likely to evaporate. Marketing people, it has to be said, are scarcely renowned for their ability to sustain a train of thought over months — let alone years. Charles Clover of the *Daily Telegraph* calls and we talk about the role of the market versus that of Government. His piece in the *Spectator* this week discussed the Tories' failure to grasp the complexity of the green agenda. The danger at the moment, with Mrs Thatcher apparently getting inadequate support for her green thrust in the Tory Party, is that she may feel that green consumerism is working so well that everything can be left to market forces. Nothing could be further from the truth. In the States, for example, market forces rule — but the regulatory framework is extremely tough and ordinary businessmen are increasingly sent to gaol as 'pollution criminals'.

Saturday 4 February
Woke this morning feeling utterly wrecked. Took the month's newspapers to the Sun Inn, where the Barnes Community Association runs a recycling scheme. Since SustainAbility takes seven or eight daily papers and any number of magazines, Gaia, Hania and I spend some time waddling back and forth between the car and two different trucks (one for papers, one for magazines) with groaning cardboard boxes.

The *Financial Times* today reports that China has quietly abandoned its unpopular — and often brutal — one-child-per-family policy. Couples with a girl are now allowed a 'spaced' second birth. From a humanitarian viewpoint, the news is welcome. The population control programmes in China and India have often been enforced with considerable cruelty. But from an ecological viewpoint, the news can only be described as disastrous.

Jonathon Porritt's article today in the *Guardian* concludes by saying that 'I genuinely like the notion of being eaten by worms. Ecologically speaking I have a huge dilemma on my hands. By and large one shouldn't take up unnecessary space, and I should probably be cremated when I die. That would be the most efficient way of ending one's tenure of life. Conceptually, I'm much happier about being gradually nibbled away, restoring to the earth part of what I've taken out.' We had spent some time trying to think of the most ecological form of departure when doing

The Guide, with burial taking up precious space and timber for the coffin; while incineration consumes fuel and adds to the Greenhouse Effect! The more of us there are, the more our ways of living and dying will become an issue.

Jonathon also notes that he has become obsessively concerned with environmental issues. Me too, perhaps, but our approach is different. Indeed, I sometimes feel that I play the Green Pollyanna to his Cassandra. But that's partly because we are addressing different audiences. He is trying to shake up the public and politicians, I am trying to wake up the business community. Most politicians respond fastest to threats, while business is more attuned to new market opportunities.

Part of our strategy is to encourage industry by spotlighting success stories. The dangers of this approach, unless you know what you are doing, are illustrated by the news story today about Rechem Environmental Services. Described last week by Virginia Bottomley as 'true friends of the earth', the waste disposal company is now being attacked because its discharges 'grossly exceeded' permissible levels.

The environmental movement must be able to tolerate a diversity of different approaches. No one has yet done what we are trying to do. We must also be willing to accept some costly mistakes. Earthlife was one of those — but it helped pioneer some important new approaches. Nothing ventured, nothing gained.

Internationally again, *The Independent* reports that Raimundo Mendes de Barros has picked up the mantle of his cousin, Chico Mendes. Once again, the news suggests that a key feature of the green movement in the Nineties is likely to be its increasingly global reach. 'The international response to Chico's death came as a big surprise,' he tells a group of US Congressmen and Senators, 'even to our enemies.'

Sunday 5 February
Interestingly, the Hotel Nelson in Norwich is apparently offering Pollution Weekends. Guests will be shown areas ravaged by acid rain, effluent and pesticides. Highlights include a beach where dead seals are washed up and (a success) the place where wild orchids have started to flourish again. A small scale green tourism venture which will be worth tracking as we begin writing *The Green Holiday Guide*.

Later go roller-skating with the children, roaring around a nearby paddling pool in the twilight — with the twin beams of Heathrow-bound jetliners cutting in and out of scudding cloud. Hit a concealed branch and up end in the sludge with what may be a pulled chest muscle, or a cracked rib. Thank heavens for knee-pads. But great to be back on wheels again — there's a price for everything.

35

Thursday 7 February
Meetings all day. Begin with David Cadman of PMA (Property Market Analysis). I first met David when we were both on the committee of The Other Economic Summit, more familiarly known as TOES, which mounted increasingly effective green counter-blasts to the inter-Government summit meetings around the world. We are talking about setting up a joint environmental service to developers of supermarkets and business parks. The property and construction industries have been slow to wake up to the threats (and opportunities) which will be created by the greening of Britain — and of their clients. But hopefully we will be able to stir up some interest in more intelligent approaches to property development.

Next: lunch with David Cope of CEED, a 'think tank' set up in the wake of the publication of the *Conservation and Development Programme for the UK* in 1983. (This was the first UK response to the World Conservation Strategy, published in 1980. I wrote the industry report for the UK programme.) David offers help on the tourism front. Thence to the Department of the Environment, to talk to Professor Don Huisingh, an American expert in clean technologies and waste reduction who I first met in Copenhagen. Don is developing a strong clean technology consultancy business with continental European companies — and we explore the potential for working together. One way or another, SustainAbility will be moving into the European market over the next year.

On to the Design Council, to talk through plans for the 'Green Designs on Europe' conference to be held at the Queen Elizabeth II conference centre at the end of March. I come up with the idea of including a display of German green products in the accompanying exhibition. Am thinking of talking in terms of an impending 'green Blitz' of environment-friendly products from the Continent. There is an irony in the fact that many of the companies that have done best out of the Green Consumer breakthrough in Britain have been German, Belgian or Dutch, with the result that some British companies could find some parts of their product ranges reduced to rubble.

The latest issue of *Management Today* notes that 'green, or sustainable, growth' will require a sea-change in business attitudes. The editorial argues that this sea-change is unlikely to happen until some time in the next century, although it stresses that accepting limits to growth need not be a depressing prospect. 'Sustainable growth means just that,' it says, 'a level of growth that can continue unimpeded.' The debate for the Nineties will be whether *any* rate of growth can be sustained indefinitely.

The magazine contains two major articles on green issues, one of which focuses on Green Consumer products. SustainAbility is extensively covered. The message is overwhelmingly favourable, although the conclusion is challenging: 'Marketeers do not think that the environment is as straightforward a concept to market as healthy eating, which clearly benefited the individual. And persuading consumers to pay more for sometimes inferior products will be far from easy.'

Thursday 9 February
Start sketching out the next *Guardian* column, on 'clean cars'. Extraordinary transformation in Rover's Peter Sellors when I call him today. Had just emerged from a presentation to the Commercial Director where he argued — successfully — that the company should aim to get the green light. 'I'm not sure the company should say it's green,' he says. 'If customers say they want high performance cars that run only on leaded fuel, we'll supply them. But we should be offering them a choice of environment-friendly models.'

I really would like to believe that Rover will get its act together in this field, but suspect that once again they will fail to spot the fact that the future of the car depends on the industry's ability to deliver a very different sort of car. At the moment, I would put my money on the Japanese.

Odd couple of invitations: to see Bob Geldof about a TV series on 21 February and to have dinner with Lord Caithness, the Environment Minister, on 28 February. I must try and remember which meeting to shave for — and which not.

Friday 10 February
Started the day with Electrolux, at VandenBurg Associates's offices in Great Portland Street. They want to use the Green Consumer logo on their fridges and other 'white goods'. We prefer to develop the Green Label scheme properly, rather than stick the logo on goods made by whoever will pay most. Electrolux agree.

Encouraging to see good write-ups today in *Design Week*, *Good Housekeeping* and the *Evening Standard*, the latter under a picture of the Queen — who has decided to convert the Royal car fleet to unleaded petrol. Elements of the message are at last getting through.

In the afternoon, drive to Sutton to work through back issues of *Super Marketing*. Enormous task, so work out a time-scale to 1992, when the Single European Market will dawn — and then work back 20 years to 1972. It's extraordinary to see how the main environmental issues have surfaced and resurfaced over the years. Looking through the 1973–74 issues of the magazine, for example, it is fascinating to see how they responded to the first OPEC oil shock. Packaging keeps popping up. Then skip forward to 1982 and — five years on — to 1987, to gauge the extent to which the supermarkets have been tracking and responding to the ever-growing green agenda.

Sunday 12 February
The *Observer* today carries a full-page, closely printed Volkswagen ad that is quite extraordinary. 'Car pollution is now heir to the publicity throne currently occupied by aerosols and the ozone layer,' says VW. 'It's hardly surprising. After pumping out noxious gases into the air for more than a century, we can hardly expect Mother Nature to keep mum.' The basic idea is that if you use unleaded petrol and have your car fitted with a catalytic converter, 'we can keep the world a little cleaner and a little healthier. And make it a nice place to go for a drive'. Not the sort of ad one would have expected from a manufacturer, even a year ago.

Slipped away from the word-processor this evening to watch 'Three-Minute Culture' on BBC2, in which Michael Ignatieff interviewed Sir Kit McMahon, Chairman of the Midland Bank. 'Most values have gone, except for the fast buck,' Sir Kit said at one stage. He also noted that: 'You need to have marble and mahogany to convince people that a bank is solid,' or words to that effect. Clearly, people are not only going to have to change their values — they are going to have to get used to different images of financial probity.

As the programme ends, Tessa Tennant calls. It sets me thinking. How, in a world of VDUs and of money that moves as fast as light do we wake up the banking world, with its chronic short-termism, to the notion that it might just be to its long term advantage to leave mahogany in the rainforest?

Monday 13 February
Interesting letter from P&G today, asking for advice on whether they should respond to supermarket requests for information on the environ-ment-friendliness of their products. They seem to have been provoked by our own Green Supermarket Questionnaire sent to the same supermar-kets. Dick Johnson says that on the face of it the requests are 'somewhat impertinent', but he seems inclined to play ball. It's fascinating to see the green market working at close quarters. Manufacturers find it very difficult to resist environmental pressures when they come direct from retailers.

Later, we are visited by Helen Fairclough from Oxford Poly, who is looking at the impact of environmentalism on the fast food sector (pretty minimal, so far) and by Paul Ekins, who runs the Right Livelihood Foundation, which awards the Alternative Nobel Prizes. Paul is increas-ingly convinced that the market can deliver much of what we want, but concerned that competition may cut down on the flow of information between people in the environmental field. At this stage, if we choose to look at it in that way, we are sitting on one of the biggest data-bases on green consumerism in the world.

Paul is working with Richard Adams, previously Managing Director of Traidcraft, the 'alternative trading' organisation based in Gateshead, on a new publication aimed at the Conscious Consumer — or New Consumer. We remain unconvinced of the near-term potential of their approach, which involves tackling a range of issues (apartheid, arms manufacture, nuclear issues, equal rights, the environment and so on) simultaneously. We feel that the more issues you strap on, the more you sub-divide your 'market'. But we are trying to be supportive.

'World in Action' on ITV this evening focuses on dioxins and furans in paper products, such as disposable nappies, tampons, tea bags, coffee filters and paper tissues. Britain is still some way behind countries like Canada and Holland in moving over to unbleached (or non-chlorine-bleached) paper products. The Women's Environmental Network's campaign against chlorine bleaching launches tomorrow.

Tuesday 14 February
The pressures, particularly on Julia and I, are building. Turn down a request to write a book for Thorsons when they call at lunch-time and duck out of the next meeting of the NCC's Advisory Committee for England. [Probably a mistake, as it turns out. 1989 will be the year that the Government decides to carve up the NCC.]

Lisa Silcock comes over in the afternoon to discuss the build-up to the Green Kitchen. She helped Phil Agland put together the Baka films and contributed some superb articles on Cameroon when I was editing *Earthlife News* several years ago. She has an extraordinary mane of blonde hair, a cross between thatch and lightning. One wonders what the Pygmies made of it! British Gas have now offered £12,000 towards the Green Kitchen, which means that the costs are just about covered. And Sucden Produce have promised at least 40 kg of brazil nuts, to point up the potential of extractive reserves in saving rainforests. Brazil nut trees cannot be grown in plantations, so brazil nuts are products — and symbols — of healthy rainforests.

Mark Edwards, a photographer who has taken powerful pictures of Third World environmental problems and developments for Earthscan and Panos, arrives simultaneously. He and I bat ideas around for a while and then the idea emerges of doing a green coffee table book on 'The Greening of Europe' in time for 1992. The idea is to provide a powerful account of the ways in which environmental trends are helping to develop the sense of a common European identity and experience. With all the other projects currently on the stocks, this one may well never get off the ground, because of the sheer level of effort we would need to inject.

The office activities surge into one room after another, colliding with the family mainly in the kitchen. The phones ring nearly continuously. And it's the children's half-term: in addition to everything else, the house fills with their noise and the aroma of the chocolate cake they are cooking. Poor Elaine retreats up the road to Lois's.

Wednesday 15 February
An extraordinary day. Endless calls asking us to write articles or to make presentations to companies. And WWF call to see whether we would consider Heinz sponsorship for Green Shopping Day. On reflection, we decide that we would prefer Heinz — who have been running a £1 million 'Guardians of the Countryside' campaign with WWF for two years now — to a single supermarket. A sole supermarket sponsor would close off all the other supermarkets, whereas a food manufacturer supplying all the supermarkets could help us get around the problem. We develop an initial proposal, and fax it through to Kate Brooks at WWF.

Internationally, *The Times* reports that the Overseas Development Administration (ODA) and WWF are launching a £2 million sustainable development programme. The flagship project will focus on the Korup National Park in Cameroon, the project which Earthlife succeeded in getting on the international agenda. The idea will be to provide a 'sustainable future' for the 30,000 people who live in the area, while stemming the destruction of the wildlife of one of Africa's oldest remaining areas of unspoilt rainforest.

The Brazilian Government announces that it will try drastic methods to protect the Amazonian rainforest. Among other initiatives, it will form a 2,000-strong National Environmental Guard and will attempt the forcible removal of 40,000 illegal gold-diggers from the northern state of Roraima. They have invaded the reserve on which 9,500 Yanomami Indians live. Radio programmes will also aim to persuade small farmers to abandon the slash-and-burn methods which are dest-roying an estimated 77,000 square miles of rainforest each year. The re-education task facing the Brazilian Government is truly gargantuan — and the Government is probably itself the target most in need of re-education.

Union Carbide, meanwhile, has agreed to pay $470 million (£270 million) in compensation to victims of the 1984 Bhopal disaster in India. More than 2,500 people were killed by the poisonous gas cloud from the plant, while tens of thousands more were seriously injured. The settlement ends four years of litigation over the world's worst industrial disaster. Union Carbide was seen as having got away fairly lightly. 'It's an incredibly reasonable settlement,' comments one New York analyst.

Closer to home, according to *Today*, the Queen was unamused by the release of 10,000 balloons (emblazoned with the message 'I love lead-free') into the skies above Buckingham Palace. The balloons may have been coloured green, but they will end up dangling from trees, impervious to weathering. Wherever you go in Europe now, the trees and hedges are streaked with tattered plastic, flapping and billowing like Tibetan prayer flags. Praying for an end to the ceaseless blizzard of trash.

But the news item that rang the strongest chord in my mind revolved around the Muslim reaction to Salman Rushdie's book, *The Satanic Verses*. Ayatollah Khomeini of Iran has called on Muslims to assassinate Rushdie as a 'blasphemer' — and all those involved in publishing the book. The news also comes through that the Iranian Government has passed a heavy prison sentence on Roger Cooper, held since 1985 on charges of spying. We met him some years ago through Emma Parsons, whose father — Sir Anthony Parsons — was British Ambassador in the waning years of the Shah's regime.

Behind these stories there lies a fundamental question. Can any religion be greened, let alone Islam? This question may well come back to haunt us in the Nineties. Apart from St Francis of Assisi, most Christians have discounted what happens here on Earth in favour of the afterlife. These problems are compounded with Islam, which is even more extreme than Catholicism. Unfortunately, greening the Pope currently looks as unlikely as greening Ayatollah Khomeini.

As a child in Northern Ireland, I was dubbed a 'pagan' or 'pantheist' by the Mother Superior at the convent school we attended in Limavady. I couldn't believe that we went to Heaven if the animals I came across in the surrounding countryside didn't. Ever since, I have been a combination of atheist and pantheist.

Maybe long term we will have to engineer the birth of a Green religion, a world-church of Gaia? It's an idea that Frank Herbert, who wrote the *Dune* science fiction novels, explored in some depth. His work — and the meeting I had with him in 1983, several years before his death — were strong influences.

Thursday 16 February
Start off at a meeting of the CEGB's Environment and Development Advisory Panel (EDAP). The CEGB is currently in the process of breaking up into the National Power Company, PowerGen and the National Grid Company — and EDAP is exploring the question of how the CEGB's

environmental activities can be carried forward into the post-privatisation world. And the CEGB announces that electricity prices will rise by 2% after privatisation to meet the costs of a £1.8 billion environmental clean-up programme designed to tackle acid emissions from coal-fired power stations. Privatising the electricity industry is going to be a real test of the Government's environmental intentions. Large parts of it are still rooted in the 1950s — with environmental standards to match. My suspicion is that once the companies are out in the private sector, their interest in environmental issues will increase rather than fall.

All energy technologies have an impact on the environment. A pressurised water reactor might take a square kilometre of land, whereas a wind-farm supplying the same energy might cover 500 square kilometres and an energy forest 4,000 square kilometres. More solar energy hits the earth every year than is stored in all the planet's fossil fuels, but — because the energy you are trying to capture is so diffuse — the renewable energy technologies often have disproportionately large impacts in terms of scale, if not in terms of chemistry or radiation.

Or consider the Severn Barrage scheme. The price-tag has now reached £8 billion, twice the costs of a nuclear facility with the same output. And it is a sad fact that half the interesting sites for wind-farms are located in National Parks, where the aerogenerators would almost certainly be unacceptable. But, while there will be difficult environmental trade-offs to be made, the potential for the renewables remains considerable.

Obviously, the less electricity we use, the better. The question is whether we can get private sector companies, competing to sell power, to see any benefit in selling energy efficiency — which will cut the size of their market.

Dr Peter Chester, who will be a Main Board Director in National Power, responsible for technical matters and the environment, notes that there is a new spirit abroad in the electricity supply industry. 'The environment is no less important,' he says, 'because the shareholder has switched from being the Department of Energy to the public.' We shall see.

The *Financial Times* today looks at what is happening in Holland, where 'a tidal wave of guilt over the destruction of the environment is sweeping' the country. Queen Beatrix recently warned that 'the Earth is slowly dying and the inconceivable — the end of life itself — is actually becoming conceivable'.

It's fascinating to see how the Royal families of Europe and Scandinavia are getting involved in the environment, not just in the Prince Philip mode of Establishment conservationism but almost as Royal Greens. King Carl Gustav of Sweden has just broken his rule of political silence

42

and called on Prime Minister Brundtland to halt the impending Norwegian seal cull. The Norwegian Government, on the other hand, says the cull is vital to protect fish stocks.

'Feelings here are running very high,' Paul Bugge of Greenpeace Norway tells *Today*. 'It is like England under threat from Hitler. Most people are very angry that the British and Americans, who they see as sentimental animal lovers, are interfering in their affairs.' We will see a growing number of such issues, which hit hard at national interests. The Royal Greens have an important role in helping nation states to recognise that international interest in how they manage their natural resources may be well-intentioned and far-sighted.

Feelings are also running high in New Delhi, where demonstrators stormed the Supreme Court yesterday, to protest at the size of the settlement for the Bhopal gas victims. They said the $470 million agreed was only a fraction of the $3.3 billion demanded by the Indian Government — and that figure only a fraction of the $15 billion the Citizens' Commission on Bhopal had decided would be fair compensation.

From the time I got back from the CEGB until 18.00, all three telephone lines burned with calls. Among those I answered was one from the *Sunday Telegraph*, who effectively wanted me to say that the Queen's support for the unleaded petrol campaign has unleashed a flood-tide of interest in what we are doing. Had to say that the pressures started last year.

But the Queen is obviously taking on something of a green tinge. With Prince Philip (wildlife conservation and population control), Prince Charles (the environment, North Sea and organic farming) and Princess Anne (Third World development and children) in the family, I said, the real surprise is that it hadn't happened sooner. Perhaps it had to wait until the environment became an all-party, or non-political, issue?

We are sounding out people in the tourism industry on our idea of a *Green Holiday Guide* — and associated initiatives. It looks very much as though our instincts are right. And with the tour operators looking for ways of 'unpackaging' holidays, and of 'trading up', very much like the supermarkets, it could well be that a campaign based on environmental quality could trigger significant changes in the industry. Roger Heape, of Intasun, has agreed to help us map out our strategy.

Friday 17 February
Julia and I drive down to Melbourn, just outside Cambridge, for a joint meeting between Brand New, PA Technology and SustainAbility. Snow has fallen and the landscape is white for much of the trip. The basic aim of

the meeting is to identify key areas for development and allocate responsibilities. SustainAbility's main problem at the moment is the fact that we have no capacity to do any more than we are already doing. But by the end of the meeting, it is decided that the three organisations will target such areas as packaging, white goods, the food chain and paper products in the first phase of developing the joint service.

All very exciting — and then things went a little flat. Had left car lights on and the battery is totally dead. Electronic central locking system, power steering and all have expired. A PA engineer tows us around the car-park while I try to jerk-start the beast, but it's a bit like trying to jerk-start a Sherman tank. Eventually, we call the RAC — but then the engineers strap the battery up to the mains and an hour later, well before the RAC arrive, the beast comes to life again.

Julia insistent that a Volvo is ugly and unsuitable for any self-respecting Green Consumer. Try to explain that family life means that safety is as important as energy efficiency. Score few points. But she proves indispensable in handling the whole crisis: cool, efficient, logical. I should take evening classes in crisis management.

Yesterday, Friends of the Earth told a House of Lords committee that energy-efficient technologies could cut the country's electricity consumption by an astounding 70%. Among FoE's recommendations, easily understood energy efficiency labels on a wide range of equipment and products.

Next, the frog spawn that spawns forests. Over in Brazil, helicopters are being used to drop 300 million forest seeds on the country's Atlantic Forest — shrunk to 5% of its original size by a combination of land speculation and air pollution. The seeds are encapsulated in gelatinous pellets and look like frog spawn. The technology was originally developed to encapsulate yeast used in sugar-cane fermentations. But it's still small beer compared with the scale of deforestation.

Saturday 18 February
'We're Nature's virus,' says artist Helen Chadwick in *The Independent*. Her (apparently) gruesome photographic panoramas, called *Viral Landscapes*, are 'painted' with a 'palette' supplied by her doctor: samples of blood, saliva, urine 'and any bits I could get that weren't dangerous'.

The viral analogy seems particularly appropriate in the light of the growing evidence on the destruction of the ozone layer. Mankind as a planetary AIDS. Using a converted U–2 spy-plane and a DC8, scientists have found 'highly significant' levels of chlorine monoxide in the high atmosphere — the chemical that scientists have described as the 'smoking gun', linking ozone destruction with the presence of CFCs.

The ozone hole over the South Pole has now been joined by a hole over the North Pole. And the chemicals associated with ozone destruction are up to 50 times more common in the ozone layer than expected.

The ozone layer is some 20 miles deep, but if you compressed it to the density of air at sea level, it would be about as thick as a £1 coin. The evidence from the North Pole suggests that this precariously thin shield against ultra-violet radiation from the sun is thinning rapidly.

'The Arctic vortex has become primed to destroy ozone,' said Dr Rod Jones, a UK Meteorological Office atmospheric chemist who was a member of the 200-person, £7 million Arctic Airborne Stratospheric Experiment. I imagine someone has thought of one obvious acronym, ARSE? With a major ozone conference due to take place in London shortly, this latest evidence will fuel calls for further controls on CFCs and other ozone-damaging chemicals.

Meanwhile Prince Philip, currently in northern Nigeria, has once again been confronted with large areas of desertification, caused by overgrazing and tree felling. 'Sometimes I'm glad that I am as old as I am,' he said, according to *Today*, 'so that it is unlikely I will still be around to answer to the next generation for leaving them a devastated planet.'

One man who must be regretting not having taken environment more seriously is Lloyd's underwriter Dick Outhwaite. His insurance syndicate is faced with claims totalling more than £260 million — and the bulk of them are to do with asbestosis and pollution incidents in America. Overall, such claims could cost Lloyds a staggering £2 billion. The syndicate say they were given too little information when offered the insurance business by other syndicates. Is it too much to hope that insurers will now ask for more information?

More positively, today's *Financial Times* looks at ethical investment funds. 'The rationale for ethical funds is enticing,' says the *FT*. 'Investors help put the world to rights and making profits becomes acceptable.' The Merlin Ecology Fund, on whose advisory panel I sit, gets an excellent write-up as one of the fastest-growing and best-performing new funds. Merlin's commitment to in-depth research on the environmental perform- ance of the companies it invests in is unique in this country — and possibly in Europe.

Monday 20 February
It's after 22.00 and a fax is still rolling in from Wide Open: the draft Green Kitchen press release. Spent most of today down at Shell's agrochemical research facility in Sittingbourne, Kent, with Janet Barber and Heather Corrie of WWF, Peter Bright, Eric Nickson and Hans den Breems of Shell International, and Hazel Barbour of Shell UK.

We were given briefings on fungicide testing, toxicity testing and environmental testing of pesticides and other agrochemicals, clonal tree propagation (Shell 'developing its green fingers', explains Dr Roger Cripps), rodenticides, agricultural biotechnology and biodegradation. Much of the research, in the words of Dr Ernie Thorpe, involves 'looking for the skeletons in a compound's cupboard'. The scientists respond well to our battery of questions.

Surprised to find how far Shell has come in the quest to find new toxicity testing methods which dispense with animals, including *in vitro* mammalian cell cultures. And the potential of biotechnology for helping us deal with such environmental problems as toxic waste treatment and soil erosion is not lost on the Sittingbourne scientists. The problem is going to be in making such applications commercially attractive.

In the end it will probably come down to politics. Interesting to see that yesterday Neil Kinnock attacked 'the claim to ecological concern made by Green Goddess, Margaret Hilda Thatcher, fellow of the Royal Society'. 'The Tories might believe that people should buy their way into private education or health,' he said, 'but no one can buy their way out of the environment. There is no such thing as an effective free market policy for the environment.' However, given the failure of many of the state socialist approaches to environmental management, it is difficult to see any ready alternative to the market. The real challenge is to develop market signals and pricing mechanisms which ensure that the market delivers sustainability alongside its other undoubted benefits.

Tuesday 21 February
Interestingly, ICI Chemicals & Polymers announced yesterday that it will upgrade its environmental standards in advance of 1992. Under new reporting arrangements, all the group's 30 European plants are being asked to submit monthly reports on chemical spillages and on the extent to which they are complying with specific laws. This is likely to be an essential step for all companies intending to put real pressure on line management to improve the environmental performance of factories and other operations.

Late for the meeting with Bob Geldof. Round-table meeting with Jonathon Porritt (FoE), Lloyd Timberlake (Earthscan), Tom Burke, Richard Sandbrook (IIED), Richard North from *The Independent*, Joss Pearson of Gaia Books, Mick Kelly of the UEA Climate Research Unit and Robert Lamb of the Television Trust for the Environment (TVE).

Elements of an environment Mafia at work here. For example, Richard Sandbrook — who I first bumped into in the mid-1970s when he was a Dirctor of FoE — is now the key man at the IIED. He and I have worked on a number of projects together, particularly in the area of sustainable development in the Third World. And I had the great pleasure of helping Joss and her team put together the *Gaia Atlas of Planet Management* in 1984.

Geldof sports what appears to be a three-week stubble and periodically runs his fingers through his long, lank hair like some rock'n'roll witch. Find myself sitting next to him, in pin-stripe suit and bow tie. In some ways it is a bit like the meetings with Prince Charles: Sir Bob holding court. But the conversation is much easier — and radically different views erupt for several hours. Geldof is bright, articulate and clearly has an eye for the media pulse.

Jonathon argues that we are hell-bent on pushing the planet beyond the brink, whereas Richard thinks we'll muddle through. Geldof's series is planned for 1992, hopefully to hit the screens before the 20th anniversary of the UN Stockholm Conference on the Human Environment — which put the environment on the international political agenda.

Good deal of discussion of James Lovelock's Gaia hypothesis, which suggests that the biosphere will survive whatever happens, but we won't.

Geldof said early on that he didn't want to give up his Saab: Tom suggests that he'll only be able to go on using the Saab if he plants enough trees to offset his carbon dioxide emissions. Jonathon argues that the Saab would cost at least £100,000 if all its environmental impacts were costed in. Overall, the meeting left me unconvinced that the series will fly. It's the right idea and the right time, but somehow it doesn't seem to hang together.

Internationally, today sees start of four-day conference called by Kayapo Indians in Amazonia. Thousands of Indians from 28 Amazon nations are occupying site of dam construction at Altamira, in the state of Para in Eastern Brazil. Hydropower schemes are central to Brazil's energy plans, but the two Altamira dams alone would flood some 7,200 square km of rainforest, including land currently occupied by some 70,000 Indians. Among the banks investing are Citibank, Lloyds, Midland and NatWest — one more example of the importance of developing green pressure points in the world of high finance. And Sting is in Brazil at the Xingu conference — hosted by the Kayapo tribe and Friends of the Earth. Although the Altamira townspeople have tended to support the huge dam project, the Kayapo are bitterly opposed to it.

The Brazilian Foreign Ministry plans to set up a human rights and ecology department. But the Deputy Foreign Minister says it will 'try to show that most of what is being said has no scientific basis. For example, it is not true that 10% of the Greenhouse Effect is caused by Amazon fires.' It sounds very much as if the Ministry is blinded by the smoke rising from the blazing Amazon.

47

Sadly, there are countries with worse problems. The *Financial Times* today carries a report on China's Yangtze River, which discharges silt equivalent to the combined total of the Nile, Mississippi and the Amazon. Soil erosion is so intense that an estimated 1.5 billion tonnes of soil are washed down the river to the East China Sea each year. If erosion continues at its present rate, the mountain topsoil in much of the Yangtze's watershed will be gone inside 50 years. Floods of Bangladeshi proportions are in prospect.

Thursday 23 February
Around midnight, animal rights activists bombed the Senate House at Bristol University, where I shall be giving a speech next week. The use of high explosive represents a new stage for the Animal Liberation Front (ALF), from a marginal group who many people saw as little more than cranks into a fully fledged terrorist organisation. Over the last two years, ALF and other groups have caused a total of more than £10 million of damage to British stores and supermarkets. My instinct is that the Nineties will see a growing trend for 'green-labelled' terrorism. In some cases environmental groups will resort to extreme measures; in others, mainstream terrorists will try to justify their atrocities by linking them to environmental campaigns. If I'm right, this is a trend that could hit the environmental movement hard.

Although *The Guide* did cover animal welfare, focusing on 'cruelty-free' products, Julia and I have often argued about whether animal welfare issues can in any sense be wrapped into the green agenda. I think they can— and should be. The use of pesticides and many other chemicals involves the use of extensive animal testing, for example. Every time we environmentalists insist that products should be safer, more animals end up in laboratories. While the ALF approach is almost certainly counter-productive, we should take a much greater interest in all the repercussions of the choices we encourage society to make. Julia thinks that endangered species are much more important, although she doesn't welcome cruelty to animals.

Today reports that acid rain has killed all the trout in Prince Charles' favourite trout fishing lake at Balmoral, while an editorial in *The Times* notes that the state of many of Britain's beaches is appalling. Sewage dumped into the sea through short outfall pipes promptly washes back on to beaches. The cost of cleaning them up to acceptable standards by 1995 is estimated at £600 million — a problem for those trying to sell the water industry to investors.

Penny at Wide Open reports that, after a good deal of to-ing and fro-ing, the *Mail on Sunday* will now do the Green Kitchen competition, which they had tried to wriggle out of. The implications would have been serious for the exhibition, given that some of the exhibiting companies came in on the basis that their products would be picked up in this way. The effort that goes into simply keeping the locomotive on the rails is enormous — but the excitement is building rapidly as the launch approaches. Also had a meeting with Richard Keefe of North–South Productions on the Green Consumer Video. He is currently editing a TV film on the rainforests, narrated by Sting. Meanwhile Sting is calling for £1 million to help fund a new Indian reserve in Brazil, which apparently would be as big as Ireland.

And Gollancz reports that the China Times Publishing Company of Taiwan has offered an advance of US$400 for *The Green Capitalists*. Apparently Taiwan has not signed any copyright convention and copyright piracy is rife. Gollancz's Japanese agent was at pains to point out that China Times has behaved very honourably in making this offer!

Take the train to Gatwick. Standing room only as we flash through endless suburbia and exurbia, rain streaking down the windows, cigarette smoke seeping in from the next carriage. Gatwick's North terminal is large, modern and almost empty. The main sound in the strikingly silent departure lounge is the whirr and rattle of air-conditioners. Are they bleeding CFCs into the atmosphere?

Out through Gate 57: a Heinz omen? Thundering down the dark runway and up into the night. By 20.30 we are over the east coast, passing the sprinkling of offshore oil and gas platforms. They glow like fireflies, plugged into fossil sunshine. A low, three-quarters moon peers in through the starboard window.

Time magazine carries a very positive profile of Body Shop founder Anita Roddick, who has also been at the Altamira conference in Brazil. 'I don't think this is a dress rehearsal,' she said. 'At 46, I think we have only got so much time.'

Americans seem fascinated by the ethical stance taken by The Body Shop group, although the article quotes a London stock analyst as saying: 'The stores may look nice, and customers may like what they say about saving the whales, but what the shops really offer is a good product at a good price.' In January, the group boasted 362 retail outlets in 35 countries and reported sales of $83.2 million in 1988, 62% up on the 1987 results.

Friday 24 February
Conference begins at 09.00 at Norwegian School of Economics and Business Administration. Theme is sustainable development, title: Global Poker, Green Joker. Professor Mikhail Lemesjev, of the Soviet Academy of Science, is an amazing figure, semi-piratical. He has a lined, humorous face, grey long hair and beard, and a stump for a right hand. From his

speech, it's clear that the state of play in the USSR is remarkably different, but *perestroika* and *glasnost* are producing some fascinating results in the environmental field. The problem for the Soviets is that for the foreseeable future, *glasnost* will mainly result in a flood-tide of bad tidings about the state of their environment. I focus on the Green Consumer as the 'Green Joker'. Once initial hiccups with slides are overcome, the speech goes well — and a considerable number of people come up afterwards. Lemesjev is asked whether green consumerism is taking off in the Soviet Union: he seems unable to engage with the question, focusing instead on technology.

The *Guardian* carries my article, 'Worries in the Wind', today. In the light of the Norwegian experience, couldn't agree with myself more. The real question for Mrs Thatcher is whether we prefer to be dragged down the clean air path or whether, instead, we embrace a greener Europe and the political and business opportunities that will inevitably follow.

Until recently, the Government's persistent downgrading of environmental issues threatened to give us the worst of all worlds. Whether or not change is now in the wind, we live in an increasingly squalid environment, are branded with an appalling international image and achieve a declining share of world markets for clean-up technologies.

Sunday 26 February
Walk to paper shop with Hania. Stunning *Sunday Times* magazine. 'The world is dying,' the front cover proclaims. 'What are you going to do about it?'

The words are supplied by Richard Girling and Brian Jackman, the aim to touch 'upon every part of the globe from the pavement outside your gate to the edge of the ionosphere'. Hania thinks I'm mad to respond so positively to the news that the world is dying, but the current level — and depth — of media coverage of environmental issues is amazing. The challenge now is to convert concerns into action.

Turn to main papers. 'Exposed: the men polluting British rivers.' The front page of *The Sunday Times* spotlights six British businessmen who chair the country's dirtiest half-dozen companies. They are: Sir Robert Haslam (British Coal), Sir Kenneth Couzens (Coal Products), Denys Henderson (ICI), Michael Hodgkinson (Express Foods), Kenneth Kemp (British Tissues) and Bernard Henderson (Anglian Water). Three of these (British Coal, ICI and Anglian Water) are covered in the audits report I am preparing for WWF. If I am any judge of human nature, the article will have sparked an extraordinary reaction. There's nothing like pinning pollution problems on individual top managers for waking them up to their responsibilities.

The latest *Digest of Environmental Protection and Water Statistics* from the DoE shows that the Norwegians are right to point the finger at us. Nitrogen dioxide emissions went up in 1987 to 2.30 million tonnes, the highest level since 1979. Carbon monoxide pollution rose to 5.26 million tonnes, a 10% increase since 1977. Hydrocarbons gases continue to rise at 1% a year, while emissions of carbon dioxide rose between 1984 and 1987 — although they did not breach the level reached in the 1970s.

The number of water pollution incidents jumped 9% to over 23,000 and imports of toxic waste also doubled. Labour's environment spokeswoman, Anne Taylor, describes the figures as 'horrific — very worrying for anyone looking to the situation for future generations'.

The mainstream political parties are certainly picking up on the language, but how deep does their commitment run — and will it hold up if Labour gets back into power?

Monday 27 February
Opening shots fired in Labour's Environment Week, a counter-blast to Mrs Thatcher's impending ozone conference. Opposition environment spokesman Dr Jack Cunningham describes the Government's proposals for water privatisation as weak, confused and incoherent. The Conservatives' free market ideology, Labour argues, disqualifies them from being true friends of the earth. Once again, while the untrammelled market is obviously going to cause environmental problems, I am convinced that a properly regulated market will deliver better results than a nationalised economy.

Just after 12.00, Julia and I drive down to Scott Paper, an American company that used to operate here as Bowater-Scott, in East Grinstead. They make products like *Andrex* and *Scotties*, so some of the conversation revolves around subjects which are scarcely the subject of polite conversation.

The disposable paper products sector is a bit more complicated than it might at first appear, however. 'We're not just in the business of wiping people's rear ends,' says Managing Director Clem Andes. 'We're in the fashion business.' The colour of toilet rolls is dictated by the colour of bathrooms.

Interestingly, Andes tried to launch a green toilet roll in the States in the 1970s. Called *Clean Scene*, the product bit the dust. But Scott are now looking for ways of understanding the impending environmental issues likely to affect their product range. Scott are in the sanitary products business which means that the WEN report has put them slightly on the spot — not least because they switched to an environmentally acceptable pulp some years back, but decided not to talk about it. However, they

51

have been involved — as we pointed out in *The Guide* — in at least one eucalyptus plantation which threatens to accelerate tropical deforestation.

Back in London give a talk to a Society of Business Economists. The main question among the economists is whether the current level of environmental concern will last. We say no, but the current tide of concern will help form new institutions which will exert a ratchet effect — holding the environment at a much higher level than before. And the cycle of concern will inevitably build again, to an even higher level.

Pick up a copy of the *Radio Times* on the way home. It's a green issue, in the build-up to Chris Baines's 'The Big E' environmental TV series. The magazine contains a green questionnaire, with the first 100 people returning their forms promised a free copy of *The Green Consumer Guide*.

Prince Charles, meanwhile, has been trekking in the Venezuelan rainforest. Speaking to reporters in a jungle clearing surrounded by fireblackened trees, he described the rainforests as 'the lungs of the world'. Their protection could not be left to one half of the world while the rest did nothing, he said, otherwise 'you will wake up one morning and find yourselves with large areas of desert'. The next question: will the rest of the world be prepared to cough up to protect these distant green lungs?

Tuesday 28 February
This afternoon, I went with Dorothy to Colgate-Palmolive, in Oxford Street. C-P interested to know how they can begin to go green, given that they are simultaneously a heavy user of CFCs — and weak in a number of other departments, too. Is there some way, they ask, that they could move towards a collaboration with groups like Friends of the Earth? How can they do what Johnson Wax have managed to do? A difficult question. The success of the small number of ethical companies to date reflects their deeply-felt commitment to their principles and it's hard to see how other companies can replicate this commitment in the sort of time-scales that make sense to marketing people.

On to the Department of the Environment for dinner with Lord Caithness. Other non-DoE guests were Professor John Knill (Chairman, Natural Environment Research Council), Sir Peter Harrop (former Second Permanent Secretary, DoE, and chaired UK committee for European Year of the Environment), Professor Tim O'Riordan (University of East Anglia), Richard Sandbrook, Robin Paul (Managing Director, Albright & Wilson) and Anthony Foster (General Business Manager, ICI Chemicals and Polymers).

Discussion started off chasing its tail on the issue of youth training and environment education for half an hour. Good airing for Third World and global environmental issues. Richard suggests the idea of a 'product stewardship' programme using volunteers, like VSO. Some interest from ICI.

Then we open up the business side of the discussion, focusing on auditing, the Green Consumer and 1992. Suggest that the bulk of British industry has simply not woken up to the threats and emerging opportunities. Also stress the need for standards and agreed criteria in this area, particularly in relation to green labelling and environmental auditing.

Discussion of Mrs Thatcher's impending conference. Feeling that it will be used by some Third World countries as a platform for hitting out at the developed countries — Richard suggests the PM should be encouraged to operate on 'a long fuse'. Tim stresses that the ozone issue is only the beginning: similar conferences will be needed on many other global issues.

John Knill says that research on the oceans is an even more important research priority than tropical forests — and so far badly underfunded. British industry, he warns, is going to have to wean itself from the 'dilute and disperse' approach to effluent and waste disposal. Instead, we will need to aim for waste reduction, coupled with the concentration of toxic materials — with more attention to the 'disarm and destroy' approach to waste treatment.

Caithness is concerned and coherent. Genuinely looking around for ways of using his position to improve matters, but very much focusing on market-solutions. It's a hopeful sign that the Department is clearly taking wider soundings, but it will be interesting to see how far the messages communicated tonight penetrate into the Department's mental woodwork.

MARCH

Wednesday 1 March
Walk through biting cold wind and drifting litter to Friends of the Earth's offices. Meeting with Jonathon Porritt and Julia to discuss plans for 1989, including Green Kitchen and Green Shopping Day. Jonathon looks deeply tired: says he generally gets into work at 06.00. Success in this area rarely comes easy.

FoE will support Green Shopping Day and are also planning to integrate a consumer dimension into all their campaigns. Like Sustain-Ability, they will be focusing on energy efficiency. Suggest a meeting to talk through reservations about green consumerism with carefully selected group of environmentalists: Jonathon agrees. [Due to pressure of events, the meeting fails to materialise.]

Drive with Julia to Queen Elizabeth II conference centre, where the DoE is launching its 'Environment in Trust' pack. Cream bun and coffee in small cafe. Unfortunately for Government, FoE's report, *The Environment: The Government's Record*, also hits the headlines today. FoE lists 55 'sins of omission or commission' — including delaying EEC air pollution controls, weakening sewage discharge restrictions and under-funding HM Pollution Inspectorate. Overall assessment: very poor.

Nicholas Ridley, according to FoE, remains one of the least-loved, most controversial Environment Secretaries ever. FoE wonders how Mrs Thatcher's Government can face up to one of the greatest challenges of the 20th century under the guidance of a man who 'holds all environmentalists in contempt and whose grasp of environmental issues remains pretty patchy'.

Other news stories include the following. Earth Resources Research, on behalf of the 'nuclear-free' local authorities, claims UK emergency plans for dealing with nuclear accidents are among the world's worst. Hardly surprising, since the nuclear industry cannot imagine the circumstances in which a major nuclear disaster would happen here.

Celebrities like Cliff Richard and Terry Wogan are criticised in the House of Lords for the 'rape' of Scotland's Flow Country, where areas of considerable conservation value have been ploughed for tax-shelter conifer plantations. Once again, the environmental lobby is trying to flush out some of the individuals behind the problem.

Pete Wilkinson, the ex-Greenpeace Director, is returning to Britain from Antarctica to launch a new campaigning organisation, Greenwave. [Sadly for Wilkinson, the name was subsequently filched by the National Front, see 18 December.]

In China, the country's first environmental group has been launched to stop the building of the world's largest dam on the Yangtse River. The $11 billion Three Gorges scheme is gargantuan: an astounding 1.1 million people would be displaced.

'We shall, of course, save the Earth,' says Christopher Patten, Minister for Overseas Development, in today's *Times*. 'There is no other option. But the hard, grinding everyday work has to start now. We have written the reports and suffered the disasters. Now it's time to roll up our sleeves and get down to the job.'

Roll up my sleeves and take the Inter-City train to Bristol, where I'm due to speak at the Green Business conference at the University. Kick off the conference. Other speakers include Dr Ian Borthwick from BP, Giles Chitty (Financial Initiative) and David Cope (CEED).

Helen Holdaway comments later how easy it is to get caught up in the environmental establishment, as embodied by the Royal Society of Arts, and miss out on what is happening with the younger generation. What strikes me most forcibly is that they are much more positive these days, at least as interested in possible solutions as they are in problems.

Thursday 2 March
Start off at PMA with David Cadman and Julia. On to London Ecology Centre, for Green Kitchen launch. Wide Open have organised it very well and the press turn-out is very good. Charles Secrett chairs and Jonathon Porritt opens, stressing the key role of the Green Consumer. He suggests that the CFC saga is a harbinger of further big changes that will be forced on industry and government. Likely target areas include tropical hardwoods and energy efficiency.

John Hume of Johnson Wax and Ian Blair of AEG briefly describe what their companies have done. Johnson Wax took CFCs out of their aerosols in 1976, losing some 10% of their turnover as an immediate result. John stresses the need for continuous improvements: today's environment-friendly product may not be tomorrow's. Ian notes that AEG has had a green 'E' (for Ecology and Economy) button on its washing machines for years. Early washing machines used 200 litres of water and 5 kilowatt-hours of electricity, he recalls, whereas today's AEG machines use 68 litres of water and 1.3 kWh. The response is good and bodes well for the future.

Watch Mrs Thatcher being interviewed by Michael Buerk on the 'Nature' programme. She really is a Tartar — and regularly distorts the facts to fit in with her world-view. But she does come across as much more committed than she would have been in 1988. She also points out that she intervened twice to save the British Antarctic Survey a number of years back — and it was the BAS that identified the first ozone hole.

Friday 3 March
Julia on TV-am and ITV's 'The Time, The Place' this morning. Good performances, although the Green Kitchen doesn't get a mention. The second programme was utterly appalling. The presenter was just about as ignorant as it is possible to be on environmental issues. He linked tropical forest destruction to the use of paper tissues to blow one guest's nose, for example. Julia picked him up on that point and a number of others. But his main aim seemed to be turn the whole thing into Christian vs. Lions, generating heat not light. It really is very difficult to judge that middle line between effective use of the media and crass over-exposure. Hopefully Anne Dimmock, who came in yesterday and seems keen on helping us out on the PR side, will help us work out a sensible strategy.

Yesterday the Market Research Society in Brighton heard a report from Cathy Hawes, a Director of Diagnostics Market Research, that while consumers may be prepared to show token support for the environment, most of them are at best pale Green. 'The stereotype of lentil chewing, open-toe-sandalled conservationists deters consumers from going whole-heartedly Green,' she concluded, 'and the feeling that we are individually powerless to change our environment makes many people feel apathetic.' She is right, of course, which is why we launched the Green Consumer. If we can get people to take small steps, they may begin to believe that the longer haul to a greener world is both necessary and achievable. Hopefully, the Green Kitchen will help on that front. It is covered in the *Daily Mail*, *Daily Telegraph* and *Evening Standard* today.

Day started with uproar: John Hume of Johnson Wax has spotted a phrase in the brochure which he hadn't previously seen, suggesting that UK household aerosols contain CFCs. I call him and David Roberts, Director of the British Aerosols Manufacturers' Association, and it looks as though it is something of a storm in a tea-cup. BAMA is in turmoil at the moment. Glaxo resigned yesterday, because of BAMA's impending announcement that it would promote a complete move away from CFCs. Glaxo, whose plants I have visited in the UK and France, uses CFCs in medical products and feels that it should be able to continue to use them. But, while the company will fight hard for CFCs, it is developing alternative methods for delivering many of its drugs.

Today's newspapers are full of the news that European Environment Ministers have agreed in Brussels to press for the phasing out of all CFCs by the end of the century. The British delegation, led by Lord Caithness, was apparently upstaged by other European countries demanding cuts of 95% — and then 100% — by the year 2000. The British Government had planned to call for an 85% ban at its 'Saving the Ozone Layer' conference this weekend.

Received an invitation this morning to a HM Government reception hosted by Nicholas Ridley on Sunday. He seems to have been outflanked by Mrs Thatcher, who is talking in terms of banning CFCs used in fridges at a time when her Environment Secretary is still saying that such bans will not be attempted. 62% of the CFCs released in Britain last year came from aerosols, a source which should have been 90% phased out by the end of 1989. Of the remaining 38%, fridges account for 8%; foams, including fast-food packaging, for 18%; and solvents for 12%.

A quirky Green Consumer campaign announced today: the Royal Society for Nature Conservation is calling for a Mother's Day boycott of daffodils. The RSNC accuses Cornish flower growers of using the highly toxic pesticide Aldrin against narcissus fly infestations. High concentration of the pesticide have been found in eels in the Newlyn River, near Penzance, and the RSNC is worried for the future of otters in the area.

Internationally, the *Wall Street Journal* reports that Greece is starting to go green. The country is described as 'the Gobi Desert of environmentalism; nary a green thing in sight'. But it now suffers from some of the world's worst smogs, which are corroding the Parthenon and other monuments, and Green factions — now numbering more than 100 — are surfacing all over the country. They include an Alternative Ecology Movement, as well as Friends of Bears, Seals, Turtles and Raptors.

Plans for Green Shopping Day are beginning to shape up quickly. The Heinz sponsorship possibility begins to look fairly hopeful. Plenty of 'Beanz Meanz Greens' humour. Still a strong sense that WWF's Corporate Department are wary of SustainAbility, seeing us as a potential competitor, but our objective is to work with a wide range of organisations.

Saturday 4 March
'We have become a grandmother,' Mrs Thatcher announces, using her increasingly regal style. Maybe the news that her daughter-in-law has given birth to a son in Dallas, Texas, will make the PM think even harder about the state of the environment we are leaving to future generations.

BAMA announces that aerosol manufacturers will be told to put warning labels on their cans, stressing that they contain ozone-destroying CFCs. This would certainly be a useful step, enabling Green Consumers to choose between ozone-friendly and -unfriendly brands.

Meanwhile, FoE are clearly on their toes. Beecham, which last week donned a green mantle when announcing that its toiletries division had stopped making CFC-containing aerosols, is accused of double standards by FoE's Fiona Weir. FoE have discovered that Beecham's *Ralgex* muscle pain sprays continue to use CFCs. A Beecham spokesman says that the chill effect used to ease the pain can only be achieved by CFCs — but that it is looking for alternatives.

President George Bush announces that he will support Mrs Thatcher's drive to phase out CFCs as fast as possible. At the same time, the news breaks that Ark is calling on all British MPs to sign its seven-point plan to save the world. Any who refuse will be exposed as anti-green and have their names published. We have used the same ploy with companies when sending out the Green Supermarket Questionnaire, so companies that reply honestly will not be disadvantaged because other companies decided to cover up by not answering at all. But the Ark approach with individual MPs leaves me rather uneasy. We should be aiming to persuade rather than coerce. Our approach is not to insist that people agree with us — simply that they express their views.

Further south, fears of neo-colonialism are rampant. President Sarney of Brazil claims that in many parts of the world, under the pretext of defending the environment, Western Governments are interfering in Brazil's internal problems — with the aim of re-establishing colonial domination. The suspicion must be, however, that he is using xenophobia to mask the fact that he doesn't want to — or can't — stop the destruction of Amazonia.

Sunday 5 March
Geoffrey Lean's 'How Green is the Prime Minister?' in today's *Observer* is beautifully done. He opens by quoting Mrs Thatcher during the Falklands War. 'It is exciting to have a real crisis on your hands,' she said, 'when you have spent half your political life dealing with humdrum issues like the environment.' I compliment him on the quote when we meet at the Foreign and Commonwealth Office this evening. He is waiting until the reception line has ended, so he can get past Nicholas Ridley without being intercepted and, by the sound of it, lynched or defenestrated.

The reception, for those attending Mrs T's Saving the Ozone Layer conference, is held in the Durbar Court. The smell of what I can only assume is Mrs T's perfume is still on my hands; expensive and persistent. She was the only woman I can remember shaking hands with during the evening.

Mrs T, Dennis T, Ridley, Lord Caithness and Virginia Bottomley all busily working the crowd. But talk to someone who has just talked to

Denis T, who had regaled him with stories of the way he dealt with environmentalists when running his own chemical company. Clearly, the greening of the Thatcher household is a patchy affair at best.

Mrs T dealt Ridley a back-hander yesterday, when she admitted that water privatisation has been mishandled. As Simon Jenkins says in *The Sunday Times*, Ridley 'has been jolted almost out of his political skin'. Once the scourge of the Shires, he must now incant 'lean-burn, greenhouse gases, CFC 114, carbon budgeting' daily before the TV cameras.

Among those I talk to, Sir John Mason, previously Director General of the Meteorological Office for nearly 20 years and now Chairman of the Scientific Committee of the World Climate Research Programme. He sees the ozone issue as a 'crackable problem', but is much gloomier about the Greenhouse Effect. If the temperature increases pan out around the bottom of the estimated range, he says, we can manage — if not, it's back to the Ark. But what alarms Sir John most is population. If China can't control its population, even using draconian methods, what hope is there for the rest of the Third World? And all those Chinese will be burning highly polluting soft coal and buying CFC-containing fridges. He complains that people like Dr Mostafa Tolba, who runs UNEP, still say that population is a taboo subject politically. But either we crack population — or it will crack us and any hopes we may hold for a sustainable future.

Monday 6 March
Papers full of the Ozone Conference. President Daniel arap Moi of Kenya warned: 'There can be no winners from the damage that man continues to inflict upon his own planet. We should all play our part in taking preventative action now. The evidence of impending disaster is already with us.' Many countries, he said, 'would be devastated even if only half the worst predictions were to come true in the next 50 years. The heatwaves in the United States of America and elsewhere, devastating droughts in most parts of Africa and the killer floods and hurricanes in most parts of Asia are signs of worse events to follow the global warming-up. With seas expanding, whole areas, even entire countries, could disappear under water. Vast areas face the grim future of being turned into dustbowls.' Welcome words, especially from a Third World politician, but Kenya's population boom renders it a prime candidate for future dustbowling.

The Third World would not find it easy to forego CFCs, he warned. Many countries are only just beginning to use CFCs in refrigeration, air-conditioning, plastics or the electronics industry. If the ozone layer is to be protected the developed nations must make sacrifices commensurate in magnitude with those expected from the Third World nations that must forego the use of these ozone-depleting chemicals. Chinese say they will sign the Montreal Protocol only if it is changed to include financial support for Third World countries.

Dr Sherwood Rowland, one of the American scientists who first identified the potential danger from CFCs in the early 1970s, warned that our level of understanding is still so poor that there would inevitably be some nasty surprises.

Mrs Thatcher has caused a storm in the fridge industry, having advised consumers not to buy fridges for 'a year or two' — or until ozone-friendly fridges come on the market. They may have to wait at least five years, the industry says. A prime example of the way in which the switch to more sustainable technologies must drive 'green growth'. Across to Earl's Court for the opening of the Green Kitchen. Excellent speech by Jonathon Porritt. Good deal of apparent media interest. But the Ideal Home Exhibition is not somewhere I would want to spend very much time!

Interesting news from Germany. The Greens' congress at Duisberg over the weekend votes in three moderates as speakers, or chairmen. The *Fundis*, who had held many of the key posts in recent years, lost out to *Realos*, or moderates, and the Green Awakening, a group which spans all factions. The endless squabbling in the party had almost blown it apart, although the latest moves may persuade some of the more radical elements to leave the party.

Wednesday 8 March
Bright sunny day as Julia and I drive down to WWF. Discussion of Green Label scheme and prospect of Heinz or other sponsorship for Green Shopping Day. They are now lobbying to have the day as the WWF Green Shopping Day, rather than Heinz Green Shopping Day. We eventually agree 'Green Shopping Day, sponsored by Company X via WWF'.

There is no question but that they are enthused about the potential, although there are some sensitivities about the simultaneous publication of *The Green Consumer's Supermarket Shopping Guide* — which could well end up criticising key companies. The subject of the need for audits keeps surfacing at WWF. On return to Barnes, complete Green Label proposal for WWF, to pass on to the DoE. Whether or not this proposal goes through, it is absolutely essential that a labelling scheme is got off the ground. If we can avoid having to do it ourselves, so much the better — but we will find it hard to keep consumer confidence without such a scheme.

Interestingly, in light of 4 March diary entry, Mrs T closed the 124-

nation ozone layer conference by saying that the birth of her first grandson had given her environmental crusade 'a greater and deeper personal meaning'. Overall, the conference has been judged a considerable success. When it opened only 33 Governments had signed the 1987 Montreal Protocol. Yesterday another 20, including Brazil, committed themselves to doing so, while a similar number said they would consider signing at a later date. India and China are among their number, but stress that the West will need to supply aid and technology to sweeten the deal.

The continuing scale of the problem is indicated by the fact that even if CFCs were banned tomorrow, it would take 100 years to replenish the ozone already lost.

Riveting aside during the press conference when Mrs T announced plans to double the UK's contribution to UNEP, which she said was £1.5 million. Mr Ridley promptly chipped in to say that the figure should be £1.25 million, which would be doubled to £2.5 million. 'Well, put it up to £1.5 million and then we can double it to £3 million,' she retorted. 'That will teach people not to give you the wrong briefing. The Treasury will have to find the money.' Even so, *Today* contrasts this £3 million with the £19 billion Britain spends each year on defence!

Thursday 9 March
The role of public opinion is underscored by three news items today. First, British Rail has said that it will put more than two-thirds of the high-speed link from London to the Chunnel below ground, either in tunnels or cuttings. Second, the Hungarian Government may consider a referendum on the controversial plan to build a hydro-electric dam at Gabcikovo-Nagymaros. People in Budapest are wearing blue and white badges symbolising resistance to the dam and concern about the environment. More than 130,000 people have signed petitions.

And third, further west, the European Commission has backed down on clean cars: growing public pressure has convinced the Commission that it might have to allow the Dutch Government to offer tax incentives (about £470 for cars meeting tougher US emission standards) to motorists who switch to cars fitted with catalytic converters. The Commission still worries that the incentives will distort European trade, however, and may take the case to the European Court of Justice.

BP launches 'Super Green' today, a higher grade of unleaded fuel which could allow an extra million drivers to use unleaded. Our Volvo has had to be retuned — and the engine now refuses to turn off when the ignition is turned off. It continues to grunt, cough and shake as though there were a herd of elephants mating under the bonnet.

In South America, meanwhile, eight countries are circling their wagons, accusing foreign powers of trying to turn the region into 'a green Persian Gulf'. The Brazilian Government has described international attempts to protect Amazonia as 'just a greener form of imperialism'. This is going to be a continuing bone of contention until Third World countries recognise that the industrialised countries are becoming genuinely concerned about the implications for their own futures of the environmental trends in the 'developing' world.

On a related issue, The Body Shop announces that it will launch a rainforest range of cosmetics by next spring. And a US ice-cream maker, Ben & Jerry, plans to launch a range of ices using rainforest ingredients! Such developments could be helpful if the ingredients came from sustainably managed rainforests.

Both *Design Week* and *Marketing Week* cover us today. *Marketing Week*'s editorial warns: 'If they avoid the temptation of short-term opportunism, manufacturers stand to benefit from consumer concern for the environment. But anybody who underestimates the potency of the Green issue, or thinks they can get by with token gestures, is heading for a fall.'

Friday 10 March
Red noses everywhere as Comic Relief hits the streets. Ten million plastic noses have apparently been made. One correspondent to the letters page of *The Times* asks readers to suggest alternative uses once it is all over. Gaia leaves for school wearing an elaborate crown made from red balls, noses and garden wire. Oxford psychologist tells the *Daily Telegraph* that the red-nosed car establishes 'a tribal connection, the publicising of an allegiance to a new value, of caring at a time when society has become more materialistic.'

See a number of clowns in the Shepherd's Bush area as I drive across to Brand New for meeting with Alberto-Culver. One pub actually sports a 10-foot red nose. And Alberto-Culver seem to want to sport a green nose: they ask how they should set about doing an environmental audit.

Out this evening for brief drinks with friends. Borne in on me the extent to which the pace of work is cutting into any social life we might have had.

Yesterday the US outlined long-awaited proposals to ease the heavy debt burden weighing on many developing countries. They are outline proposals, rather than blueprints, but a hopeful step nonetheless. Total developing country debt amounts to $1,200 *billion*, half of which is owed by countries with debt problems. Result: an accelerated pace of environmental destruction.

In the Hague, meanwhile, 24 countries call for a stronger UN body to enforce environmental standards for the atmosphere. A French initiative on Dutch soil. The US, Soviet Union and China were excluded from the invitation list! In Berlin, a Red–Green coalition Government is finalised for the city, linking the Social Democrats and the Alternative List – or Greens.

Sunday 12 March
The Sunday Times today leads on 'Britain's water rats', putting the spotlight on 'guilty' chairmen of water authorities with sewage works with the worst pollution records: John Bellak (Severn-Trent), Bernard Henderson (Anglian), Sir Michael Straker (Northumbrian), John Elfed Jones (Welsh Water) and Roy Watts (Thames). Piece is titled: 'Water bosses who let sewage pour into rivers.' The total bill for ridding rivers of raw and substandard sewage could exceed £1.6 billion. If it does nothing else, privatisation is certainly turning up the heat under the water industry.

According to Alan Vedgley in the *Observer*, *The Sunday Times* editorial conference a couple of weeks ago suddenly realised that almost an entire issue of the paper had 'gone green'. Four feature articles had to be pulled at the last minute to restore some sort of balance!

A worrying example of the feeding frenzy which develops in media-land. The faster the publicity bubble expands, the sooner and more devastatingly it will burst.

Internationally, the conference in The Hague ends up calling for major new moves to tackle the Greenhouse Effect. The international leaders present — including Brundtland, Kohl, Lubbers, Mitterrand, Mulroney and Mugabe — warn that the very conditions of life on our planet are under threat. A global response is needed. But, following intense political pressure, they backed away from calling for the launch of 'Globe', a new global pollution control body.

Strong political pressure would be appropriate in Tanzania at the moment. The country looks set to be the first African country to call for an international ban on the ivory trade. According to John Merritt in the *Observer*, 200 tusks were discovered last month in a container owned by the departing Indonesian ambassador. The seizure, said Tanzania's Wildlife Conservation Society, was just 'the tip of the iceberg'.

In the afternoon, take the family across to the Ideal Home Exhibition in Earl's Court. Verging on rain, streets seething with traffic, nowhere to park. An explosive car-crash happens right alongside, with bonnets and boots erupting into the air. Late for book-signing session, so finally park on a yellow line over ten minutes' walk away.

Get lost in the gormless, burger-munching throngs inside, but finally battle way up to the comparative oasis of the Green Kitchen stand. Very busy and *The Guide* is selling well. Sign a couple of box-loads of books, with the help of a production line set up by Gaia and Hania. Lisa seems to be doing well, but tired like everyone else.

Monday 13 March

SAVE OUR POLLUTED PLANET PLEA BY GREEN QUEEN reads the headline in *Today*. In her annual broadcast to the Commonwealth today, the Queen calls for a common partnership to conserve the world 'not only across the oceans but also between generations'.

Can Mrs Thatcher keep up? Lovely piece on green politics in *The Independent* by Jill Tweedie. The real message of the last 20 years, she says, is that: 'Our elected leaders, of whatever political hue, had somehow managed to walk blind and deaf through two decades of a green revolution and emerge with the foresight of moles, the future timescale of mayflies, and less knowledge of environmental issues than a shoal of dead fish. We must not be bamboozled. Whatever our politics and however content we may be with other policies, we should not be seduced by the efforts of politicians to convince us that the planet is safe in their hands.' Timely advice.

In France, meanwhile, the first round of the municipal elections suggest that the Greens have arrived as a serious force in French politics. They may hold the balance between left and right in many communes in the second round, next Sunday. Perhaps this is also the shape of things to come in Britain — but I have an instinct that the Greens won't get genuinely airborne until Doomsday arrives.

Fascinating call from Australia this morning. Kevin Condon is a marketing man who has worked for many of the big supermarket groups there, including Woolworth, and sees the environment as a rapidly building wave in Australia. He says that over the ten years he has lived in the country you could actually feel the sun's rays becoming more intense. One in three or four Australians have melanoma, or skin cancer. The thinning of the ozone layer is acutely felt there. And the pollution of coastal waters is beginning to hit back. Fish sales at the Sydney fish market dropped 40% over the last few weeks, following scares about sewage pollution. With *The Guide* coming out over there, he may be a very useful ally. Must fax him with suggestions of how we might work together.

Talk with Association of Metropolitan Authorities about July conference at which they want me to help run a Green Purchasing seminar. Suggest idea of questionnaire survey of all local authorities to see what they are doing — and might do — to specify environment-friendly goods when purchasing. The idea looks as though it might fly.

Wednesday 15 March

Yesterday's *Financial Times* reports on launch of new Green Party in Egypt. Having worked there in 1975, am particularly interested. The new party's founder is Dr Bahaadin Bakri. Says one aim is to help Egyptians appreciate their environment. 'People have to be educated how to see beauty and how to feel it,' he says. 'They have become too used to an environment full of ugliness.' Having spent some time in Cairo, I was not surprised to learn that this city of 14 million people has an average of just ten square centimetres of green space for each inhabitant!

The Chancellor, reports *The Times*, has put Britain's motorists on the road to a 'green revolution' with a decisive cut in the duty on unleaded petrol. It's now 10p cheaper. Press is full of full-page unleaded ads by Esso, Volkswagen and Tesco. 'We live on a vulnerable planet,' says Esso's ad. 'We must learn how to care for it.' The company's Unleaded Airship will be throbbing overhead in the coming weeks.

Meanwhile the garage, having tried to retune the Volvo to help it run on unleaded without 'pinking' so much, stun us by saying that it probably never should have been run on unleaded. Conversion, they say, will cost over £160 and the performance will be noticeably worse. The main Volvo garage are appalling. They say they don't know anything about unleaded. The local garage say if we convert the car we'll be the first Volvo owners to do so. Seems utterly incredible — most of these people seem utterly ignorant and prepared to lie between their teeth as long as the problem will, please, go away.

Meeting with Jeyes Fluid. They have been in business for 110 years and are well established in the niche markets where they operate. Now the supermarkets are asking Jeyes to make them 'own brand' green products. Jeyes seem keen, but want to know how they should set about it. We agree to meet them again in April. Dorothy describes environmental issues as 'spongey' issues — with a tendency, I add, to turn to the consistency of breeze-block overnight.

Pick up a copy of the latest issue of *Marketing Week* during the day and find myself on the front cover. The profile, entitled 'Pragmatist with a Green Belt', is very positive, but does quote one unidentified — but not unidentifiable — environmentalist who has this to say of me: 'On the one hand I would say that he is a very good thinker and has got a good grasp of the various issues involved. But from the environmental pressure group point of view he is considered a bit of a sell-out. He is a bit like the Polyfilla between the environmentalists on one side and industry on the other, and as such he comes in for some stick; the environmentalists think that he is not doing enough, while companies think he is dark Green.'

The piece goes on to say: 'That said, there is little doubt that his heart is in the right place and that he is trying to make companies take a more responsible attitude towards the environment.' Suspect that the supermarkets at the moment wish we were behaving rather more like Polyfilla! People like Denis Hayes are fascinated to know more about how we have managed to catch industry's ear.

This evening chair a conference organised by the Chemical Industries Association at the Society of Chemical Industry, in Belgrave Square. Lively debate, with a number of industry people effectively calling for a Green Label scheme.

Julia has left for the States and Canada.

Thursday 16 March
Yet another fax from lawyers representing manufacturers of cling-film, who say we are libelling them in *The Guide*. Our latest wording, which does not give the plasticizer DEHA a 100% clean bill of health, is challenged. Something else for tomorrow. Gollancz ring during the morning to say McDonald's are already challenging what I have said about rainforests and the 'Hamburger culture'. Read through the English text and decide there is no problem: let McDonald's bleat.

Feeling half-dead by end of day. Interesting to note in today's *Times* that British preference for being cremated saves an estimated 200 acres of land every year. Since 1950, the number of crematoria has increased from 58 to 223 and cremation accounts for 70% of all funerals. But now, presumably, we should also be thinking of cremation's contributions to carbon dioxide emissions and global warming!

Friday 17 March
Long telephone conversation with Janet Barber of WWF about the Green Tourism project, where I insist we are in danger of failing to exploit the potential for changing hearts and minds in the industry unless we can get WWF funding in short order. She says she will have another look at the proposal and try it out on her WWF International Conservation Review Committee.

Exhausted to the point of near-collapse. Am experiencing mild heart-pains, but a sense of being borne along on a constantly accelerating conveyor. 1989 is turning us all into green workaholics. Am assuming that the pains will go away.

Afternoon spent mail-merging all the letters for the environmental audit report consultation process. Also do interviews with *Daily Express* and *Business Week*. Denis Hayes, who is organising Earth Day for next April, calls late afternoon. Invites me to join international board of sponsors of Earth Day 1990; agree in principle. One of the first generation of environmentalists — and strange to talk to him after an eight-year gap.

Over in Norway, meanwhile, Gro Harlem Brundtland is under fire because the latest draft of an eagerly awaited Government white paper has been leaked — and is denounced by opposition parties and environmentalists. It contains 'no concrete actions for sustainable development' and emissions of carbon dioxide are not to be reduced before the end of the century, while energy consumption — among the highest in the world — is likely to increase by 30%.

And another whaling nation, Japan, is incensed that Greenpeace has successfully disrupted its 'scientific' whaling operations in the Antarctic. The Japanese are calling Greenpeace terrorists on the high seas, and have so far caught 'only' 220 Minke whales, rather than the 300 they set out to catch. Most environmentalists see this 'scientific' whaling as simply a ruse on the part of a nation of whalemeat-eaters to get around the International Whaling Commission's 1982 moratorium on Antarctic whaling.

Saturday 18 March
This morning's *Guardian* carries my piece on fridges and the ozone layer. The cartoon shows a junkyard of fridges, with a vaporous wraith of CFCs, topped off with a bird's skull head, rising from the scrapped fridges and freezers.

Interesting article by film-maker David Puttnam in *The Independent*. He fears that the advertising industry is playing into the hands of the Government, which is in the process of identifying the citizen with 'that most identifiable object of the 1980s — the consumer'. This, he suggests may be convenient 'and even invidiously accurate', but 'it is also dangerously reductive. Consuming, be it goods or services, is only *part* of what we do. More importantly, it is only a small part of what we are, certainly as thinking individuals'. The challenge for the advertising industry in the 1990s will be not just to 'force-feed' its creation, the consumer, but also to begin to address some of the wider issues — including environmental issues — which increasingly concern all of us.

Interestingly, CBI President Sir Trevor Holdsworth has just told companies that they should seize the environmental initiative, to avoid being forced into action by pressure groups. Too many firms, he says, are 'keeping their heads down in the increasingly forlorn hope that the public and the media will not be interested' in the environmental impacts of their activities and products.

The same message has been brought home to the Brazilians. Charles Clover reports in the *Daily Telegraph* that the controversial $500 million World Bank loan for energy projects, including the Altamira dam complex, has been killed. Instead, President Sarney's government has accepted a new $300 million 'environmental' World Bank loan, which will be used to fund a new 'super environment industry' in the debt-ridden country.

Work on proposal for Rolex Award for Enterprise. Suggest a Green Tourist Award, with millions of brochures handed out to tourists during 1990, inviting an essay on the environmental pressures affecting the country, region or resort they are visiting — and suggesting ways of greening tourism.

But one of the most interesting new developments is the news that City investors, including the Norwich Union, Refuge Assurance and Pearl Assurance, are writing to the companies pilloried in 26 February's *Sunday Times* and asking what they intend to do to clean up their act. They, and the Church Commissioners, may 'disinvest' if they are dissatisfied with the response. The Norwich Union alone holds 1.6% of ICI, 4.6% of Coalite, 1.43% of RTZ Chemicals, 4.3% of Grand Metropolitan (which owns the Express Foods Group) and 2% of Coats Viyella.

Nicholas Ridley, admitting that Britain is a 'dirty nation', is now trying to lay the blame wholly on the country's town halls. 'We are declaring war on litter,' says Mrs T. 'Bag it and bin it and that way we'll win it.' Adspeak for 'leave it to the citizen-consumer'? Like many other environmental problems, litter needs new legislation and a commitment to enforcing tough penalties. Will Mrs T grasp this green nettle?

The real horror of today, though, was the news that Julia's flight back from Toronto was delayed by 24 hours. Will have to try to get her green suit to her at Heathrow tomorrow morning. Problem is that Heathrow won't accept packages for obvious reasons.

Monday 20 March
Get to Terminal 4 at 07.40, but flight delayed another hour. Toss bag to Julia as she runs out of Customs. Get her into cab for Terminal 1. She gets her flight to Newcastle with seconds to spare.

Meanwhile, Greenpeace are talking of risk of a 'marine Chernobyl' off Guernsey. Six tons of Lindane have gone adrift from a Panamanian freighter which went down last Monday. Dr Paul Johnston says all marine life could be devastated in a strip of sea 440 miles long and 25 miles wide. Greenpeace grab the headlines — but may have got their science slightly in a twist. *Daily Telegraph* quotes a NERC marine toxicologist, who admits that the effects could be felt over 10–20 miles, 'but in terms of everything being eradicated in the English Channel, that is preposterous.'

Another example of Greenpeace exaggeration — or a genuine catastrophe in the making? There is a real possibility that if environmentalists continually over-exaggerate, the media and public will simply switch off.

Talk of spectre of a new dustbowl — and worldwide food shortages in the *Guardian*. Dust clouds have been sweeping across the American Midwest, whipped up from drought-parched fields by 60 mph winds. The Worldwatch Institute is asking whether global warming will bring more droughts in the States? This is one area where it is hard to exaggerate the threat. The combination of exploding populations and an eroding agricultural resource can only spell long-term trouble.

Tuesday 21 March
Martin Stott calls from Oxford City Council to say that they have voted unanimously to launch a fridge collection and CFC recycling scheme, apparently the first authority in the country to do so. Apparently my piece in Saturday's *Guardian* sparked off the idea.

Call Tessa Tennant to congratulate her on appearing on the front page of the second section of the *Wall Street Journal* today, warning that the rapidly growing investor interest in the shares of ecologically sound companies could well come to grief. 'There are many fund managers and investors who are acting like cowboys,' she says, 'and spreading a lot of misinformation. If you want to speculate and play the market, that's fine, but if you're concerned about the issues, and want to invest in stocks that are profitable as well as clean, then there are only certain carefully selected stocks.'

Fascinating profile in the *Guardian* of Maggie McCaw, a long-time Greenpeace campaigner currently serving as a deck-hand on the *Gondwana*, which is re-supplying Greenpeace's base at Ross Island. Has been to prison in Canada (for parachuting into a nuclear power plant), California (for trespassing in a nuclear weapons factory) and Norway (for chaining herself to the crow's nest of a whaler). Contrast between her background, working for 11 years at the 'sharp end', generally for no pay, and the new Greenpeace, with three million members worldwide and a mountain of cash. The organisation's 17 national offices are 'stuffed with armchair campaigners,' she says, 'who see Greenpeace as a career move, a stepping stone to other better jobs.' Real clash of cultures, but we have got to work out of ways of recruiting — and keeping — a much broader mix of people in the movement.

69

Wednesday 22 March
Meeting with Dow Europe at 15.30. Roger Fawdry who has been parachuted in as Dow's Manager, Environmental Affairs, asks what the company's image looks like from outside. Pull no punches: say Dow is in many ways still seen as the 'Great Satan' by environmentalists, because of the napalm (Dow made it), 'Agent Orange' herbicide (used in the jungle defoliation programmes) and dioxin (which contaminated the herbicides) controversies during the Vietnam War, plus extremely hard-nosed approach to PR since. They turned US Environmental Protection Agency officials off their sites and one manager leaked the (false) information that a Greenpeace activist had VD to the media.

Once Dow could get away with playing 'hard-ball', because its name didn't go on its products in the same way as a consumer products manufacturer's name might. Dow made commodity chemicals bought by other companies, who bought on the basis of price. Today, however, chemical companies are all trying to move into 'speciality' chemicals — and a company's name and image counts.

Dow appears keen to think through how it might start to green its image. Agree that Roger will send us a brief and that we will then put together a position paper, to be followed by a presentation to senior people in the company.

Next, Merlin Ecology Fund meeting. Fascinating interplay between investment and ecological priorities. With £3 million already in, Tessa is confident that at least another £2–£3 million can be raised this year.

Prepare Alberto-Culver proposal.

Thursday 23 March
Strange day: *The Sunday Times* calls to say that British Telecom has announced that it plans to sign a contract with us next week, opening up a complete District to us for an environmental audit. First I have heard of it. Ring Guy Dauncey, who chases the story through the system, and finds that it's based on fact. I call BT, who say they want to proceed to a pilot exercise, with the possibility of going national later. Part of the reason for all this activity has been the announcement by two big city firms, Touche Ross and Coopers Lybrand, that they plan to break into environmental auditing.

Turn down Channel 4 Green Consumer slot. Even though it would have been on a fortnightly basis, all these commitments are piling up. Even if we have an unusually high failure rate on the proposals that we currently have out, we are going to be overwhelmed with work.

Politics here: Nicholas Ridley admits that about 14% of sewage in England and Wales is discharged untreated into the sea, whatever Mrs T may have adamantly claimed the other day. The French are still looking for the Lindane: what they thought was the container turned out to be a block of concrete. In a letter to *The Times*, Sarah Gretton suggests that all toxic chemical containers should carry signalling devices, in case of shipwreck. An excellent, practical, timely idea. Which probably means this will be the last we hear of it.

Financial Times profiles Rentokil, which has been pilloried for using wood treatment products based on Lindane. 'Environment is the buzz-word,' the paper says. 'Rentokil now has about 60% of the third-party pest control business so future growth is likely to come from overseas or from newer green interests, ranging from servicing tropical plants to disposing of waste medical equipment.' *Green?*

The UN convention controlling the trade in hazardous wastes has been agreed by 116 countries meeting in Basle, subject to final vetting by lawyers. Insists that countries exporting waste should have the written assent of importing countries for each specific cargo. But waste producing countries have not been made responsible for the ultimate disposal of such wastes. Nor will there be automatic inspection of Third World disposal sites. There should be.

Friday 24 March

In the States, a new report from the Environmental Protection Agency shows that around 2.4 billion pounds of toxic chemicals — 60 of them potentially cancer-causing — are being pumped into the air each year. 'The magnitude of the problem exceeds our worst fears,' said Congressman Henry Waxman of California. The figures, which are a considerable shock to ordinary Americans, do not include car emissions, factory emissions or toxins produced by waste dumps.

Meanwhile Professors Martin Fleischmann of Southampton University and Stan Pons of Utah University claim to have carried out controlled nuclear fusion in a test-tube. Fusion power, which has been the great white hope of the nuclear industry, has looked more attractive as fission has hit one problem after another.

Fusion could prove to be a cleaner and much more abundant source of nuclear power, but the approaches used to date have been enormously complex, exceedingly expensive and depressingly unsuccessful. Fleischmann and Pons claim that they have tricked deuterium, a type of hydrogen atom, into fusing. Previously, scientists thought that fusion was only possible at temperatures of more than 100 million degrees Centigrade.

Although there is widespread scepticism among those who have been failing while throwing much larger sums of money at the problem, which has to be cracked if nuclear fusion is ever to become a viable source of energy, the implications of the latest announcement are potentially profound. *The Times* today says that it could be the 'great breakthrough of the century' — which is saying a great deal in a century which has seen the launch of gene-splicing and the development of computers which can just about sit on a pin-head.

Saturday 25 March
In Alaska, an 11-million gallon oil spill threatens an ecological catastrophe. A giant oil tanker has run aground near the Valdez oil terminal, near the migratory routes of 13 species of whale. The tanker, the *Exxon Valdez*, was apparently taking an unauthorised route to avoid ice floes when it hit a reef clearly plotted on the charts.

Monday 27 March
Bank Holiday Monday. Beautiful day, predominantly spent at the word-processor. Julia ploughs on through the supermarket questionnaires. Despite the fact that it's Easter, the new environment correspondent of *Scotland-on-Sunday* calls to interview me for next weekend's paper. They plan to launch a regular Green Consumer column.

Janet Barber comes to lunch. Coincidentally, she is quoted in the *Guardian* today, in an article on the threat posed to wildlife by such projects as winter sports developments, hydroelectric dams and fish farms funded by EEC regional aid. 'Unless positive action is taken,' she says, 'the valuable wildlife of southern Europe and Ireland could be irreversibly damaged by inappropriate developments.' £35 billion in aid will be spent over the next five years: can Europe's environmental assessment resources keep pace? Interestingly, WWF are repositioning themselves as an environmental organisation, rather than a wildlife organisation.

State of emergency declared in Alaska. Hear the Governor of Alaska on Radio 4 at around 23.15, while finishing off the draft detergents section for *The Supermarket Guide*. The captain was apparently not on the bridge when the *Exxon Valdez* hit Bligh reef last Friday. Ship was one-and-a-half miles from approved shipping lane and has spilled 11 million gallons of oil into the heart of one of the richest marine environments in North America.

Tuesday 28 March
The economic boom of the Nineties will cause massive destruction of both the countryside and wildlife, according to the Council for the Preservation of Rural England (CPRE). While there may well be recessions, the impact of the Single European Market from 1992 looks set to fuel economic growth Community-wide.

Renault, the state-owned French car firm says it will break ranks with other European car makers and produce all its cars with catalytic converter systems from 1993. The decision is seen as a question of make-or-break for the company. The company produces two million cars a year and estimates that 'clean cars' could be up to 10% more expensive. I wonder.

Exxon, meanwhile, admits that the man at the helm of the *Exxon Valdez* was the third mate, who wasn't qualified to navigate in such waters.

And Edward Abbey is dead. He wrote *The Monkey Wrench Gang* in 1975, a book that advocated 'ecotage', or sabotage of polluting industrial plants by environmentalists. Groups like Earth First! and (the clearly-not-humourless bugbear of the biotechnology industry) Mindless Thugs Against Biotechnology have continued to carry the torch he lit. The role of environmental vigilantes may become more of an issue in the 1990s.

A boom of rabbits here. Gaia and Hania now have three baby rabbits, whose long ears and wide eyes often interrupt work. Something of a struggle to convince the girls that rabbits don't need central heating and that their hutches can go outside.

Wednesday 29 March
Day starts at 07.30 with meeting with Stephen Ronaldson, possible new lawyer for SustainAbility. Seems very much on the ball. Like it or not, lawyers are indispensable even to a small business like ours. And as we go international and companies become more sensitive to what we say, our need for legal advice can only grow.

On the political front, the Green Party hit the headlines today: they announce they will run a full slate of 78 candidates for election to the European Parliament in June. No Green candidate has so far succeeded in saving his or her deposit, either in elections for Westminster or the European Parliament. The June elections will be an interesting litmus test of the greening of politics.

Unfortunately, the news coincides with news of a West German Green scandal. Alfred Mechtersheimer, the Greens' star peace campaigner, proves to be linked with a $10 million MAG (an acronym which apparently stands for Muammar al-Gaddafi) 'Foundation for Peace and Solidarity', set up with the help of Libyan funds. Mechtersheimer vigorously denies that he has become a lobbyist for Colonel Gaddafi. 'The petro-dollars of a North African country are no shadier than the profits of a Swedish explosives producer who founded the Nobel Prize,' he is quoted as saying by *The Independent*. 'What is important is what they are used for.' Other Greens are appalled by the accusations, remembering a speech by Mechtersheimer in February in which he claimed that the Libyan plant suspected of making chemical warfare weapons was only making pharmaceuticals.

Thursday 30 March
Working day begins with interesting meeting here with Marks & Spencer's new manager for green issues, David Morgan. M&S, though coming from behind, seem to be determined to get ahead of the game if they possibly can.

Later Carlo, the decorator, is stunned when he opens the door mid-morning to find Anne Diamond on the threshold. She had come to see Julia. I disappear at 12.00 to a lunch hosted by Bob Worcester, Chairman of MORI, the opinion poll people. Also at the lunch are George Medley of WWF, Stephen Mills, Deputy Secretary General of the International Social Science Council (ISSC), Jonathon Porritt of FoE, Professor Luis Ramallo, ISSC Secretary General and Des Wilson of CLEAR. The ISSC is planning a research programme on the Human Dimensions of Global Change.

Hot afternoon, so windows have to be opened. Some sort of unrelated demonstration going on outside, which gives the occasion an extra dimension. Luis describes the ISSC as a big sombrero — it gives you no sense of the size of head, or brain, underneath. His introduction to the Council's work is competent, but leaves the question hovering as to whether social science can ever do anything but *post mortems* on what has already happened? I have become increasingly disillusioned with social science research, despite — or perhaps because of — having taken a first degree in sociology. But suspect that this area of 'science' will really take off in the early years of the 21st century, for better or worse.

Jonathon argues forcefully that the scale of change needed means that we should be wary of mere reformism. Bob and Des disagree. Des points out that the (ultimately successful) campaign for unleaded petrol moved through a succession of small steps to achieve its goals — and in doing so helped give credibility to other environmental campaigns.

Later, the conversation moves to the likely spiritual and religious responses to the big global problems. I suggest that the response is likely to come from outside the established religions and that if it comes it could run like a prairie fire around the globe. Luis notes that Catholicism has contributed to ecological problems by persuading believers that this world is simply a stepping stone to the next. This world, as he summarises the Catholic perspective, 'is just a bad night in a bad hotel'.

Interesting, but ultimately unsatisfactory meeting. Social scientists may have a role to play, and Jonathon noted that we need new economic indicators of wealth that reflect sustainability. But on this showing, the real movement is going to come from elsewhere, with social scientists bringing up the rear.

Friday 31 March
Feeling better, if still exhausted. Working day starts with Guy Dauncey at BT, near St Pauls. Lovely weather, but with just a hint of an LA-style haze building up. BT seem very open to suggestion as to what they ought to do generally in the environmental area. Their size is extraordinary, with an annual turnover in excess of £10 billion, over 220,000 staff and handling some 25 million telephone calls a day.

Not surprisingly, they are interested to know what staff resources *we* can bring to bear. It looks as though we shall also have to think in terms of staffing up on the consultancy side. In the afternoon, buy three new word-processors for the office, and another — plus printer — for Barnes. The basic cost of scaling up is clearly going to be substantial, but we must invest to ensure that we can cope with our escalating work-load.

This week *City Limits* has an interesting front cover, titled The Big Green Sell and showing a man besuited brandishing green plastic bottles, a green burger, green cans and so on. Inside there is a feature entitled How Green is My Wallet? and a photograph of Julia and I, taken in the garden here last summer. Big stir about the fact that AEG, one of the Green Kitchen sponsors, is involved in advanced electronics for the weapons industry. 'It is very unfortunate that they slipped through our net,' says Charles Secrett of FoE, 'just because we don't have the staff at the moment, or the money, to carry out a full environmental audit.'

Our view is somewhat different. Yes, we want better information about companies, but we certainly don't want to rule out companies too readily. In some senses we have to be like the early Christians: the biggest sinners present us with our biggest challenge. Just as Saul became St Paul, there is real hope of converting some of the big industrial battalions to our cause.

Given the political stance of *City Limits*, it is something of a surprise that SustainAbility gets a good write-up as 'paramount' among the 'new breed of brokers whose job it is to mediate between big business and the green movement.'

Bad news, meanwhile, from the NCC end of the universe. The new environment correspondent on *The Times*, Michael McCarthy, reports that Nicholas Ridley's latest appointments to the NCC's governing council have caused uproar among NCC staff members. The new members appointed to the 12-man council include two landowning earls, a gamekeeper and a forester who disagrees with the NCC over the conflicting priorities of forestry and conservation. 'There is grave disquiet over these appointments,' one senior NCC staff member is quoted as saying. The disquiet is justified. There is no doubt that the Government has had the NCC in its sights for some time.

In an interesting move, Rod Perriman, a refugee from the Department of the Environment, has joined ICI's Brixham environmental laboratory. Perriman was chief pollution inspector until his resignation last November, because of his dissatisfaction with the way the Government was tackling pollution. A spokesman for Greenpeace told the *Guardian*: 'Rod Perriman is a guy with principles and I can't see him selling out to ICI or anyone else. His appointment looks a very progressive step.' But it would take more Perrimans than we have at our disposal to turn ICI around in this area in a sensible time-scale.

In London yesterday, Prince Philip arrived for the launch of WWF's biodiversity campaign in an electric-powered car. 'The inescapable conclusion,' he said, 'is that this planet Earth, as the habitat for humanity, is itself being threatened. If we do nothing it will mean disaster in the long-term. What we do not want to do is reduce this planet to something like Mars.' One in five animals, insect and plant species could disappear by the year 2000 if present trends continue. He wants £35 million internationally, £10 million to be raised in Britain, for conservation projects.

The wreck of the container ship which was carrying the Lindane has been found 35 miles off the Devon coast, but the main container is still missing; and the *Exxon Valdez* spill, dubbed 'America's Chernobyl', now covers over 600 square miles. *Exxon*, the world's largest oil company, seems to have been totally unprepared for the scale of the disaster. So far, it has recovered only 225,000 gallons of the 11 million gallons of crude oil spilled. Blood samples taken from the captain's blood seven hours after the wreck showed that he had been drunk — and was still one-and-a-half times over the limit.

APRIL

Saturday 1 April
At the Green Party's Spring conference in London yesterday, BBC sports presenter David Icke estimated that during the three days it would run, tropical forests the size of the Isle of Wight would be destroyed, 600 million tonnes of topsoil would be lost through erosion, three species would become extinct and 300,000 people starve to death. 'The present system,' he said, 'is geologically and ecologically unsustainable and morally unjustifiable. It cannot go on.'

On a more practical note, the *Guardian* reports Jonathon Porritt as saying: 'The Green Party has got to gear itself up to what I would describe as Green Machiavellianism over the next three or four years. An engagement in what is actually going on out there, in shaping the policies that will directly shape people's lives over the next five years, is terribly important.' The Green Party is certainly on a roll at the moment, but it is in no shape to win genuine power in the foreseeable future.

FoE launch a campaign aimed at cutting the permissible amounts of particulate pollution from diesel engines. Hundreds of FoE supporters are out on the streets today, reporting on vehicles which they believe are breaking the law in an attempt to spotlight the inadequacies of the present legislation.

The *FT* and *Independent* both have a go at Exxon, in the wake of the Alaskan disaster. The *FT* argues that 'the sight of one of the world's biggest oil companies screwing up on such a cosmic scale — and then being slow off the mark in cleaning up — will have done untold damage to the entire industry, at a time when it is trying to present itself as the guardian of the world's nature resources.'

In the evening we go for a walk in Richmond Park. Masses of deer about, streaming like bison through the evening, plus jackdaws, rabbits, a kestrel and a bat. Bitterly cold wind and old jets thundering and smoking up from Heathrow, banking away to the east and south.

Monday 3 April
In the continuing Exxon saga, the Governor of Alaska, Steve Cowper, is now threatening to shut down the 800-mile oil pipeline that crosses the state unless the oil industry improves its safety and environmental performance. The sheer scale of the spill is becoming clearer. Fish, birds

and sea mammals are now threatened in an area the size of Switzerland. Sea otters, of which there are an estimated 12,000, lose buoyancy when just 10% of their body is covered in oil. The risk to wildlife is extraordinary. A state Government biologist, Michael Wiedmer, told the *Financial Times*: 'There simply are not enough zeroes on the calculator to show how small a fraction we can save.'

Over the weekend, the Green Party opted for Jonathon Porritt's 'Green Machiavellianism', with the aim of manipulating the structure of the European Parliament 'to bring about the profound and radical changes that are necessary'. An essential step if they are to have a real impact. The Party, which currently has nearly 10,000 members, plans to spend more than £250,000 contesting the June 15 European elections.

Oak trees, birds and plants are dying because of acid rain in Britain, according to a new report from Wildlife Link, the body which links 16 organisations, including WWF, the RSPCA and FoE. Britain's power stations, cars and lorries, the report concludes, emit more sulphur dioxide than those of any other country in Western Europe.

Alaskan weather today. Wind whistles and howls through the gaps in the oldest kitchen window.

Tuesday 4 April
A 10.00 meeting on environmental auditing at WWF's offices in Beauchamp Place, with Janet Barber, Tessa Robertson and Kate Brooks of WWF; Georgina McAughtry (ENDS); Steve Robinson (Environment Council); Richard Sandbrook (IIED); Charles Secrett (FoE); and Tessa Tennant (Merlin Ecology Fund).

Considerable support for greater use of environmental auditing by environmental groups, leading to suggestion that Environmental Auditing Bureau be set up. Both ENDS and Merlin may provide a focus, but a great deal remains to be sorted out.

Different organisations likely to use similar techniques, but then operate different ethical principles. FoE have been drafting a set of guidelines to govern fund-raising — the latest draft is so rigorous that it would even prevent FoE taking money from Greenpeace, because of Greenpeace's undemocratic decision-making procedures. Conclusion is that NGOs need a five-year strategy, to ensure that they are not 'bounced' by the pace of events in this field.

There is a danger that environmentalists will feel that they should jump on the train because it is just pulling out of the station — whereas we should be out ahead, changing the points or even laying the tracks in a different direction. As usual, though, it has to be a combination of tactical responses developed within an overall strategic framework.

The Government is challenged today, by CPRE, FoE, WWF and ACE, an industry association, to show its new commitment to environmental protection by 'greening' the Electricity Bill. The Electricity Bill is a bigger environment Bill than any Bill that has gone through Parliament in the last decade. CPRE sees it as the biggest single test of the Government's commitment.

The electricity supply industry (ESI) is Britain's biggest polluter, churning out 233 million tonnes of carbon dioxide annually, which contributes to the Greenhouse Effect; 2.8 million tonnes of sulphur dioxide, which contributes to acid rain problems; and 809,000 tonnes of nitrogen oxides, that contribute to both. Carbon dioxide emissions from the ESI, which accounts for 39% of all such emissions in the UK and which are not covered by European Community regulations, could increase over the next 15 years.

Cutting energy consumption by 20% would cut carbon dioxide emissions by 60 million tonnes. The best available technology used for lighting, domestic fridge-freezers and industrial motors alone could achieve savings of 11.5% in electricity demand, which could cut carbon dioxide emissions by 24 million tonnes.

Financial Times reports that West Germany's ecology-conscious citizens who recycle more rubbish than almost anyone else in the world, have been dismayed to hear that less than 3% of the glass, paper and tin they collect is in fact recycled. The Government, on the other hand, has disputed this figure, aired by the ARD TV network Panorama programme, claiming that more than 20% of recyclable household rubbish is re-used. Still seems very low! Presumably, most of the rubbish ends up in landfill sites. Let's hope that in 20 years such scandals will appear little more than hiccups in a steady progression towards the closed cycle economy.

In the States, meanwhile, Minneapolis has passed a new law outlawing plastic food packaging, including egg boxes and meat wrappings. 'The absurdity of selling a five-minute hamburger in a wrapper that endures for 500 years' has spurred the new law, according to the *Daily Mail*. It will be interesting to see if the Americans can make such legislation stick. If they can, there is some hope that elements of it can be imported to Europe.

Wednesday 5 April
Snow, although it doesn't settle. Some of the papers carry a full-page open letter to the public from Exxon Chairman Lawrence Rawl about the Alaskan disaster. 'We believe that Exxon has moved swiftly and competently to minimise the effect this oil will have on the environment,

fish and other wildlife. Exxon cannot, of course, undo what has been done, but I want to tell you how sorry I am that this accident took place.' A text-book case of too little, too late.

Guy Dauncey comes to talk through the proposal to BT. He is very bright and visionary, suggesting — among other things — the donation of solar-powered faxes to some of the Amazonian Indian tribes campaigning against tropical forest destruction. Julia disputes the need for such machines, even though the Indians themselves have asked for them, convinced by the Sting visit and other recent developments that they simply have to plug into the Global Village. Julia sees communication technologies as part of the problem, because of the lifestyle and other messages they convey, whereas Guy and I tend to see them as solutions, particularly in cases such as this.

Gaia talks this evening of her long-held ambition, to collect animals like Gerald Durrell. Yesterday I put together a glass cabinet for her new bedroom, to hold her extensive collection of skulls, from deer skulls with antlers right down to a sparrow's skull. On occasion she has even had me down on the Thames foreshore with an axe, chopping the head from a dead, considerably decomposed heron corpse.

I point her to a piece in *The Times*, by David Nicholson-Lord, which suggests that Britain may set up the world's first electronic zoo, in which the latest advances in video, holographic and computer technology will show visitors simulations of everything from an Alaskan salmon river to slugs copulating. This last act, according to one expert, is absolutely riveting. Gaia is unmoved: she wants to collect real animals.

'Ironically we know more about the workings of distant galaxies, or monolayered films on silicon, or the internal workings of atoms, than we do about the fragile film of living organisms that is the life support system of our planet.' That was the background, Professor John Lawton (Director of NERC's new population biology research centre) told Tim Radford of the *Guardian*, to the plan to create 30 sealed, self-sustaining worlds, called 'ecotrons'.

Each miniworld will be two metres square, being filled with sterile soil, pure water, filtered air, and selected plants and small animals, and it will aim to uncover some of the ecological secrets of planet Earth. The largest animal in any of the ecotrons, however, is likely to be the slug, although their copulation will probably be low down on the list of priority areas of interest. 'If we are going to harvest in a sustainable way populations of wild organisms,' says Professor Lawton, 'be they fish, or whales, or red grouse, or trees in a forest, then the science that allows us to do that in a sustained and rational way is the science of population biology.' A great idea and one, I suspect, that could come up with some real insights into the necessary, if embryonic, art of planet management.

Thursday 6 April
More than 20,000 people a month are now joining environmental pressure groups such as Greenpeace and Friends of the Earth, according to *The Times*. In one week last month, Greenpeace signed up over 4,000 new members and is now recruiting at an average rate of 3,000 a week. 'I fall off my chair when I think about it,' says Charlotte Grimshaw, Greenpeace's head of fund-raising. FoE is receiving 800 applications a week, while more than 500 people are apparently applying to Ark. The Green Party is signing up 150 new members a week. It remains to be seen whether the no-growth party can handle such growth.

Lord (Peter) Melchett, the Labour peer who is Chairman of Greenpeace, thinks the green organisations are on the verge of a boom: 'I think we are at the beginning of a period of growth,' he said, 'rather than peaking.' Meanwhile, seven in ten British electors say that a party's environmental policy will be an 'important' factor in deciding who to vote for at the European elections in June, according to a MORI poll just published. The fact that the Euro-elections are not yet seen as 'serious' elections by most Britons may help the Greens.

A Foreign Office Green? Minister of State Mrs Lynda Chalker said last night that an international convention may be needed to tackle the Greenhouse Effect. She also, according to the *Financial Times*, urged that UNEP should be radically altered and strengthened to help it deal with the global warming trend.

But will the Government ever have the nerve to tackle environmental problems caused by key supporters, for example Britain's farmers? Farm pollution is rising, with over 4,000 farm pollution incidents reported in England and Wales last year, 6% up on 1987. Undiluted farm slurry is up to 100 times more polluting than untreated human sewage, while silage liquors can be up to 200 times more polluting.

In what *The Independent* describes as a 'remarkable gesture to the Green movement', the European Commission has pledged itself to proposing much tougher, US-style emission standards for cars, which could cut the exhaust emission fumes produced by small saloon cars alone by as much as 75% before 1993. The evidence suggests that the 'clean car' debate is up in the air again, which will delight the environmentally 'hawkish' countries like Denmark, The Netherlands and West Germany, but is likely to infuriate France and Spain.

28 Latin American intellectuals and writers have written to President Sarney of Brazil, protesting against the Amazonian holocaust. They

include the Nobelist Gabriel García-Márquez of Colombia, Guilhermo Cabrera Infante of Cuba, Carlos Fuentes of Mexico, Marío Vargas Llosa of Peru and Isabel Allende of Chile. Their letter, according to the *Daily Telegraph*, calls for a tribunal to judge 'barbarian acts of ecocide and ethnocide'. A spokesman for the Brazilian Foreign Ministry says it was 'being analysed'.

Friday 7 April
Launching a new environmental programme yesterday, President José Sarney claimed that the destruction of Amazonia is being exaggerated. Only 5% has been destroyed, he says. Environmentalists say the figure is more like 12%. Whatever the facts, a new supreme environmental council is being launched, together with a rainforest university. The entire Government programme of tax incentives and low-cost credit for Amazonia farming projects is being reviewed and the use of mercury by gold-panners will apparently be banned.

Meanwhile, Sarney is in dispute with French Premier Michel Rocard. Rocard apparently rang Sarney last week to persuade him to sign the so-called Hague Declaration. When the French text was published, however, the implication was that Sarney was 'ready to surrender a part of its national sovereignty for the common good of all humanity'. Sarney says he isn't!

News comes through that the *Exxon Valdez* was on automatic pilot: the crewmen tried to stop the 987-ft tanker running on to Bligh Reef, but were prevented from doing so by the automatic pilot. It remains to be seen whether this latest rumour is true, but it raises some interesting questions about the increasing computerisation of some many high-risk operations and systems. The appalling disaster is giving environmentalists powerful new ammunition in their fight to prevent the oil companies opening up the vast Arctic National Wildlife Refuge to oil exploration. Another judge today cut Captain Hazelwood's bail to $25,000.

The Whole Thing's green catalogue, due to be published in May, gets something of a mauling in *The Times*. NOT QUITE THE WHOLE THING reads the headline. The products offered range from a waterproof, solar-powered Walkman to a humane mousetrap. William Pryor and his partners, *The Times* concludes, 'hope that "The Whole Thing" logo will become the European green label. But will it survive, as the sum of such superficial parts?' We feel that they have used Julia's name in a pretty under-handed way: suggesting in their prospectus that she would be reviewing their product lines, but subsequently refusing to give her a chance to comment on their product choices.

An article on Sweden in the *Financial Times* called: Fertile territory for the rise of green capitalism. It's a strange feeling when a phrase you coin, like 'green capitalism' or Green Consumer becomes part of the language. Offers come in for *The Guide* from France and Sweden.

Saturday 8 April
'Greening capitalism' is the title of an editorial in the *Daily Mail* today, commenting on a 'green summit' of Cabinet Ministers Mrs Thatcher has called for the 26th at Chequers. The message they will be given, the *Mail* predicts: 'The free enterprise way to advise the cause is to convince our businessmen that where there's pollution there's profit in removing it.' Jack Cunningham, Labour's environment spokesman, describes the proposed 'teach-in' as 'window-dressing'. He may be right, but — whether the Tories or Labour are in power — the market must be greened.

A giant Soviet nuclear-powered hunter-killer sub erupts into the headlines: it is thought to have sunk in the Norwegian Sea, after a major fire on board. The Norwegians are concerned that they may have a mini-Chernobyl on their hands. Meanwhile President Gorbachev was busy tipping his hat to the environment in his Guildhall speech yesterday. 'As regards environmental issues,' he said, 'the Soviet Union will faithfully abide by existing agreements and co-operate in international programmes, and will soon adhere to those it is not party to.'

Although the Soviet Union is a signatory of the Montreal Protocol, which seeks to cut CFC use by 50% by 1998, the Soviets have so far refused to accept a total ban on CFCs by the year 2000. The Soviet Union has still to make a formal response to the Brundtland Commission's report, *Our Common Future*, and owes over £500,000 in payments due under the Convention on Trade in Endangered Species, which the Russians signed in 1976.

Good piece by Christopher Booker in the *Daily Telegraph*. 'The ultimate question,' he concludes, 'is whether we can realistically go on looking for unlimited economic growth, as almost every nation in the world is still doing. Where do we start to cut our expectations? How do we persuade the rest of the underdeveloped world not to want to join in the potentially fatal race, so long as we remain in a position of material privilege and unwilling to make any real sacrifices ourselves?' The Green Consumer is a first step in this direction, but the challenge for the Nineties is far greater than anything we have faced to date.

President Bush failed to pull *his* finger out yesterday. Although he pledged to send troops — to help in the clean-up — and financial help to Alaska, he has certainly not done nearly enough to convince environmentalists that he is prepared to impose sufficiently rigorous controls on the

83

oil industry. Interestingly, though, he proposes that thousands of young Americans might volunteer for the summer, to help in the clean-up. An ecological version of the Peace Corps. An idea which could well surface elsewhere.

Profile of Exxon Chairman Lawrence Rawl in the *Financial Times*. 'I'd like to have your Mr Rawl come up here,' said one local man in Valdez this week. 'We'd roll him in his oil and cover him with bird feathers and send him down where he came from.' The Exxon response to the disaster shows an appalling lack of imagination and panache.

Sunday 9 April
Came across a very large duck torn apart by a fox on the way to pick up the papers with the children. Gaia fascinated, craning around the gore-spattered ground in search of the head, for her skull collection. She hasn't got anything which came with a bill!

Western experts say that the captain of the 10,000-tonne Soviet submarine that went down off Norway probably scuttled his ship to prevent a marine Chernobyl. According to Captain Richard Sharpe of the US Navy, there is an obvious comparison with Chernobyl. Both incidents resulted from working to a set of safety standards that wouldn't have been allowed in the US. In the USSR, Defence Minister Dmitri Yazov confirms that the nuclear reactor is shut down and rules out radioactive contamination of the environment. The death toll stands at 42, including the captain.

The US believe that the fire on the submarine, driven by two unusual and highly dangerous liquid-metal-cooled nuclear reactors, caused major damage, possibly even setting fire to the titanium hull. Apart from the vessel's reactors, a range of nuclear weapons are thought to have been aboard and are now lying on the sea-bed.

Meanwhile, the controversy over the 'fusion in a test tube' announcement continues to rage. The politicking between rival researchers is streets ahead of anything experienced in the environmental field — as yet. And if the Fleischmann-Pons results do turn out to be true, overturning physics as we know it, the chances are that one of the first things anyone does with it is build a new submarine around it!

Whales have taken over *The Sunday Times* colour supplement today. A humpback breaches on the front cover. The text focuses on the campaign to force Japan, Iceland and Norway, the last of the die-hard whaling nations, to stop. Despite the fact that two of the Icelandic whalers were sunk by environmental activists in 1986, the Icelandic fleet continues with 'scientific whaling'.

As Brian Jackman and Richard Girling point out in their article, this is a vile prostitution of science. 'Icelandic scientists have found that Sei whales in the North Atlantic are about the same shape as those in the North Pacific,' as observers at the 1988 International Whaling Commission acidly put it. What about *sustainable* whaling? The problem, as Jeremy Cherfas stated in *The Hunting of the Whale*, is that: 'Sustainable whaling will never happen because money in the bank grows quicker than whales in the water.' So it will probably always make commercial sense to kill the whales as quickly as possible and invest the profits in something else.

Gruelling tales also from the tuna-fishing fleets of the Eastern Tropical Pacific. For some reason, dolphins and tuna swim together, the schools of dolphin on the surface, the yellowfin tuna a few feet below them. The tuna fishermen catch $1 billion of tuna a year by hunting the dolphins, spreading their purse-seine nets to catch both. As a result, many dolphins are horribly mutilated and butchered; an eerily Holocaust-like six million are estimated to have been killed over the last 30 years.

Monday 10 April
The NIMBY (Not-in-my-backyard) syndrome comes to Ambridge, as developers decide they want to build 1,500 homes as a 'satellite village' to Hanbury, in Hereford and Worcester. Hanbury provided the inspiration for the BBC Radio 4 series, *The Archers*, which began in 1951. Symptomatic of the growing rural concern about development pressures, particularly in the South.

Parliament gives a second and last reading to Commission proposals to cut emissions from small cars, with engine capacities under 1.4 litres. The resulting Directive will soon be out of date, though, because of the Commissions' plans, announced last week, to introduce much tougher car pollution controls from 1993.

Good piece in the *Guardian* by James Erlichman on the need for a UK eco-label scheme, offering the fact that *The Guide* has sold over 200,000 copies as proof that the consumer cares about the environment. The Consumers' Association call to say that they have seen my latest *Guardian* article, on detergents, and want a meeting to discuss what they — and *Which?* — might be doing in this field. We had tried to get them interested before Green Consumer Week, but, while the Consumers' Association produced a press release welcoming the Week, the impression was that it was worried that its one million-plus members would see an environmental campaign as too political. Another indication of the way in which the green wave is reaching ever-higher up the beach.

Tuesday 11 April

The Government is planning to launch a campaign to encourage the recycling of newspapers, which account for about a fifth of the volume of household rubbish. Since about three-quarters of Britain's newsprint consumption of almost two million tonnes a year is imported, this initiative could help cut our trade deficit. It remains to be seen whether the Government can effectively mobilise the public in support of recycling and energy conservation.

The Times reports that the Green Party will field 643 candidates, nearly double the number standing for Dr David Owen's SDP, in the county elections on 4 May. 'We are now providing a real challenge, not only in terms of philosophy and ideas, but also at the ballot box,' says Chris Rose, who is acting as the Green Party's elections co-ordinator.

Many of the papers report that researchers at Texas A & M University have duplicated the 'fusion in a test-tube' experiment. The process also generated more (40–60%) energy than was put in, although it is still not at all clear whether this is a new nuclear process or an unsuspected chemical reaction. A key reason why there is so much enthusiasm for cold fusion is that if it were ever to become practicable, it could help to tackle the Greenhouse Effect, because it doesn't produce carbon dioxide.

In Australia, meanwhile, Environment Minister Graham Richardson warned yesterday that millions of Australians will be forced to move away from coastal areas in the next 30–50 years, because of flooding caused by the Greenhouse Effect. 'The coastline is going to change radically,' he predicted. 'In a lot of those areas, people who were seeking waterfront views are going to get a bit more waterfront than they ever bargained for.'

Shirley Gear of the World Resources Institute, in Washington, DC, faxes through WRI press release for *Cleaning Up*, the report Jonathan Shopley, an Associate with John Elkington Associates for three years, and I wrote last year. This, the release says, explodes the myth that waste and pollution are predominantly problems of highly industrialised nations. Population growth and rapid urbanisation in many developing countries will dramatically increase pressure on both local and regional environments. In fact, the most pressing problems are going to be in the Third World, which has the least capacity to deal with them.

Wednesday 12 April

Ark get on to the front cover of *Today* with a campaign based on the Greenhouse Effect, but attract a barrage of criticism from environmental scientists. 'Parliament may have to move to Birmingham because vast areas of central London will have disappeared beneath water. In the year

2050, Doncaster and Peterborough will be seaside towns. Grantham — the Prime Minister's birthplace — will be a bike's ride from the sea. Blackpool will be an island.'

Ark's predictions that global warming will cause a sea-level rise of five metres over the next 60 years led to immediate criticisms from leading scientists. They said the forecasts were wild and irresponsible. But, while it's clear that the group has chosen to follow Greenpeace's line in terms of exaggerating problems, it's interesting that Ark has chosen to campaign on this issue. Earthlife, too, planned to launch a series of maps showing the likely extent of flooding some years ago.

The conflict between energy and environmental objectives will become acute in the 1990s. *The Times* today reports that the lights have gone out on Tiananmen Square, in the heart of Peking, for the first time since 1949. Even senior Communist Party leaders are experiencing power cuts. 'If energy is the lifeblood of modern society,' said the *Guangming Ribao* in a long front-page article on Monday, then 'China is sickly and anaemic.' The cause of the anaemia is a critical coal shortage. Solve that, though, and China's contribution to the Greenhouse Effect will sky-rocket.

Meanwhile, a second American research team — at Georgia Tech — has announced that it has repeated the cold fusion experiment. One company that is already benefiting from the fusion bandwagon is Johnson Matthey, which refines and markets a third of the world's platinum and a sixth of its palladium. The price of palladium has leaped 21%, to about $170 an ounce, since the 23 March cold fusion announcement.

Fiona went to an event at Lloyd's yesterday, where the National Trust spotlighted its Enterprise Neptune campaign to save Britain's coastline — and unveiled its plans for its Silver Jubilee Year in 1990. Apparently, just after Sir Archibald Forster, Chairman of Exxon subsidiary Esso had apologised to the audience for the Alaskan disaster, all the lights suddenly went out and he was left speaking in the dark, without a microphone.

Thursday 13 April
The greening of Europe moved into the fast lane last night when the European Parliament voted overwhelmingly — by 309 votes to five — to push through dramatic cuts in the exhaust emission levels to be achieved by small cars. Car manufacturers will now be forced to adopt standards at least as tough as those prevailing in America and Japan. The vote is seen as a major reverse for the UK and French Governments, which have consistently opposed such cuts.

The British car industry has argued that it would be best to wait for 'lean burn' engine technology to reduce emissions, rather than fitting catalytic converters. But, while catalytic converters may add a further

£500 to the cost of a small car, lean burn technology is unlikely to be available in an acceptable time-scale.

The Ministry of Agriculture announces an urgent review into the safety of Alar, also known as daminozide, which is sprayed on apples and pears and is suspected of being a carcinogen. The Advisory Committee on Pesticides is expected to report within ten weeks. Alar is sprayed on apple blossom to help the fruit set and the Government has refused to ban the spraying of blossom expected to bloom in the next three or four weeks. Yesterday Sky TV phoned wanting someone to respond to a news item in the *Guardian*, which said that millions of British apples are being sprayed with Alar. In the States, the Environmental Protection Agency said in February that it planned to ban Alar within 18 months. The pesticide cannot be washed off apples, because it gets into their flesh. If processed apple juice is heated, it is claimed, Alar breaks down into a more carcinogenic substance, UDMH.

'Any fool can grow a big crop of apples the size of golf balls,' said Peter Holmes, Chairman of the apple and pear committee of the National Farmers' Union, 'but Alar helps to produce the sort of apples 65–75mm in size which the supermarkets and customers want.' But Sainsbury's is now ordering all its suppliers to deliver Alar-free apples, to allay public concern. The apple blossom is about to open on the tree in the garden here.

Tesco announces that it achieved sales of £5 billion in the year to 25 February, attributing some of its success to its new green image, which Managing Director David Malpas says 'has captured the public imagination and is commercially important'. The scale of Tesco's turnover illustrates the importance of greening such companies, although it would be interesting to think through what a full-fledged green strategy would do to Tesco's long-term profitability.

In the evening Fiona and I go to a reception at the *Observer*, building up to the launch of Green Book Fortnight. The Fortnight's catalogue contained three of our books, but it is *The Guide* which is up there in the Top Twenty.

Among the other books that are to be featured are Heathcote Williams's *Whale Nation*, Ben Elton's novel *Stark*, *The Greenpeace Story* by Michael Brown and John May, *The Gaia Atlas of Planet Management* (which I helped to edit), Karen Christensen's *Home Ecology*, Paul Harrison's *The Greening of Africa*, Guy Dauncey's *After the Crash*, John Seymour and Herbert Girardet's *Blueprint for a Green Planet* and Marion Shoard's *This Land is our Land*.

Talk to dozens of people. Towards end, talk to Francis Miller, who first came up with the idea for Green Consumer Week. He is now thinking of a one-minute silence to mark New Year's Eve and the transition into the 1990s. Green Book Fortnight was another of his ideas.

Friday 14 April
Abbie Hoffman was found dead on 12 April. The Sixties' activist was arrested over 40 times in a radical career spanning several decades, organising countless demonstrations, many tongue-in-cheek. In 1967, for example, he was among the group who scattered dollar bills from the visitors' gallery on to the floor of the New York Stock Exchange, causing a near-riot as the traders rushed to pick up the money.

Later, he was instrumental in provoking one of the most influential riots of recent times. Having founded the Youth International Party ('Yippies'), he was one of the Chicago Seven accused of conspiring to disrupt the 1968 Democratic Convention in Chicago. The result was what was described as a 'police riot', with Mayor Daley's police launching bloody attacks on peaceful demonstrators. Ironically, some political analysts have since claimed that the Chicago riots cost the Democrats the election, letting in Richard Nixon.

The subsequent trial was an astounding cause *célèbre* and had a considerable impact on those of us whose main contribution to the cause of protest had been seeing how long we could grow our hair at school before being sent to the barber by the headmaster. Dismissed by President Nixon as a 'long-haired bum', Hoffman developed the use of humour as a weapon against the Vietnam War and the military-industrial complex which was the beating heart of 'Amerika'. He was also an active environmental campaigner. While on the FBI's most-wanted list, he met President Carter under his alternative identity as a representative of an environmental action group!

Of 1968, Hoffman once said: 'They don't make years like that anymore. If it weren't for our efforts we'd have a president today sending troops off to exotic countries like Lebanon and Grenada and bombing cities like Tripoli.'

On a slightly different tack, maybe there's hope for the Greens here, too. Ex-Goon Spike Milligan is among the party's supporters, along with David Bailey, who has agreed to direct the Greens' party political broadcast for the European elections. This afternoon, Duncan McCanlis — Secretary of the Green Party — came through. With a background in industry, he is looking for ways on helping the Greens to find a more realistic route to power. We are also talking about an environmental audit of the Iceland Group.

Other news: The *Daily Telegraph* reports that statisticians expect China's population to reach 1.1 billion today; WWF says Japanese imports of tropical timber will destroy the remaining forests of South-East Asia within 20–30 years; Professor Bo Doos of the International Institute for Applied Systems Analysis tells a conference in Stockholm that about 50 animal and plant species will disappear every day between 1990 and 2020 unless something is done to stop the Greenhouse Effect.

Saturday 15 April
Drive down to Gloucestershire early in the morning to visit friends and family. As I leave, wood pigeons wing across my shoulder, carrying twigs to a new nest in a hole in the building opposite. Sad: the building is being refurbished, which means that their nest will be bricked in. Weather is almost Californian, driving — once off the M40 — a pleasure. At least three dead foxes on the motorway verges. Two crashes on the way out. Beyond Burford, rooks chase each other up into the sky.

Ford — long a champion of lean-burn engines, rather than catalytic converters — announced yesterday that it is to introduce a range of catalyst-equipped cars in the UK within the next year. The latest EEC developments have convinced Ford that it risked being left behind in the race for the emerging market for clean cars. But Greenpeace's campaign also had a major impact. 'Ford gives you more,' Greenpeace's ads said. 'A Ford in Britain pumps out 100% more toxic fumes than a Ford back home in America.'

In the States, Ralph Nader is calling for a 'citizens' crusade' against Exxon. 'There should be a consumer boycott,' he says. 'That's the only penalty those bastards are going to pay. Everything else is insured and deductible. It's conceivable that, given the publicity and the anger of the people, you could drain off a couple of billion dollars in the next six months. That's just 2% (of the company's value), but that's a kind of penalty.' TV stations are suggesting consumers return their Exxon credit cards to the company in plastic bags filled with waste oil. Greenpeace has decided not to join the boycott, while FoE are wavering.

Fashion designer Katharine Hamnett, a new recruit to the Green Party, is about to launch 'Green chic', according to *Today*. 'I decided there was only one way it could look,' she says. 'Baggy, red and spotty to match the baggy eyes and horrible complexions that the people who are wearing (the clothes) will no doubt have. How else could they look when they are being poisoned by polluted water, breathing in chemicals, and eating food that contains terrible things?'

The fashion industry, she points out, is the fourth largest industry in the world. 'I thought we should do something to prevent that happening. I already insist that our jeans are stone-washed without bleach. Acid-washed jeans pollute the drainage system.' She says she wants to help the

Green Party raise £100 million. 'I might even design a Green Party T-shirt.'

Sunday 16 April
Main news of the day is that 94 people were killed, many of them crushed to death, at yesterday's FA Cup semi-final between Liverpool and Nottingham Forest.

Julia and I work most of the day, but with a sense that we are falling badly behind with *The Supermarket Guide*, because of other pressures.

Endorsement today for Fleischmann and Pons from Sir Graham Hills, Vice-Chancellor of Strathclyde University and a former colleague of Professor Fleischmann. 'People still haven't appreciated the full implications of this discovery,' Sir Graham says. 'This means goodbye to carbon and dangerous waste. We are going to live in a pollution-free world that will be run on hydrogen. This discovery is the saviour of our planet.'

If cold fusion were ever to prove feasible, a virtuous cycle might well operate. The main source of 'heavy water', which would be likely to be the fuel of such reactors, would be sea water. Large-scale electrolysis of sea water would produce hydrogen as a by-product. And that hydrogen, whether as a liquid or gaseous fuel, could power transport, industry and heating systems. Hydrogen is an astoundingly clean fuel: it simply produces water vapour when burned.

Tuesday 18 April
Go across to our new lawyers in Gower Street to run through our agreements with foreign publishers and Brand New.

Stephen Ronaldson feels we are horribly exposed, particularly in the US market, where our book is being adapted by others, yet we have no veto on the content and are ultimately liable if companies issue writs. In the US climate this is almost guaranteed. Stephen has pulled in a Dickensian-looking lawyer, Richard Gallivant. He sports a straggly greyish beard which grows from just beneath his jawline. Both he and Stephen react with delight as we uncover one new project after another, almost all of them rich in legal complexities and challenges. It strikes me that they must see us as a factory churning out cans of worms.

One area we consider is whether we can get any protection on the Green Consumer concept, which I first dreamed up in 1986 while helping to develop the Design Council's Green Designer exhibition. My feeling has always been that we want the phrase to become part of the language, to help open up people's minds to the books and services we offer. Stephen and Richard finally conclude that it would be far too expensive to attempt, in any event, although we agree to go for trademark registration of SustainAbility and of our logo — which I originally scribbled out on a plane back from Brussels.

Work on writing an article on the Greenhouse Effect commissioned by *The Sunday Times*. There was a considerable tussle over whether I should do it, with Julia stressing the need to get on with *The Supermarket Guide*. But the opportunity, at a time when Mrs T is banging her Ministers' heads together on this issue, simply too good to miss.

Wednesday 19 April

Explosive detonation as plane drops towards Frankfurt: lightning. Picked up at the airport and driven in a sleek BMW to the spa town of Wiesbaden for the launch by publishers Orell Fussli of the German edition of *The Green Capitalists*. The book's German title means 'The Environmental Crisis is an Opportunity'. PPA, the Munich-based PR company which organised the launch, were told by many of the companies they approached, that it would be too dangerous to share a panel with the Greens. And Klaus-Peter Johanssen of Shell confided before the meeting that he, too, would have refused if he had known the *Exxon Valdez* disaster was in prospect!

I am asked to kick off the panel discussion. Do my normal spiel. My approach is characterised by several speakers as based on many small steps rather than a great, revolutionary leap forward. Although there is concern that the problems are closing in too fast, just about everyone who speaks supports what we are doing. Joschka Fischer, a Green who is a past State Environment Minister, says I'm an optimist, to which I reply that I can see the problems as well as the next person, but that if you simply give people the bad news the chances are that they will switch off completely.

Dinner at the Kellermeister restaurant. Particularly interesting conversation with Monika Griefahn, a director of Greenpeace International. Greenpeace have been invited to start greening Russian youth. When the Party speaks out on environmental issues, it seems, people are no more likely to believe it than on other issues. Monika has been at the heart of many of the Greenpeace campaigns and is something of a Green celebrity in Germany. When a Greenpeace pop compilation LP went on sale for the first time in March in Moscow, there was bedlam outside the Melodia record shop on Kalinin Prospekt. They expect to sell three million copies at around three times the usual price of an LP. Meanwhile, the million-selling Soviet paper *Za Rubezhom* is running an environmental award scheme very much like that run here earlier in the year by *The Times*.

In today's papers: Labour promises a £12 million crash programme to clean up Britain's water; Chancellor of the Exchequer Nigel Lawson is apparently battling environment ministers to prevent some of the proceeds of the £7 billion water privatisation going to fund clean-up measures; scepticism prevails as Exxon Chairman Lawrence Rawl unveils a plan to clean up 300 miles of Alaskan coastline — using 4,000 workers and 200 vessels — by September 15 (the day after Green Shopping Day, as it happens); and Tesco starts running a full-page ad in the nationals, dubbing itself The Greener Grocer. Visit Tesco's stores, and we are told 'You'll find that you won't just be shopping for yourself. You'll also be shopping for your great-grandchildren'.

Thursday 20 April
100th anniversary of the birth of Hitler today. Up at 06.00, to get to airport. Travel by S-bahn, with slashed seats and a fair number of loutish young people with driving heavy metal music hissing from their head-phones. Stark contrast with the chic inhabitants of Wiesbaden. The train snakes back and forth over the Rhine bridges, passing a line of tall red brick industrial chimneys in Mainz which dribble yellow smoke into the dawn.

Flight back badly delayed by air traffic problems.

Gorbachev has sent the world's largest oil-skimming vessel, the *Vaido-gubsky*, to Alaska to help clean up the spill. The goodwill gesture echoes the despatch of Soviet ice-breakers to help free the three whales trapped in the Alaskan ice. The vessel can scoop up 84,000 gallons of oil and sludge a day, more than the recovery capacity of the entire US fleet of hundreds of boats currently at work on the spill.

Meanwhile, as petrol prices soar in the wake of the disaster and Tuesday's gas explosion which has shut down the South Cormorant A platform, the lead-free TV ads knock coffee and burger ads off their pedestals to become the most effective ads. Vauxhall announces that it plans to become the first car manufacturer to fit a catalytic converter to all cars sold in the UK. Some will be launched this autumn, with the company's entire fleet converted by 1993.

Research published by the Plymouth Marine Laboratory suggests that the Greenhouse Effect is warming the planet's temperature by 0.1°C a year. Christopher Patten, Minister for Overseas Development, argues that the UN may have to step in. 'I don't envisage people in blue berets being parachuted into countries to save their forests,' he told *The Independent*, 'but these are matters of such consequence that I should have thought the international community would wish to address them at the highest level. They are about our security.' Suspect that this idea of a global 'green beret' task force will take root in the coming years.

Continued con-fusion on the Fleischmann-Pons front. Two teams say they are withdrawing their claims to have repeated the cold fusion experiment, while a Stanford University team says that it *has* duplicated the experiment. The results are thought to be important because the experiment produced 50% more energy than was fed in both when heavy water and ordinary water were used. This appears to eliminate the possibility that cold fusion is a previously unknown electrochemical reaction.

The Government bans the release of detailed data about the water industry's compliance with European Community standards, fearing that investors might turn tail.

Friday 21 April
British salvage teams have recovered most of the pesticide cargo from the Panamanian wreck off Guernsey. All 12 drums of cypermethrin and 15 out of 20 drums of permethrin were found. The search continues for the missing five drums — and, on the French side, for the separate container of five tonnes of Lindane.

Two endangered species stories. The Japanese whaling fleet has now left Antarctica with 241 frozen Minke whales, instead of the planned 300. Japan says it is killing the whales to see if the Minke populations are in danger of extinction! Unfortunately, too, the whaling ban is now increasing hunting pressures on dolphins in Japanese coastal waters. Meanwhile Sotheby's react to pressure from conservation groups — particularly the Friends of Animals and the African Wildlife Federation — and withdraws two African elephant tusks due to go on sale in New York today. They were expected to fetch £10,000 each.

On the home front, Labour yesterday pledged itself to create Europe's strongest environmental protection agency when next elected to power. 'There is a bewildering diversity of managerial, advisory and regulatory agencies with overlapping powers and responsibilities,' says Shadow Environment Secretary Dr John Cunningham. 'But there are also significant gaps, particularly with respect of independent monitoring and freedom of information.'

National Power says up to 10% of Britain's electricity could be produced by 'greener' gas-powered generating plant by the mid-1990s, producing around half the amount of carbon dioxide emitted from conventional coal-fired stations.

I go to LBC to tape a radio interview on the theme of the 'green office', linked in to an exhibition at the London Ecology Centre, which will coincide with Environment Week.

The industry and environment supplement appears in the *Financial Times* today, carrying a major piece entitled Emergence of the Green Consumer (which mentions the SustainAbility/Brand New link-up) and my article on the emergence and commercial significance of green consumerism. 'Green Consumer markets now look set to boom across Europe,' my article concludes, 'with most British companies starting the race from behind.' The task now is to wake up our companies to the impending threat to their products and services.

Saturday 22 April
Ozone Help, a new organisation discussed in today's *Independent*, proposes to rebuild the ozone layer by launching balloons, each carrying 100 ionisers and powered by 300 solar panels made by West Germany's Siemens. Launched in the Arctic and Antarctic, the balloons would be funded by putting a levy of £1 on every refrigerator sale, 2p on every aerosol canister and 1p on every take-away food carton. Britain alone would produce 600 giant balloons a year. But 'back-of-the-envelope' calculations suggest that five *billion* balloons would be needed to replace the ozone destroyed each year!

An equally extraordinary, but perhaps more achievable plan, is outlined in the *Daily Telegraph*. Norman Myers, who I worked with on the Gaia Atlas, recalls a recent World Bank meeting at which he and a couple of colleagues were asked to cost the task of saving a large proportion of the species currently threatened with extinction. 'We did some overnight arithmetic,' Norman says, 'we drew a deep breath and proposed $1 billion (£590 million) a year for the opening five years. The Bank people didn't blink.'

Exxon, meanwhile, has done it again. One of its barges has spilled 400,000 gallons of waste (90% water, 7% alcohol, 3% oil) into a river next to a wildlife reserve in the Mississippi Delta.

The *Guardian* carries my piece on recycled paper products. British Alcan Aluminium announces that it will build a £20 million plant to recycle aluminium cans, while Coca-Cola says it will at last switch to non-detachable ring-pulls on cans in Europe which have been used for years in the States.

One in the eye for Environment Secretary Nicholas Ridley, launching the Civic Trust's Operation Eyesore in London yesterday. Trying to remove graffiti from a wall, he managed to squirt liquid detergent into his eye.

Sunday 23 April
The Sunday Times runs my greenhouse piece, entitled How Green is your House? It is huge, with a couple of illustrations, taking up most of the front cover of the paper's New Society section. Must check the calculations of the carbon dioxide output from white goods like cookers and fridges. Earth Resources Research apparently said my estimate of

two tonnes per household sounded to be in the right ball-park, but better safe than sorry.

Government ministers apparently want a 'green charge' shown on water bills, to explain to consumers that they will be paying £3 billion over the next six years to bring Britain's water industry up to new EEC standards. Labour retorts that the move is a green gimmick, designed to hide the true costs of privatisation.

And anyone who doubted the potential of the lost Lindane to damage the environment should be pointed to a small item in the *Observer* today. A small quantity of the chemical leaked into Poole harbour in Dorset yesterday from a timber storage yard: hundreds of dead fish have been seen.

Monday 24 April
We move the office to Holland Park. Raining as the boxed office is loaded into a lorry and trucked away.

News in *The Times* of the flight of a manned balloon from the North Pole. A team of five from an organisation called Global Concern manhandled the equipment to the North Pole, where the balloon then ascended to 1,000 ft in temperatures of −40°C, collecting air samples for testing at the University of California and NASA. The expedition was got off the ground by Paul Lavelle and his girlfriend. He was so concerned about the ozone layer that he sold his house in Swindon to raise the £100,000 needed for the flight. His aim: to publicise the damage being done to the ozone layer and encourage shoppers to stop and think before buying their next aerosol.

The Times also reviews the recent greening trend in the Soviet Union where *glasnost* is spurring the trend in some surprising directions. The reviving nationalism in many parts of the Soviet Empire, the Samizdat Press Agency says, is closely tied to worries about pollution and past destruction of cultural heritage. And the *Financial Times* carries a supplement on Italy, containing two articles on the environment and environmentalism. 'Nowhere in Europe,' it concludes, 'is the environmental pendulum swinging so fast, from neglect to acute concern, as in Italy.' The latest convert, apparently, is the Communist party, which has plastered Rome with posters lamenting Brazil's vanishing rainforests.

Tuesday 25 April
Julia, Annie Dimmock and I drive down to Heinz in Hayes, Middlesex. Jams most of the way: due to arrive at 10.00, actually get there closer to 10.30. Then there is a long walk from the car-park, the latter stages of which we effect by walking across the carefully mown grass in front of the

office complex — under the eyes of scores of Heinz executives. Sense of having committed every corporate sin in the book, and enter the building with our shoes covered in grass cuttings.

The meeting goes well. Several senior Heinz people keep dipping in and out of the meeting — we are told something fairly major is happening. We are asking Heinz for a total of £125,000, £75,000 for SustainAbility. This would give them a close identification with Green Shopping Day and the other £50,000 would give them, via WWF, a Heinz Green Advice Bureau, to run for a year. They seem concerned about the possibility that we might attack brands and companies in such a way as to bring them into disrepute, but seem reassured by our presentation. It is inevitable that they will be criticised, but in the current climate their participation will be seen as pioneering.

The climate across the water in Holland is suggested by the news that, after months of bargaining, a National Environment Plan will shortly be published, designed to cut pollution there by 70–90% by the year 2010! If the Plan is adopted, it will be an important model for the rest of Europe.

Meanwhile, the air over the North Pole, it appears, is often more polluted than in many British cities and some places in northern Europe. A new £2 million NERC research programme will focus on the Arctic haze discovered some 30 years ago — and at first thought to be a natural phenomenon. It now looks as though a great deal of it is industrial pollution.

Interesting fact in relation to our planned *Green Holiday Guide*: travel and tourism now represent the world's largest industry, reports the *Wall Street Journal*, employing more than 100 million people — or one of every 16 workers.

No wonder Russians do not trust the Party: it now appears that some of the 20 civilian deaths when demonstrators in Tbilisi were charged by troops earlier in the month were caused by the use of poison gas. Something distinctly more unpleasant than tear gas. 'There can be no justification for the tragedy,' said Mr Givi Gumbaridize, Soviet Georgia's new Communist Party leader. 'You cannot talk to people by means of force.'

Wednesday 26 April

The Heinz mystery is cleared up: the news breaks that 'consumer terrorism' has hit Britain in a big way, with baby foods made by Heinz and Cow & Gate being contaminated with broken glass, razor blades and suchlike. The food industry is effectively being held to ransom. No wonder there was such to-ing and fro-ing yesterday.

Tesco has announced that it would impose a total ban on products containing CFCs by July. But Tory MP Sir Richard Body says that the attempts of the supermarkets to out-green each other are just expensive hype. They are deceiving the public, he claims, particularly in their willingness to buy meat from British abattoirs where hygiene standards are inadequate. Certainly, the major chains have a long, long way to travel before they can legitimately fly the green flag.

Letter from Alison Costello of the Women's Environmental Network in the *Guardian*, pointing out that the government report on dioxin contamination of products like tampons is not out until the end of the month. In my article on Saturday I suggested that the report would give the 'all clear' to such products on health grounds, as indicated by a number of sources recently, but that the environmental issue is likely to remain extremely important.

Mrs Thatcher is hosting the all-day Seminar on the Global Climate at Downing Street today, looking at what can be done to halt — or at least slow down — the global warming trend. All the indications are that she is going to come out pushing nuclear power for all she is worth. Sky TV call late this evening to ask whether I will go on tomorrow morning to react, but refuse, for a number of reasons. Am tired, committed to getting *The Supermarket Guide* properly under way rather than engaging in media jaunts, and still not sure that TV is my medium anyway.

The CEGB announces a £1.25 million research programme on four subjects related to the Greenhouse Effect. Dr Peter Chester notes that UK power stations generated only 0.7 kWh of electricity for every kilogram of carbon dioxide discharged in 1950, but improved efficiency and an increased use of nuclear power have meant that they now generate 1.2 kWh for every kilogram of carbon dioxide. A huge new effort will be essential if we are to tackle the Greenhouse Effect, while restoration of the world's forest will certainly require international co-operation.

Meanwhile, Sting and Chief Raoni, leader of the Kayapo tribe, are hard at work trying to raise £3 million for their Rain Forest Foundation. They have already met President Mitterrand and the Pope, and on Friday go to see Prince Charles. Sting says he is prepared for criticism from all shades of the political spectrum. 'But this is not a political movement — it is something which affects us all.'

The French have abandoned the search for the Lindane container in the Channel. Transport Minister Michael Portillo explained that 'the physical nature of the Lindane, the packaging, the depth of water in which the container was lost, water currents and other factors, are such that the likelihood of contamination is much less than at first feared'. Ho hum.

Hungarian-born Italian MP Ilona Staller, better known as La Cicciolina, released a white dove in Kiskunhalas yesterday to mark the withdrawal of large numbers of Soviet troops from the country. The first Soviet tank to roar up a ramp towards a tank transporter succeeded in mashing the bird of peace into the concrete.

Home by bus: in total, it takes around one hour 30 minutes for a trip you could drive on a clear day in less than ten minutes. London's traffic is showing increasing signs of seizing up entirely. The worst of all worlds: the cars, buses and trucks spew their carbon dioxide into the air and get precisely nowhere. And the only solution the Government can imagine is building new roads.

Thursday 27 April

As expected, the main result of Mrs T's seminar yesterday was to give a 'green light' to nuclear power. She hopes to seize the high ground by presenting a report on the Greenhouse Effect to the Commonwealth summit in Kuala Lumpur in September. Meanwhile, Peter Melchett, Executive Director of Greenpeace, retorts that: 'Nuclear energy is an inherently dangerous, wasteful and expensive way of generating electricity, which carries with it enormous environmental costs, such as the generation of waste which we don't know what to do with.' Yes, but if the Greenhouse Effect takes hold, we may be viewing nuclear power in a rather different light.

Interestingly, a Gallup poll reported in *The Independent* shows that most people are not interested in investing in the privatised electricity industry, but 50% say they are willing to pay for a cleaner environment. Ironically, the James Howden Group announces that it is pulling out of wind-power, following losses caused by repair bills for faulty wind turbines it built in California.

In the afternoon, across to the Royal Institute of International Affairs at Chatham House, for a roundtable discussion with Amory Lovins of the Rocky Mountain Institute. He says his case, filled with energy-efficient light-bulbs and other products, contains the equivalent of 200 Chernobyl-sized nuclear power stations and the North Sea. Energy efficiency is now six times as cost-effective as it was in 1984, he says. 'You can save twice as much electricity as five years ago, at one-third the cost,' he told the *Guardian*. 'Savings can be made at a cost far below what just finding the oil or operating the nuclear power stations would cost, even if building them cost nothing.'

While with FoE over here in the early 1970s, Lovins fought RTZ's plans to mine copper in Snowdonia. Now he sees himself working with industry. 'I have learnt Aikido politics, a non-violent martial art in which instead of fighting an opponent you dance with a partner. A better idea

emerges than either would have thought up and either can take the credit.'
One energy-efficient light-bulb could prevent the release of a ton of
carbon dioxide over its life-time.

Friday 28 April

Work on next article for *Guardian*, on the Green Office. Call Managing
Director of Tipp-Ex, who are now selling a 'green' correction fluid — but
not advertising the fact. They are approaching it on a softly, softly basis,
planning to let the market decide. But it's difficult to see quite how the
market can decide in favour of 'New Formula' Tipp-Ex when it doesn't
know it exists. Tipp-Ex, apparently, fear repeating Coca-Cola's mistake
of launching a new formula and then being forced by consumer demand
to reintroduce the original product.

In his speech to the Civic Trust's Building a Better Britain exhibition
yesterday, Prince Charles launched a major attack on Romania's
President Ceausescu, who has embarked on the wholesale destruction of
his country's cultural and human heritage. To achieve this plan, some
8,000 villages could be demolished, together with churches, ancestral
graveyards and every connection with the rural people's past. By
demolishing traditional homes and replacing them with pokey flats in
looming tower-blocks, Prince Charles said, President Ceausescu is
striking 'not only at the soul of the people but also at the patrimony which
belongs to all mankind'.

Elsewhere in the Communist world, and cheered on by hundreds of
thousands of Chinese workers, a human tide of students surged through
Peking yesterday — ignoring threats of reprisals. 'Whoever has the
backing of youth has the backing of the future,' they told the Party. 'Long
live democracy. Long live the people. Down with corruption.'

The *Guardian* carries a report by Paul Webster on the fight by the
French Greens to save one of Europe's last untamed rivers, the Loire.
Tours has frequently been hit by devastating floods and a new dam is seen
as the first step of an ambitious programme to control the 620-mile Loire
and its tributaries. Perhaps surprisingly, the dam project has been
approved by Environment Minister Brice Lalonde, the former French FoE
leader who ran as a Green presidential candidate in 1981. The decision
has not made him popular in the Green movement.

Saturday 29 April

Some good news, though. On the third anniversary of the Chernobyl
disaster, the Soviet Environment Minister Dr Feodor Morgun said
yesterday that the Russians plan to increase their environmental protection spending and to cut pollution over Northern Europe by up to 40% by

1993. But they have a long way to go. Dr Morgun admitted that many European countries and the United States allocate twice as much money to the environment as the Soviet Union. The pace of change in the Soviet Union is breathtaking. Will it last?

Both *The Green Consumer Guide* and *The Green Consumer's Supermarket Shopping Guide* get a mention in *The Times* today. And *Business* magazine reports on the Ecology Building Society's progress: with assets growth of 32% last year, it is Britain's fastest growing building society. With assets of £3 million, the business is still small, but the Society — run by Bob Lowman — is unique in that it will only lend on properties which 'conserve resources, save energy or preserve communities'. Lowman recalls: 'When we started, people thought we were nutcases'.

The challenge facing these small green pioneers is to withstand the competitive pressure once the big financial institutions wake up to the need to 'go green'.

Sunday 30 April

Various participants at Mrs T's Greenhouse Effect seminar are now expressing outrage that they have, in effect, been used to 'rubber-stamp' her nuclear push. The main thrust of the meeting was that greater energy efficiency was the way forward. David Cope of CEED told the *Observer*'s Geoffrey Lean that Energy Secretary Cecil Parkinson's later report on the meeting was 'very, very partial . . . I was very surprised and very shocked'.

In *The Sunday Times*, Robert Harris neatly sums up the Government's water privatisation plans — now the subject of a £1 million-a-month advertising campaign. 'People are being forced to pay for adverts they do not notice,' he says, 'in order to buy shares they do not want in an industry they already own.' Gallup says three-quarters of the population oppose water privatisation.

Evidence of a deeper threat to urban society in New York this week, where a savage gang-rape left a young investment banker brain-damaged and in a coma. The attackers, black youths aged 14 to 17, were engaged in what they call 'wilding'. *Going to do a little violence*, as one put it. Urban America, says *The Sunday Times*, is sitting on a time-bomb: 'The emergence of an illiterate, illegitimate, poverty-stricken, crack-plagued, crime-ridden, AIDS-infested residuum, which shares none of society's opportunities and few of its standards.'

If there is ever to be a sustainable green revolution, equity issues will have to be addressed. But it will be interesting to see whether Greens are happy to set and enforce — or see enforced — standards in areas other than environmental protection.

MAY

Monday 1 May

Overcast Bank Holiday Monday. Someone has tried to repeat the Hungerford massacre, killing one man and injuring more than a dozen others. Thank God he only had a shotgun, not an automatic rifle or a machine gun.

Meanwhile, it turns out that the poison gas the Russian troops used on demonstrators in Georgia last month was chloroacetophenone, last used by Germany in WWI, with devastating effects. Are the forces of reaction trying to discredit Gorbachev?

Writing in *Pravda*, Grigory Revenko, First Secretary of the Kiev region of the Soviet Union, says that safety is taking a back seat at Chernobyl, with trained specialists in short supply and workers still struggling to find the best way of sealing off the damaged No. 4 reactor. With aging nuclear rectors around the Soviet Union, I suspect we have not seen the last of nuclear disasters there — and it is clear that their capacity to respond is already taxed to the limit.

In a letter to the *Daily Telegraph*, Tom Burke notes — on the subject of Mrs T's Greenhouse Effect seminar — that political seminars resemble computers: prejudice in, prejudice out. The Government, he argues, has consistently refused to carry out an evaluation of the carbon emission reduction benefits likely to flow from investments in nuclear energy and energy efficiency, despite the repeated urging of Select Committees and other public bodies. 'I am, therefore, not optimistic that anything more sophisticated than familiar prejudice from No. 10 will be the driving force for British policy on the Greenhouse Effect.'

Tuesday 2 May

Profound gloom. Feel a dire case of flu building. Even the news that Heinz have signed on for Green Shopping Day fails to help. By end of day am convinced that I want to throw the whole thing in.

Two reasons for a wider sense of depression: it looks as though the Dutch Government is going to fall this week, having failed to attract sufficient support for its tough anti-pollution stand, and Greenpeace releases a report saying that the sunken Soviet sub will leak radioactivity for 1,000 years. Radioactivity aboard the Mike class vessel is estimated to be somewhere between 10 and 20 million curies — 20 times the total amount dumped in the sea by Britain and other European countries before the practice was stopped because of pollution fears.

More hopefully, environment ministers from more than 70 countries are meeting in Helsinki to begin strengthening the Montreal Protocol, the international treaty governing the phasing out of CFCs. Apparently, since Montreal, ozone layer depletion appears to be occurring twice as rapidly as predicted. This one is going to be a long, long haul, testing the tenacity of agencies like UNEP.

Unleaded fuel sales have doubled in the last month, says Virginia Bottomley, Under Secretary of State for the Environment, now accounting for 14% of total sales. 'This is equivalent to saving 200 tonnes weight of lead in the atmosphere,' she points out.

And the UK Register of Organic Food Standards (UKROFS), set up by the Government in 1987, publishes the first truly national standards today for organic farming. It's not yet clear if the scheme will be backed by the pioneers in this field: the Soil Assocation, in particular, and British Organic Farmers and the Organic Growers' Association. Currently thought to account for around 1% of domestic consumption, extremely optimistic estimates suggest that organic farmers could perhaps meet 10% of our needs by the early years of the 21st century.

Wednesday 3 May
Off to Holland Park, walking, as usual, from the Commonwealth Institute up to Holland Park Avenue. At the moment I have to carry a large brief-case and a shoulder bag containing my Toshiba computer, plus the day's post and a dozen newspapers. Spines weren't made for this. In the background, the despairing cry of peacocks.

The Dutch Government has fallen, after seven years in office. First time an environmental issue has brought down a Western government. Politically, the 1990s could be a rough ride. Mrs Thatcher, on the other hand, is now apparently giving serious thought to the idea of a 'green' ministry. It's difficult to know whether such a ministry would carry quite as much clout as the DoE, but the chances are that it would least keep its eye on the ball.

Meanwhile, Paul Lavalle and Mette Larson, the balloonists who soared above the North Pole, say that a yellow smog is wreathing the Pole. 'It used to be said that the North Pole was somewhere God goes to escape mankind,' Lavalle told *Today*. 'But he may have to change his destination in the light of what we've discovered so far. When you are in the balloon you have a 360° horizon, but when we looked towards Europe all we could see was a sort of yellow fog.'

A declaration supporting the banning of all production and consumption of CFCs by the year 2000 has been backed by 80 countries at the UNEP meeting in Helsinki. Norway says it is prepared to allocate 0.1% of its GDP (which would mean about £60 million) towards a fund on climate change, if other industrial nations will follow suit.

America's drought last year continues to undermine the country's rural economy. The *Daily Telegraph* reports that a 'bitter harvest of homelessness' is spreading across America's farming belt, echoing John Steinbeck's classic novel of rural poverty, *The Grapes of Wrath*. 'Rural homelessness is growing faster than we can keep track of it,' said Bill Faith of the Ohio Coalition for the Homeless, 'and people are living in railroad cars and tar-paper shacks, as shelters in tiny towns we have never heard of fill up and turn people away.'

Thursday 4 May

'The environment is no longer a fringe issue in any European country, and perhaps not in any industrialised country anywhere,' says the *Financial Times* in an editorial on the fall of the Lubbers Government in Holland. In Helsinki, meanwhile, Nicholas Ridley promises swift aid to developing countries to help them phase out CFCs, but raises question marks over the proposed world climate fund — which he describes as 'rather simplistic'. Britain really is going to have to take a more positive, supportive line on all of this.

Today carries a 12-page pull-out section on the environment. One section of the supplement is titled 'So much owed by so many to these few', focusing on David Bellamy, Gerald and Lee Durrell and Sir David Attenborough. 'Our planet is now on the critical list,' says a full-page ad from the Co-op. It concludes: 'We're working on the principle that no product or package should damage the environment, whether in manufacture, use or disposal.' A tall order!

In West Germany, the world's leading producer of diesel cars, diesel sales have been badly dented by environmental concerns. Particularly hard hit have been Mercedes-Benz, Opel, Peugeot and Volkswagen. Mercedes-Benz counter that laboratory animals breathing air 300 times more polluted than that found in the average street showed no ill-effects. But the push for 'clean cars' is going to be a key trend in Europe.

Afternoon meeting with Procter & Gamble. Dick Johnson, Director of Marketing Services, suspects that Britain will follow the lead of other European countries by switching to phosphate-free detergents by this time next year. He doesn't believe it's necessary in order to protect the environment, but he suspects that one or more manufacturers will break ranks and launch phosphate-free products.

Fiona goes to Asda Festival of British Food and Farming, which takes up more of Hyde Park than any previous show. Among the green groups which have taken stands are the Vegetarian Society, Compassion in World Farming and Animal Aid. Apparently, the public interest in the show has been very strong.

Greenpeace announce that they are launching a campaign to save Britain's vanishing dolphins. Strikes a chord: we used to go down to stay with my godmother in Solva, Pembrokeshire, and there was a dolphin that would turn up in response to drumming on the side of a boat. Recall Hania and Pat, my mother, standing in the waves with their dresses rolled up, 'calling' the dolphin. He turned up the next day. Greenpeace is convinced that over-fishing and pollution are pushing dolphins and porpoises to the verge of extinction.

Friday 5 May
Catch early bus in. Beautiful weather and masses of rabbits scampering through Holland Park.

Greenpeace is attacked by Dr Margaret Klinowska, a specialist in dolphins at Cambridge University, who argues that there is no evidence of a decline in dolphin numbers — because no formal surveys have been undertaken. All good grist for the Greenpeace publicity mill.

Among the news stories today one of the most interesting focuses on Du Pont, the US's biggest chemical company, which says it now aims to become the world's most environment-friendly manufacturing business. The company's chairman and chief executive, Edgar Woolard, says that Du Pont planned to cut the amount of hazardous waste produced by its factories by 70% over the next two years. 1,000 square miles of land around the company's plants will be set aside as wildlife refuges. And there will be special cash incentives for staff who excel in environmental performance. Wonderful stuff for the book I plan to do next, *The Green Business Guide*.

In the afternoon, Kevin Gover and Andrew Litchfield of Volvo Concessionaires come in. They want SustainAbility to carry out an environmental audit of their operations, and they say I should visit Sweden to see what elements of the Scandinavian approach to environmental protection might be imported to the UK. My presentation interrupted by periodic paroxysms of coughing and wheezing.

Saturday 6 May
Green Office piece appears in the *Guardian*. They render SustainAbility in the credits as SurvivAbility! Afternoon spent at the National Theatre seeing *Hamlet* — with Daniel Day-Lewis, Judi Dench, John Castle and

Michael Bryant. Extraordinary staging: and my brain takes some elements of the play's message as a warning to try and avoid the emergence of power-politics in our own operations.

Fascinating profile of EEC Environment Commissioner Carlo Ripa di Meana in the *Financial Times*. Despite early concerns among environmentalists that he would be too light-weight, his first 100 days in office suggest otherwise. Four main issues concern him: the need for a European environmental agency; the integration of environmental policy into the Single European Market programme; the need to take the environment into account when formulating other EEC policies; and the threat posed by the loss of the tropical rainforests. 'My ambition,' he says, 'will only be completed if I can persuade the member states to devote adequate resources to the environment. I don't say that we necessarily have to have a European fund administered in Brussels — but without money everything that is said is hot air.'

In Helsinki, it looks as though the idea of setting up a world fund to save the atmosphere might even get off the ground at some stage. A working party will be exploring the potential for such a fund and considering the need for a world-wide 'carbon tax', based on the size of each country's annual production of carbon dioxide. The working group will report in 1990. 'We simply can't handle these huge problems, especially the Greenhouse Effect, without some kind of international fund,' said Kaj Barlund, Finland's Environment Minister. 'I would have preferred a stronger commitment, but I think it will happen sooner or later.'

It looks as though the next meeting of the Organisation for Economic Co-operation and Development (OECD), the 24-nation club of rich industrial nations, will be dominated by environmental issues, particularly the quest for market-based solutions. The meeting, scheduled for the end of May, may prove an interesting barometer of the trends in environmental politics. One diplomat told *The Independent*: 'There is a great head of steam building up on the environment, but there is no sense of what can be done.'

The greening of money inches forward with the announcement of a new ethical fund, the Sovereign Unit Trust Managers' Ethical Unit Trust, which will invest in UK companies that 'have a positive attitude to, and have committed resources to, the protection of the environment, environmental issues and the rights of mankind'. And Henderson Financial Management launches what it calls the world's first 'green' PEP, or personal equity plan. Its managers argue that companies with a significant position in environmental markets will grow faster than the industry average.

Sunday 7 May

Cold fusion — at least on Fleischmann/Pons lines — is declared missing, presumed dead. Optimists of the 'And in one bound he was free' school — and anyone who had hoped that a miraculous new energy source would solve our energy and environmental problems at a stroke — will have to look elsewhere. Scientists at Harwell, the Oxfordshire-based nuclear laboratory, have been trying to reproduce the cold fusion results but, says team-leader Dr David Williams: 'We have spotted neither heat nor radiation.' As *The Sunday Times* reports, the verdict is regarded as definitive because the checks were carried out with the help of Fleischmann and Pons.

Time runs quotes from scientists who went over this same scientific Niagara Falls. In 1956, for example, US physicist reported achieving low temperature fusion. It turned out he hadn't, but he recalled the 'short but exhilarating experience when we thought we had solved all of the fuel problems of mankind for the rest of time'.

So it's back to the grindstone, to difficult accommodations to new realities. In Holland, the Labour Party has agreed in principle to back the controversial environmental plan that toppled the governing Christian-Democrat-Liberal coalition last week.

The Sunday Times launches a campaign against litter, arguing that it will hit Britain's tourism receipts. 'Conservation without tourism is not possible,' says Peter Moss, Managing Director of EcoSafaris. 'But tourism without conservation would not work either, because there would be nothing to see. They need each other and, as long as tourism is controlled, it can work.'

An interesting fact in relation to our planned *Green Holiday Guide*: travel and tourism now represent the world's largest industry, reports the *Wall Street Journal*, employing more than 100 million people — or one in every 16 workers. Meanwhile, the British Tourist Authority have warned that Britain's annual £6.2 billion income from foreign visitors could go down the drain because of litter and pollution.

Monday 8 May

In early, to avoid disruptions caused by Tube strike today. In the event the roads are clear and the sun dazzling. The *Wall Street Journal* carries a long story on the impact of growing environmental concerns on the US auto industry. DEBATE OVER POLLUTION AND GLOBAL WARMING HAS DETROIT SWEATING the sub-head runs. Even though individual cars run much cleaner than those Americans drove in 1970, the year Earth Day first hit the streets and the Clean Air Act was passed, traffic has increased 70%, so the air is far dirtier than anyone reading the Act would have predicted.

In Brussels, the idea of a European Environmental Agency is gaining growing support, while an even more radical idea promoted by Carlo Ripa di Meana is getting an airing. The suggestion is that billions of dollars should be raised from a carbon dioxide tax, with the money invested in tropical forest conservation. The paper currently being circulated among senior officials points out that the Community is threatened by the loss of the rainforests directly, via the contribution to the Greenhouse Effect, and indirectly, 'by the potential collapse of development efforts locally and regionally, due to environmental disruption, with attendant threats to food supplies and hence political stability'. The Agency is a good idea, but on current evidence it is not at all clear that it will have sufficient teeth.

In Brazil, scientists say that President Sarney was wrong about the scale of rainforest destruction: instead of 5% destroyed, the actual proportion was 9.3%, or 215,000 square miles. The World Bank, on the other hand, says that an eighth of the forests have gone.

Leaders of eight South American countries at an Amazon summit in Manaus have linked rainforest protection with a better deal for their massive foreign debts. Only better debt terms, they say, would permit economic growth and thus enable them to afford environmental conservation. Brazil continues to resist 'debt-for-nature' swaps, which run down debt burdens in return for large areas being turned over to conservation. Will it come up with a viable alternative?

More and more companies are ringing us up and asking for environmental audits. Dow Europe rang back today to say they were delighted with the meeting the other night and promptly booked a couple of days of my time to talk through the next steps. Valin Pollen is one of the companies that called today asking for an audit of one of their clients, a regional electricity board on the road to privatisation.

It's extraordinary how many people these days comment that we are riding the crest of the 'green wave', on a 'green roll' and so on. We are, of course, and it will be interesting to see whether we can steer this thing, or whether we will simply be carried along and dumped wherever the wave is bound. At this stage, I think we have a good chance of steering it.

Wednesday 10 May
Day starts with a meeting with Ian Blair of AEG, Werner Zickerman (an AEG Director) and Charles Secrett of FoE. AEG have been shocked by FoE's reaction to the news, brought to their notice by *City Limits* during the life of the Green Kitchen stand, that AEG is involved in defence electronics. I suggested the meeting to Ian so that AEG could hear a little more about the FoE perspective — and vice versa.

To begin with Zickerman cannot understand why FoE can't simply accept that AEG is keen to work for 'the cause' and fails to see where weaponry and so on fit into the picture. We explain that there are all sorts of reasons why Greens disapprove of the military. Not only is it a question of the impact of military activities, and of war, but also of the opportunity cost of defence budgets, the massive diversion of resources — including trained manpower — from the central tasks that now confront us.

FoE are in a difficult position: on the one hand they want to promote green products, but they don't want to be seen as endorsing companies like AEG across the board. Charles explains that it would be like holding up a green-painted fingernail on a horrendous beast and insisting that because the nail looked attractive, the whole beast was beautiful. He explains that FoE want to look at the whole beast and are moving towards environmental auditing. He notes that there are 'many things we can do privately, and some things we can do publicly, to help industry go green'.

After an hour and a half, the conversation has become much more relaxed. I mention that the same chips that are used in automatic bank tills can be used to guide rockets and Zickerman notes that AEG has even supplied washing machines for use on nuclear submarines! There are a nest of writhing issues here which environmentalists are going to have to address, but equally it is essential that companies like AEG understand the very different — but potentially complementary — perspectives prevailing in different parts of the Green movement.

On the subject of submarines, Greenpeace claims that the USA and Soviet Union between them have littered the ocean floor with at least 48 nuclear weapons and 11 nuclear reactors — most of them lost by the Soviet Union.

And a UN survey just published suggests that China, Japan, Argentina and Mexico are starting to share the same green concerns as countries like West Germany and Norway. There is less concern, unsurprisingly, in the poorer developing countries, such as Kenya, Nigeria, Senegal, India and Jamaica.

Mrs T is showing every sign of attempting to seize the initiative on the Greenhouse Effect. In New York on Monday Sir Crispin Tickell, Britain's permanent representative to the UN, told the UN Economic and Social Council: 'The British Government has long been concerned at the prospect that the steady increase of the so-called greenhouse gases in the atmosphere — especially carbon dioxide, chlorofluourocarbons and methane — could lead to a rise in average temperature with incalculable consequences for human society.' This is surely going too far? The UK government resisted controls on CFCs until very recently. But, then, they say a week is a long time in politics!

Thursday 11 May
Now even the white cliffs of Dover are apparently threatened by the Greenhouse Effect. Soft cliffs on the Channel and North Sea coasts have already been eaten away by wave erosion at the rate of up to five yards a year, says Professor Keith Clayton of the University of East Anglia — and the Greenhouse Effect could accelerate that rate by about three times by the year 2030.

Meanwhile, Nicholas Ridley was warning Britain's farmers of a pending Government crack-down on pollution caused by the use of nitrate fertilizers and the careless disposal of farm waste. *The Times* saw the Minister's speech as strong evidence that he is trying to go green, but there were signs that this leopard is going to find its spots impossible to change. 'Public concern for human health and the environment is manifesting itself increasingly in demands for organically-grown produce,' he said. 'I personally view it as a way for you to rip off the customer by charging more for identical produce. But you need a break sometimes!' Some Ministers need their necks broken sometimes.

The Government has cleared Alar, the apple spray suspected of causing cancer in children. The product has been banned in New Zealand and the same evidence that has persuaded MAFF to clear Alar has persuaded the US Environmental Protection Agency to reach the interim conclusion that Alar does pose a cancer risk. Here, Tesco has banned the use of Alar in its apple and pear suppliers.

Sukey Firth, Davy Sims and Dymphna Flynn of Radio 1 are putting together an Environmental Week for 26 June–1 July, dubbed The Green 1. Since as many as 17 million people listen to Radio 1 every week, the main audience being aged 16 to 30, it's a worthwhile target. They have asked me to do some fact sheets to send out to listeners who write or call in. Last time they did something like this, some 17,000 young people wrote in.

During lunch one of the issues we discuss over the battered octopus rings is the state of the seas. The scale of the problem is indicated by a House of Commons written reply last night. The area in which the container of Lindane was lost in the Channel, it turns out, was used by the UK for the disposal of surplus explosives from 1946 until about 1971, and for the disposal of low level radioactive waste from 1950 to 1963! We really do live in a planetary dustbin.

'All the signs are that the 1990s will be a decade of tighter environmental controls and of growing consumer pressure for more environmentally-friendly products and practices,' Lord Young said yesterday. The market for pollution control technology is worth between £100 million and £150 billion a year, he concluded. 40,000 copies of a booklet on the ways in which DTI can now help firms 'go green' are being sent out.

Friday 12 May
First copy of *Cleaning Up* comes through. This is the third in a series of reports I have written — the last two with Jonathan Shopley — for the World Resources Institute. This one looks at the potential for the US waste management and pollution control industry to help push forward Third World sustainable development. Our aim has been to build a constituency for sustainable development in key emerging technology sectors in the United States.

The Times runs an editorial welcoming Nicholas Ridley's challenge to the farming community (telling them to move away from artificial fertilisers) and mentioning the key role of the Green Consumer. The NFU, on the other hand, calls Mr Ridley's remarks 'ill-timed and inopportune'. But change is in the wind. ICI says it plans to launch a range of nitrogen-free fertilisers for arable crops, called Cropstart.

Marketing runs a front-page story, VIDOR BLOWS A GREEN FUSE. Battery manufacturer Vidor's Sales and Marketing Director, Barry Wells, has sent a letter to both trade and press claiming that so-called green batteries are nothing more than marketing hype. Consumers and the trade alike, he says, are being duped. Ever Ready retorts that this is simply a case of sour grapes, because Vidor sees its market share being pinched. I am quoted to the effect that Vidor may find that this strategy backfires — since the controversy may help cut battery sales by persuading consumers that mains electricity is much greener (it takes up to 50 times as much energy to make a battery as you ever get out of it) than even the greenest of batteries.

Chase WWF on the Green Label proposal. Incensed to hear that they haven't even sent it in to the DoE yet. Apparently they are rethinking their whole strategy. Insist that unless we can get a labelling scheme off the ground, the whole Green Consumer initiative could be undermined. WWF promise they will send it in immediately and keep the pressure on.

Saturday 13 May
Writing in *The Independent*, Duff Hart-Davis suggests that to help curb the Greenhouse Effect governments should decree, every now and then, a Day of Zero Excursion (or DOZE). Everyone, except the emergency services, would switch off their engines for the duration. 'With aircraft grounded, cars, trains and buses at a standstill and the population back on foot or two wheels, we should not only give the environment a break,

but also return ourselves to a state of tranquillity that has long since gone away.' Nice idea — maybe we *will* see the emergence of a Green Sabbath?

And a tongue-in-cheek piece by Andrew Freeman in the *Financial Times* who, anxious to be a model citizen, tells how he tried to dispose of his fridge.

'We duly lugged the fridge out of our first-floor flat and manoeuvred it into our car. At the dump we were shown where to leave the fridge —by the side of a large skip which was full of twisted metal. Before unloading it, I made a final check on its fate.

'"You do break this up safely, don't you," I asked.

'"I dunno what you mean, guv'nor," came the reply.

'"Well, draining the CFCs, protecting the environment, that sort of thing."

'"Listen mate, all we do is put it in the skip and flog it to a scrap merchant. For all I know, he drinks the CFCs. You don't want to worry about it."

'And that was that. Home went the fridge,' and so on.

Great fun, but a useful reminder that the infrastructure for Green Consumers generally is still non-existent. Also ends with a great plug for *The Green Consumer Guide*. The main problem is that our recommendations on fridges are now somewhat out of date. We are going to have to update, one way or another.

The Independent carries a massive, two-page ad for British Nuclear Fuels on the Greenhouse Effect which, it says, 'has become one of the world's hottest topics'. The answer, not surprisingly, turns out to be nuclear power.

Environmentalists will not be amused — indeed, we can expect a strong riposte. A few pages on is a photo of the Greenpeace vessel *Beluga* and several other small boats surrounding the aircraft carrier *Ark Royal* during its visit to Hamburg. One of the boats carry a banner, in German, saying: 'Warning: atom bombs on board.'

In the States, Exxon — under massive pressure from ethical investors — says it will appoint an environmentalist to its board, to advise on future policy. Harrison 'Jay' Goldin, who for some reason apparently wants to be mayor of New York, accomplished the turn-around by threatening to stir up a revolt among shareholders who held a total of $1 billion (£600 million) of Exxon shares.

Sunday 14 May
On the day that Chico Mendes was murdered, Karl Zeigler read a news item which he found equally appalling. Brazil's 1988 coffee crop was

expected to fall 35–40% below the previous year's — because of climatic changes brought about by clouds of smoke from the country's burning forests. According to a report in *The Sunday Times*, Zeigler was a banker who played a leading role in the 'lending frenzy' era of the 1970s, persuading Latin American and African governments to accept loans they had no hope of repaying. Now he has converted — and has come up with a plan for saving Amazonia.

Instead of 'debt-for-nature' swaps, which Latin Americans view as little more than 'gringo blackmail', we should try a 'Something for Nothing' strategy. The Amazon represents a far more valuable resource to Brazil than oil does to Saudi Arabia, because it's renewable. The West, Zeigler suggests, should write off Brazil's debt in return for determined action to save the rainforest. 'Brazil would be charging rent, so to speak, because the forest helps to keep the world a cleaner place. The rent would be servicing Brazil's debt.'

The Zeigler plan is now being considered by Brazil and other Governments. Zeigler appears to be collaborating with ethnobiologist Dr Conrad Gorinsky, who was involved in the Earthlife and Bioresources ventures in Cameroon and Latin America. It is difficult to exaggerate the importance of tackling these problems, but the solutions are not going to be easy ones.

British Aerospace, meanwhile, has built a new scanner to monitor damage to the ozone layer and the build-up of the Greenhouse Effect. Called Isams, it will be blasted into space on an American space shuttle early next year — if all goes to plan.

Dutch researchers say they have proved that the DoE's claim that lean-burn engines are better than catalytic converters at cleaning up vehicle exhaust emissions is wrong. They have found that, while lean-burn engines use a fifth less fuel than conventional engines, the cleanest emissions are from exhausts fitted with three-way catalytic converters, which cut harmful emissions by up to 90%.

A tougher MoT test is in prospect in the UK from 1991, which will measure emissions of carbon monoxide, unburnt hydrocarbons and nitrogen oxides. Fail the test and you will have to fit a catalytic converter. Older cars will be exempt. 'The situation will be self-solving,' says the Department of Transport, rather lamely. 'Older cars will not last forever.' But will the problem be 'self-solving' in time? I think not.

Monday 15 May
Julia flies to Leicester for the Co-op's launch of its £2 million 'going green' initiative, starring David Bellamy. A Harris poll of 1,000 adults apparently showed that, while most were concerned about the impact of

products on the environment, they didn't know how to choose environment-friendly products.

The environment, Prince Charles told Selina Scott yesterday on CBS TV, 'is the biggest issue of our day'. Although he said his advisers often advise him to tone down his speeches, he said he would continue to speak out on environmental and architectural issues. 'I had been talking about the environment for quite a long time when I was just dismissed as a crank,' he recalled. 'Now I'm going to go on talking about it. I'm not stopping just because it's become a political issue, I can assure you, and I'm going to go on even more — because now at last there's an audience.'

In the States, President Bush has bowed to pressure from environmentalists and is now accepting that the US should commit itself to work towards an international convention on global warming. East European environmentalists won a big victory at the weekend when the Hungarian government suspended all work on the giant Nagymaros dam; and in Australia, 'Greenie' environmentalists won 17% of the vote in the Tasmanian state elections and now hold the balance of power.

Tuesday 16 May
Wonderful set of massive headlines in today's *Times*: A DEADLY HARVEST OF THE LAND (second major feature on river pollution) and STORM GATHERS OVER BUSH INACTION ON GREEN ISSUES. The Government is slammed by new House of Lords Select Committee report for its 'inaction' on hazardous waste. Meanwhile, ironically, Mrs T's greening is getting a good press across the States, while President Bush — who said he would bring environmental issues to the top of the political agenda — is having a rough ride.

'It is no exaggeration,' comments Michael Oppenheimer of the Environmental Defense Fund, 'to say that the global environment may become the over-reaching issue for the next 40 years in the way that the Cold War defined our world over the past 40.' Spot on: have been saying the same in recent speeches.

Over here, a 5,000-word *Blueprint for a Green Europe* is launched by FoE, WWF, CPRE and the Green Alliance. It sets a series of environmental goals for the European Community in advance of the European elections on June 15. Perhaps the most interesting aspect of the exercise is the collaboration between the various groups — a signal in itself.

The Government announces that Britain's oil bonanza will continue for another 25 years. Given that the North Sea oil has pumped an estimated £70 billion into the UK economy over the last decade, that has to be good news, but what happens when it's gone? Fusion scientists think they have the answer, again: a US committee is now arguing in favour of a strong acceleration of research on 'hot', high-temperature fusion. The report was completed before the uproar over 'cold fusion'.

Birds swoop over the bluebells, nettles and campions as I walk back through Holland Park around 20.00. Skateboarders blur past the 'No Skateboarding' signs. Hot evening as I work at the Toshiba. But it's even hotter for African elephants; 300 are slaughtered each day by poachers. Elephant populations are down two-thirds from the 1950s, to less than a million. Four more countries (Austria, Chad, Hungary and Niger) have joined Kenya, Tanzania and the USA in calling for a total world ban on the ivory trade. WWF and IUCN, the two biggest conservation organisations, remain unconvinced that a ban would work, however, but unless something fairly drastic is done most of Africa's elephants will be little more than bleached skeletons and novelty sculptures by the turn of the century.

Wednesday 17 May

Elaine commented to a seven-year-old friend of Hania's today that she, Tara, looked as though she had caught the sun. 'No,' said Tara, 'it's the Greenhouse Effect.' Meanwhile, an American immunologist warned that AIDS victims could die faster if they get too much sunlight — and that the ozone hole is almost certainly making matters worse.

Start off by cutting business papers in the office. Germany's Blue Angel labelling scheme for environment-friendly products features on the front cover of the *Wall Street Journal*. A recent survey suggests that 75% of German consumers prefer to buy one of the 2,500+ Blue Angel products, if the choice is available.

In the States, the *Daily Telegraph* reports, apple growers have bowed to consumer pressure, with widespread concern about apples and apple juice, and have voluntarily abandoned the use of Alar. The chemical is used to stop apples dropping off the tree, to improve their redness and crispness, and to extend their shelf-life. But the consumer is King/Queen — and not prepared to rely on the advice of Government tasters. Losses to apple growers and juice processors could reach $100 million this year.

In Britain, according to the *Guardian*, comedienne Pamela Stephenson, actor Ben Kingsley, opera singer Kiri Te Kanawa and director Terry Gilliam are among those backing a new pressure group, Parents for Safe Food. They will petition Downing Street for food labelling to name pesticides used on apples and other food crops. 'Apples are supposed to be the symbol of health,' said Stephenson, 'and it made me angry to think I may have harmed my children.'

In Alaska, the evidence suggests that some of the major fisheries have escaped destruction by the Exxon oil. 'This is not to say that there has been no ecological disaster here,' said one Fish and Game Department spokesman. 'The birds and sea otters and wildlife that depend on the beaches and the land-sea interface have been devastated, but the fishing seems to have been less affected than expected.' However, first-of-the-season sockeye salmon, usually flown south like August 12 grouse or Beaujolais Nouveau, failed to command any sort of premium this year. Environmentalists are expected to call for Exxon president Lawrence Rawl's resignation at the company's annual shareholders' meeting tomorrow.

In Scotland, meanwhile, 7,000 mature salmon escaped from a fish farm into Loch Aline, near Oban, on Monday. The propeller of a boat taking stocks of young fish out to sea hit nets holding the salmon. Millions of fish, mostly smolts, are thought to escape each year, raising fears of 'genetic pollution' of wild salmon stocks.

Flexible polyurethane foam makers say they will drop CFC blowing agents sooner than expected, by 1991 rather than 1993. The foams are used in car seats, furniture and bedding. Fascinating piece in the *Guardian* yesterday about Thomas Midgley, an American inventor born 100 years ago in 1889. He gave the world both leaded petrol and CFCs!

At the time, both looked like miracle products, one helping to trigger the massive growth of the auto industry, the other that of the refrigeration and air-conditioning markets. The ultimate comment on the man's life was the manner of his death. He contracted polio in 1940 and was partially paralysed. He promptly devised a system of pulleys to help him get in and out of bed — and succeeded in strangling himself with the apparatus in 1944. Has he done the same for the planet's ozone layer?

Thursday 18th May
In Britain, *Today* publishes a public opinion poll sponsored by paint-makers Crown Berger which shows that one in two Britons believe that cleaning up the environment should be the nation's top priority. Pollution is top of the list of concerns, followed by litter and the 'disappearing countryside'. The Government announces today that it plans to double expenditure on road-building, an announcement which will send shudders down many green spines. The Thatcher administration increasingly seems to be suffering from an advanced case of schizophrenia.

The *Wall Street Journal* runs a massive piece on organic agriculture, although it quotes one farmer who predicts that the reduction of agrochemical inputs would simply result in a 'nightmare of weeds'. In the *Financial Times*, Professor Martin Parry of Birmingham University argues that British farmers could well benefit from the Greenhouse Effect. 'We should not rule out the possibility of northern and central Europe increasing its role as a producer to the world food market,' he says.

But the big news today is China, where massive protests against the

Government have overwhelmed the Chinese–Soviet summit. More than a million demonstrators have brought Peking to a standstill. The epicentre is Tiananmen Square where many of the 3,000 hunger-strikers continue to fast. A sense of profound changes in the air around the world. But echoes of Poland in the early 1980s; the reaction will presumably come before long. Will the Western correspondents stick around to see what happens after Gorbachev has gone? Too often, we encourage people to stand up for their rights, but fail to stick around to see the same people punched senseless — or worse.

Call Volvo Concessionaires this afternoon. We have won the environmental audit contract with them.

Leave the office at 21.30. A hazy, May moon hangs in the sky and in the warm evening air the plants give off an almost Mediterranean scent. See two No. 9's racing each other into the distance. Kick my heels for 20 minutes. Not sure I can put up with the vagaries of public transport, particularly if I am going to be working late at Princes Place.

Friday 19 May
Beautiful summer weather. Off to Covent Garden for Packaging and the Environment conference. Heaving, packed Tube train from Hammersmith. The windows between the cars are open and a long mane of hair streams through from a girl in the next car up. The Connaught Rooms are also heaving at the seams with delegates: there must have been over 400 and the heat was New Yorkish. Some good papers, but also a great deal of special pleading by manufacturers of competing materials like glass, paper and plastics. But one thing is clear: the environment is becoming an intensely competitive issue for business.

Robert Swan, the British leader of the international Icewalk team which has reached the North Pole on foot, arrives back in London today. 'What does it mean, this broken body? It means a commitment,' he says in a diary extract published in *The Times*. 'We must fight to press home our message of environmental concern and call to action. I haven't slept in 70 hours. I sit alone in my hotel room, on the telephone 24 hours a day speaking to the world media. It is our role, the team's that is, to engage the public in their own quest for survival. The effort we made to survive in the Arctic must be reciprocated on a global basis. We have been to the North Pole; we have come back. I know there is hope. Now the real fight begins.'

In New York, Exxon seems to have got away with it. 'We will be there as long as it takes,' the company's chairman, Lawrence Rawl, says of the Alaskan disaster. 'We will pay whatever it takes.' The *Wall Street Journal* reports that Exxon has already lost $115 million because of the spill. 7,000 people are now working on the clean-up, along with 700 vessels, 56 aircraft and more than 90 miles of booms to contain the oil. The company rejected a proposal put forward by environmentalists, that it should launch a $1 billion environmental trust — and the idea that actor Robert Redford should replace Rawl got short shrift at the shareholders' meeting!

In Colorado, 200 people living near the Rocky Mountain Arsenal have filed the first private lawsuit against the Shell Oil Company over land and groundwater contamination at a former pesticide manufacturing site near Denver. If they win, it could add tens of millions of dollars to a clean-up bill that will already total an estimated $1 billion.

In Brazil, where half the cars (and three-quarters of all new cars) run on alcohol rather than petrol, emergency measures have been decreed to ration fuel alcohol — which is produced by fermenting sugar cane and is 25% cheaper than petrol. The Government is now apparently looking at ways of *cutting* long-term alcohol demand.

Here the Green Party has launched its Euro-election campaign. Its manifesto, *Don't Let Your World Turn Grey*, argues that the emergence of the Single European Market from 1992 will cause untold environmental damage. It derides the vision of Europe as '320 million shoppers in a supermarket'. The Greens want a much greater degree of self-reliance, with 'local goods for local needs'. They say they would abandon the Chunnel, nuclear power stations, the Common Agricultural Policy and agrochemicals. The imagination boggles at the scale of the task they are setting themselves.

The Government has at last banned the pesticide Aldrin, made by Shell among others, because it was found to be building up in the tissues of fish in the River Newlyn, Cornwall, where it is used to treat narcissus bulbs and in potting compost.

Saturday 20 May
The turmoil in China goes on as millions wait to see if Deng Xiaoping and his colleagues will resign. No one seems to know what will happen if Deng has other ideas.

All the motorways into the capital have been blocked by peasants who stopped five columns of army trucks on their way to restore order. Workers say they are planning a general strike. The Government's attempt to impose virtual martial law may have backfired. Tiananmen Square, dominated by massive statues of Mao's revolutionary heroes, has become a 'state within a state'.

Hot, hazy weather. My plastics piece appears in the *Guardian*. On the eve of the launch of Sheffield's new guise as 'Recycling City', I note that if recycling can be made to work nationwide, the plastics industry could still surprise us all by becoming a green industry of the 1990s.

Full-page Co-op ad in *The Independent*, asking: Is the world being destroyed? Interesting to see how the language of *The Guide* has been picked up, from 'products that don't cost the Earth' through to the Co-op's use today of the phrasing of its policy that 'no product or package should damage the environment, *whether in manufacture, use or disposal*'.

Elaine, Gaia and I happen upon a tasting of Southern Hemisphere wines, at the Barnes Wine Shop today. Some wonderful wines — real sense of the fruits of the earth. Bump into Robert Handyside there, who set up the Real Cheese Shop, both in Barnes and elsewhere. He says he is going greener, with biodegradable plastic bags on order. He also plans to ask his customers to bring their own plastic bags, but isn't sure what the response will be!

Sunday 21 May
In China, although tanks move towards the area of insurrection, the threatened confrontation doesn't come. In the *Observer*, Jonathan Mirsky notes that while this is people power in action, 'this is not the Philippines, where the people knew that Marcos had to go and that they wanted Cory Aquino. Here they know which leaders they want to get rid of, but they cannot tell you the name of a single hero'.

The paper also makes the point that the Chinese word for crisis is *jiwei*, which is made up of two other words, meaning danger and opportunity. The danger is incontrovertible, but can some members of the Central Committee seize the opportunity and, by moving the world's most populous country towards a form of democracy and greater economic stability, defuse the current crisis?

1989, says Norman Macrae in *The Sunday Times*, could well turn out to be as momentous a year in human history as 1789 was. The turmoil now going on in some of the leading Communist countries could be the beginnings of a new world order. On the other hand, the sheer scale of the crisis could bypass the opportunity and leave us in a situation where one of the big Communist superpowers was run not by a Gorbachev, but by a Galtieri! Democracy without massive monetary and economic reforms can result in the sort of hyperinflation (6,000% a year) seen in Argentina, where the Peronist candidate, Menem, has just been elected.

A different form of cloud is at the heart of Conrad Gorinsky's plans, outlined in *The Sunday Times*. Conrad, a British biochemist born of Amerindian extraction in Guyana, near the Brazilian border, has carried out pioneering research on the medical use of plant compounds by indigenous peoples. Last year he established the Foundation for Ethno-biology, in the wake of the liquidation of Earthlife and Bioresources. 'The

Amazon basin,' he says, 'holds a fifth of the world's fresh water. It acts like a heart. Airborne moisture is brought in from the Atlantic on a blanket of water, half of which is then locked into the Amazon's trees — each being a powerful pump. They distribute it across the Andes to the northern and southern hemispheres. This system is now being destroyed to meet Brazil's debts. We have perhaps ten years before the point of no return is reached. Then it's irreversible: the heart dies.'

His suggestion: write off Brazil's $50 billion national debt and launch a Green Bank funded by $50 billion of Green Bonds, with a mandate to rehabilitate and conserve the environment. The best people to consult on 'forest technology', he stresses, are the Amerindians themselves. 'They will be our barefoot professors.'

The sun begins to drop into the late afternoon haze; the children and I take to the streets on skates and cycles. A number of other children join in as we cause traffic havoc. Pied Piper on wheels.

Monday 22 May
Downpour as we awake. The world smells pulsatingly damp, almost tropical. In the park, the foxgloves are just coming into bloom. In Peking, amazingly, the protestors have staved off the Chinese army for the third night running and there are signs of deep divisions in the highest levels of the government. According to *The Times*, the students are chanting 'Handcuffs are useless' and 'Bullets won't penetrate us'. Strong temptation to touch wood!

Meanwhile, Moscow is back to its bad old ways of the Cold War days. There are clearly some parts of the Kremlin which *glasnost* and the new thinking hasn't yet penetrated. It has expelled 11 Britons in a tit-for-tat for the earlier expulsion of 11 suspected Russian spies. 'For a journalist to leave Moscow at a time like this is the cruellest possible punishment,' says Angus Roxburgh, the expelled *Sunday Times* Moscow correspondent. 'Perhaps only here, over the past couple of years, has there been a sense of history in the making and journalists have the excitement of reporting not just the making of a new Russia but possibly of a new world order.'

Ark is apparently one of the Western environmental organisations now trying to forge links with like-minded organisations in the Soviet Union. Today Julia and I went to the Ark launch of seven environment-friendly household cleaners. They have enlisted the help of Paul and Linda McCartney, Bob and Paula Geldof, Lenny Henry, Dawn French and Cliff Richard. The whole thing leaves us feeling slightly uneasy about the ratio of celebrities to real message. The products, made in Germany, are available through Tesco, Safeway, Gateway, Superdrug and other stores. Fears of a new outbreak of the distemper plague which killed two-thirds of the seals in the Wash and 17,000 in northern Europe have been revived by the discovery of several infected carcasses in Norfolk.

The witches of Kent have had a go at BR. They met at the Countless Stones or Little Kity Coty Stones, which BR's Channel Tunnel rail link threatens to obliterate. After the incantations, the *Guardian* reports, a small plastic train carriage was doused with methylated spirits and lit. The High Priest, called Kevin, and his wife led the chant: 'BR begone! BR begone!'

Wednesday 24 May

Stand in the queue, waiting for the bus and watch the goslings, ducklings and baby coots parading back and forth on Barnes Pond, leaving a wake through the pollen-dusted water. A carp periodically breaches, leaping right out of the water, occasionally right in front of a startled water-bird.

Horribly hot, with the sun grilling Annie, Fiona and Isabelle under the glass roof.

With 1.5 million tonnes of air for every human, says an Australian paper, 'it isn't easy to pollute the entire atmosphere. But mankind has finally done it.' In Sydney, there have been an extraordinary 73 wet days in the last 90. Central Australia is in danger of turning into a lake. In Britain, scientists are now predicting another sweltering, waterless summer like 1976. London temperatures yesterday were the warmest for May since 1939.

SEVEN OUT OF TEN MUMS FEAR SWIM IN FILTHY SEA, runs the headline in *Today*. A MORI survey carried out for ICI has found that seven out of ten mothers believe that sewage pollution has made the traditional seaside holiday unsafe — and 60% think our beaches are even dirtier than the Mediterranean's. In Southampton, Greenpeace's *Moby Dick* is blockading the Southern Water authority's sludge tanker, the *Mancunium*, which dumps sewage sludge at sea around the British coast.

There are a number of sub-texts here. For one thing, ICI has always said that its massive effluent discharges into rivers and seas pale into insignificance when compared with water authority sewage discharges. And ICI has also developed a strong new sodium hypochlorite disinfectant, called Coast Guard, which it says should be used to disinfect sewage before discharge to the sea. According to some of the press reports, ICI also intends to use the product in the sea itself. Unbelievable.

And in the States, investigating the *Exxon Valdez* disaster, Federal Government wildlife officials say their body count to date includes 17,043 birds, 706 sea otters, 80 deer, four killer whales and two young seals.

Mrs T is urging a complete ban on the sale of new ivory, to try to slow the slaughter of the African elephant. Britain, according to *The Independent*, plans to call for a Europe-wide ban at the next meeting of Community environment ministers on June 8.

Thursday 25 May
Strange weather, like a seaside town, with a cool summer haze.

The world's population is growing faster, according to the *Daily Telegraph*, reporting the latest statistics from the Population Reference Bureau. By midsummer, there will be 5.24 billion of us, nearly 250 million more than there were in 1987. Our numbers are rising by 90 million a year, which means that at current rates the world's population will double in 39 years — by 2038, or by the time, God willing, I am 79.

Britain, meanwhile, has decided to back EC proposals to require catalytic converters on all new small cars by 1993. Bad news indeed for UK manufacturers, who had been relying on 'lean-engines' to bail them out. Although catalytic converters will boost carbon dioxide emissions, with pollutants like carbon monoxide, nitrogen oxides and unburnt hydrocarbons broken down into nitrogen, water vapour and carbon dioxide.

Information technology, the *Daily Telegraph* reports, has done nothing to save paper. Instead, a new Princeton University study concludes, 'the paperless office, the bookless library, the cashless, chequeless society, all have gone the way of the Empire State Building's dirigible mooring, the backyard helipad, the nuclear-powered convertible and the vitamin-pill dinner'. The UN headquarters in New York alone printed and distributed 676 million pages of documents last year. Since 1959, annual US consumption of writing and printing paper has risen from less than seven million tons to more than 24 million tons — a 243% increase.

Saturday 27 May
The rumoured arrest of Zhao Ziyang, leader of the Chinese Communist Party, signals the end for China students, according to *The Times*. The number of students in Tiananmen Square dropped to its lowest since the protests began as the news went around, although student leaders say they are still confident that they can mobilise the people if necessary.

Whatever happens, though, there is a real sense that the protests — even if they themselves haven't changed the world — symptomise the deep-rooted changes now taking place, particularly in the Communist world. The coverage of the demonstrations shows how the communist nations are being absorbed into the Global Village. Massacres look bad on TV, although it looks as though some very senior Party heads are going to roll.

More top heads should also roll in industry following major disasters, says solicitor David McIntosh in *The Times*. His firm has represented the drug company involved in the Opren case and the water authority involved in the Abbeystead disaster in Lancashire. He believes such recent disasters as the Piper Alpha oil-platform explosion and the King's Cross fire would have been less catastrophic if safety and evacuation measures had been properly focused upon and provided by those in power. 'Surely justice demands personal answerability where senior management has abrogated its safety responsiblities in favour of production and profit.' Increasingly, management seems unwilling to accept that a major disaster is the sort of failure that should trigger resignations.

Meanwhile, the Dutch Cabinet presented the world's first costed, multi-year national programme to Parliament. 'This is not a consultation document,' Environment Minister Ed Nijpels said of the National Environmental Policy Plan. There is cross-party support for the measures, which aim to cut pollution by at least 70% by 2010, but the Plan will be a major issue in the elections. The proportion of the country's wealth devoted to environmental protection will almost double by 1994, putting a further £10 a month on the cost of living for every Dutch household.

Sunday 28 May
It's a helter-skelter year. Cold fusion will solve our energy problems, then it won't. Then a thousand flowers bloom in Peking, only to be ground into the soiled paving of Tiananmen Square. Deng Xiaoping appears to have triumphed over the demonstrators and the counter-revolutionary coup is now well under way. 'Deng may be 84,' one academician told Jonathan Mirsky of the *Observer*, 'but he is in overall charge. His followers are terrified that if he goes China will fall apart. So they obey any order, no matter how crazy it seems.'

Dark pessimism prevails and many Chinese now live in expectation of a knock on the door. Indeed, it looks as though the Western media have misjudged some elements of what was going on outside the Square.

But, whatever happens in China and the Soviet Union in the short term, there is an interesting link between the push for greater democracy in the Communist world and growing environmental awareness. As the *Observer* reports, the Chernobyl disaster sparked a new wave of environmental concern in the Communist bloc — and green issues have since become an officially acceptable channel for protest. The number of environmental and green organisations is exploding in Eastern Europe and the USSR. With Warsaw Pact environment ministers meeting tomorrow in Prague, there are many who see progress in this area as an important barometer of progress towards democracy.

Strong words in *The Sunday Times* from Teddy Goldsmith, whose *Blueprint for Survival* helped catalyse the early Green movement in Britain. 'They are *lapdogs*, these bastards,' he says of the developers and politicians driving development in the Third World. 'You are dealing with gangsters. Politicians with criminal records. The international institutions are no different. If we are going to ensure that man survives the next decade, we need *massive* changes. Everything that's happening today we predicted in *A Blueprint for Survival*. I was somewhat *naif*. I thought that if we publicised these things, the politicians would take the right action. But they briefed their scientists to rationalise their decisions. The Government has lied. And scientists are like lawyers: they say what their employers tell them to say.' Over-stated, perhaps, but Teddy is right about the need for radical changes. The key question now is not whether but *how*.

Finish the latest piece for the *Guardian*. Sparked off by the Earthworm Awards, a green literary prize backed by FoE and Save & Prosper. Suggest a Children's Environmental Crusade. By the time the younger generation reaches retirement age, the world's population will have doubled. Use the Greenpeace three-continent children's campaign as an illustration of the potential. Talked to Monika Griefahn of Greenpeace International in Hamburg last week; says the project is going ahead well. Six cities each in North America, Europe and the Soviet Union will develop pilot projects. Amazing to see the Soviets, in this post-Chernobyl world, inviting Greenpeace to turn their children into environmental campaigners.

Monday 29 May
Brilliant sunshine. After lunch, lie on lawn, skin itching with aphids and assorted mites and read advance copy of the Diagnostics report *Project Green II*, by Oliver Murphy, Cathy Hawes and Gillian Sin. Based on eight group discussions in London, Birmingham and Manchester in May. The idea: to see to what extent ordinary people have taken environmental issues on board in the time since Green Consumer Week — and the publication of the first Brand New/Diagnostics Green Consumer report. The tortoise sidles up and tries to bite my hand and then my bare feet. Distressing to be eaten by something one has rescued, housed and fed.

The Diagnostics report concludes that not only is consumers' knowledge about environmental issues deeper than before, but embraces more issues. One young man said: 'It's not just a minority any more. I haven't met anybody that says it doesn't matter. Everybody's life is at stake.'

The most active Green Consumers are mothers with children aged either under five or 13–18. Interestingly, retired men and women 'perceive the problems of the environment almost as akin to the wartime enemy of the 1940s, and adopt a similar style Blitz-like approach in response (i.e. we've all got to chip in and do our bit).' Awareness of the issues has grown substantially among groups like pensioners and young mothers, but remained static among young girls.

The EEC is seen as a Good Thing. 'By 1992 we'll have had to move in line with Europe,' said one young woman, 'and they (the Government) will be doing more.' As far as industry is concerned, there is a sense that, as one young man put it: 'They should change, but they'll wait till they're caught and then pretend they didn't know.'

There is a concern that some green products are not up to scratch. And recycled paper clearly has an image problem to overcome with young people, who expect it to be 'grey-looking, soggy-looking, with running colours, unhygienic'.

But the overall conclusion is that consumers are beginning to get the message — so Green Shopping Day could turn out to be well timed.

Tuesday 30 May
First meeting of the day with Jules Trocchi of Air Call, to discuss potential for setting up a Green Consumer Line in time for Green Shopping Day. This would be a phone-in service for consumers, giving them the latest product information. There would seem to be a fair amount of potential for doing something useful.

The European Commission is taking legal action against Britain, France and Spain to protect the environment. France is being taken to court because of its importing and re-exporting of 6,000 rare animal pelts from Bolivia four years ago, despite an international ban. Less exotically, Britain has been sent a final warning because of our failure to deliver a promised plan to reduce air pollution levels in Sunderland.

Anyone who thought that the recent nice weather was a hint of pleasures to come as the Greenhouse Effect takes hold, has another think coming — according to John Gribbin in the *Guardian*. Jim Hanssen and colleagues at NASA's Goddard Institute for Space Studies and the US National Oceanic and Atmospheric Administration have concluded that there is no evidence that there will be regional 'winners' if greenhouse gases continue to increase rapidly. Regions that do not suffer increased droughts seem likely to suffer from too much rain, often in the form of devastating storms and floods. They also calculate that the destructive power of the worst hurricanes of the 2030s could be 40 to 50% more devastating than today's worst.

Meanwhile, according to *New Scientist*, Soviet scientists at the Krzhizhanovsky State Energy Institute in Moscow have developed a new pumping system, which could make it economical to extract hydrogen sulphide from the bottom of the Black Sea, where a polluted layer is accumulating and rising at the rate of two metres per year. As matters stand, they believe, even a small earthquake could send the gas racing to the surface, starting huge fires.

Wednesday 31 May
Off to CBI. Green Consumer, Green Business conference. Start with TV interview for the one o'clock news. Opening speeches by CBI Deputy Director General John Owens and Trade and Industry Minister Tony Newton. The day was chaired by Consumers' Association Chief Executive John Beishon, who summed up by saying that he had previously been aware that environmental issues were important, but that he now recognised that they were urgent.

Apart from my own speech, calling for a UK Green Label scheme, the green banner was carried by Rob Holdaway of Brand New, Tessa Tennant of Merlin and Charles Secrett of FoE. But stirring 'we're going green' presentations were also made by companies like Volkswagen and Sainsbury's. The audience was perhaps 200-strong and the interest intense. Many companies — including British Airways and Courtaulds — came up to ask whether we might be able to help them go green.

Charles says FoE's next campaign will be against consumerism itself. It's certainly the logical next step, but a much more difficult message to get across to the ordinary Briton.

Afterwards, Julia and I walk down to Covent Garden for the launch of the Women's Environmental Network's Green Home exhibition at the London Ecology Centre. Talked to Stuart Boyle, ex-FoE and now at ACE. He wants to discuss the potential for an energy-saving efficiency labelling scheme for products like fridges, cookers and dishwashers.

In the European elections, there is a good deal of interest in whether the Greens can boost their 10,000 UK membership to overtake the 11,000 figure reported by the SDP. The Greens are standing on a Europe-wide platform agreed with their colleagues in 14 other countries.

In Tasmania, the five Green independents now sitting in the state's parliament have failed to force the resignation of the Liberal Party leader following their link-up with the Labor Party, giving them the barest of majorities. They plan to move a vote of no confidence.

In New Zealand, entomologists apparently now worry that the country could fall victim to a locust plague because of the Greenhouse Effect. But fear not, help is at hand. In a wonderfully worded communique, energy ministers from 21 countries — members of the International Energy Agency — stressed 'the need for a balanced, integrated bundle of realistically implementable and cost-effective energy-related and other responses, without losing sight of the need for energy security.'

America's space agency, NASA, hopes to help save the planet by launching a 'Mission to Planet Earth'. In a project first suggested in 1987 by Sally Ride, America's first woman in space, this new mission's objective, says *Time* magazine, is 'to understand the planet's dynamics well enough to anticipate ecological disasters — and find ways to forestall them.' The programme of work, which NASA hopes will start in 1996 with the launch of a pair of 15-ton unmanned space platforms called the earth-observing-system (EOS), would cost $20 billion over two decades.

Today claims that Prince Charles plans to turn every Royal and their palaces Green. In an interview to be broadcast next Monday, World Environment Day, as part of a programme called 'Climate in Crisis', he apparently will call for a wide range of Green Consumer-style actions, from using energy-saving light-bulbs to banning pesticides in the Royal gardens.

And, according to CPRE, land equivalent to four counties (presumably not the biggest) has disappeared under concrete and tarmac in the last 40 years — and 109,000 miles of hedgerows have been destroyed. Meanwhile, dairy farmers are being encouraged to go organic by Unigate, the dairy group. It is offering farmers a premium for organically produced milk. 'More and more people are going green,' says the group's farm liaison manager, 'and we believe that if we can get a supply we will have no trouble selling it.'

JUNE

Thursday 1 June

In Berlin yesterday, Mr Bush called on the Russians to tear down the 'brutal' Berlin Wall. Responding to what he called the terrible lesson — that environmental pollution knows no borders — he offered the Eastern bloc access to Western pollution control expertise in the battle to save Europe's forests and rivers. (One symptom of the trends there: Bulgarian dissidents have set up a new environmental organisation called Ecoglasnost to campaign for environmental clean-up.)

Japan, according to *New Scientist*, is thinking of recruiting a 'green corps' of young experts in environmental protection to work overseas 'to rescue their country's dismal ecological image' — as the world's largest importer of tropical timber and poached ivory, and operator of the world's largest whaling industry.

An interesting step in the right direction, but culturally Japan is still light years away from a green worldview.

We also make the front cover of *The Ecologist*, whose latest issue focuses on 'The Limits of Green Consumerism'. An article by Sandy Irvine, a co-author of *A Green Manifesto*, accepts that green consumerism is a fast-emerging trend, but notes that it is 'wide open to being cynically hijacked by the established interests in business and politics'. The Green Consumer boom, he suggests, is designed to give the idea that careful housekeeping will mean that we can somehow have our cake and eat it. He concludes: 'Only the holistic perspective of the deep Greens provides both an adequate definition of and policies for ecological sustainability.'

In the same issue, Sara Parkin of the Green Party complains that, 'whatever Elkington's motives might have been at the outset, he has not so much turned confrontation into co-operation by his "bridge-building" exercise as delivered the Green movement into the lap of the industrialist.'

We should probably reply, although I do not expect to change either the hearts or minds of the Parkins of this world. It is not in their interest to make any serious attempt to understand the more positive dimensions of what we are doing. If the world population were stable or in decline, the prescriptions of the deep Greens might have some chance of working, but in the real world of rapid population growth and Third World industrialisation, I fear they are spitting in the wind.

Friday 2 June
WWF is talking of an 'elephant holocaust'. Reports that the African elephant population has crashed 'catastrophically' by more than 125,000 in the past two years. Only 625,000 elephants are left, compared with 1.3 million a decade ago. WWF says the species could be extinct in 15 years — and calls for a total ban on ivory trading.

In Brazil, the *Guardian* reports, the world's greatest-ever gold-rush has seen hundreds of thousands of *garimpeiros*, or prospectors, swarming into Indian territory. They use mercury to amalgamate the particles of gold washed out of gold-bearing muds, with as much as 1,800 tonnes of mercury now being dumped into the Amazon ecosystem each year. There are signs that there could be a spate of deformed babies, like those born in the Japanese fishing village of Minamata in the early 1960s. The impact of such toxins on the unborn was the subject of my book *The Poisoned Womb*. 'What we fear,' Professor Geraldo de Assis Guimaraes told the *Guardian*, 'is a generation of "Japanese monsters" in the rainforest.' And it is already clear that the Chernobyl radiation has caused genetic mutations in both plants and animals — and some chemicals can have the same effect.

Early meeting with Patrick Veale, to plan filming of video for NCC and Shell. Julia goes to the launch of the Green Grocer Awards, sponsored by Varta and *The Grocer* magazine. Heinz are voted the Best Company. The CBI speech has sparked a good deal of interest, and am called upon to do interviews with the *Financial Times*, *Daily Mail* and *Daily Telegraph*. Also do an interview on information technology, based on *The Shrinking Planet*, our report for the World Resources Institute, for the Hewlett-Packard magazine.

The annual gathering of Women's Institute members — of whom there are some 340,000 — yesterday spent a fair amount of time on environmental issues. 'I don't think there are any members here who are not ozone-friendly,' one WI member told the *Guardian*.

Saturday 3 June
In Peking, protestors succeeded in turning back thousands of soldiers as they tried to march into Tiananmen Square. The same chant went up: 'You are the people's army. Don't hurt the people.' Some of the soldiers had their heads in their hands, the *Financial Times* reports, and appeared to be crying. Scarcely surprising — and another humiliation for the Chinese authorities. How long will they put up with it?

The Soviet Union's new Congress of Deputies howls down Dr Andrei Sakharov, for daring to suggest that Soviet troops were responsible for atrocities in Afghanistan. He has also claimed that Soviet helicopters gunned down Soviet troops to prevent their being taken prisoner. Almost certainly true, but Sakharov is uncommonly brave to apply *glasnost* to the Afghan war while the wounds are still raw.

'Green Consumers, so recently considered a faddish appendage to the mainstream market-place, are fast becoming a force which industry ignores at its peril,' says *The Times* in an editorial today. 'Their forebears, the "healthy eaters", were prepared to pay extra for additive-free; the Green Consumers demand more, the health of the world.' The paper describes green consumerism as a market revolution in the West and notes that consumer guides now help (Green Consumers) to select 'best buys' not just in terms of price, but of environment friendliness.

But there are flies in the green ointment. An extraordinary full-page colour ad in the paper is built around a pulsing headline ENVIRONMENT FRIENDLY. 'To help keep Britain a green and pleasant land,' it says, 'Panasonic Green batteries have had all the traces of mercury removed but still retain more power than any ordinary battery.' Unfortunately, batteries can never be 'environment friendly', given that they take up to 50 times more energy to make than you ever get out of them.

Sunday 4 June

In tears this morning as the news comes in on the radio that the People's Liberation Army has crushed the demonstrators in a bloodbath in Tiananmen Square. It is odd that one should be surprised after all the violence of this century, but this massacre by fresh, ultra-loyalist troops both underscores the moral bankruptcy of today's Communism and the extraordinary heroism of the students and ordinary people who continued to resist even when the firing had started.

It's impossible to really understand what has been going on, but these latest events — ordered by Li Peng and Deng Xiaoping's Government — can only feed the flames of resentment and the desire for greater freedom.

And history also rolls on with the news that Iran's Ayatollah Khomeini is dead. It's unlikely that he will be followed by anyone radically better-intentioned towards the rest of the world, but his death does not make the world any darker. I wonder where he's gone?

Monday 5 June

World Environment Day . . . and sense of outrage as the scale of the massacres in Peking becomes clear. The Red Cross estimates 2,600 dead, 10,000 injured. Giving the order to attack the protestors, Deng Xiaoping — from his hospital bed — apparently said: 'In China . . . one million people dead is still only a small number.' The cynicism of Communism and state socialism is mind-numbing. Extraordinary frustrations in seeing such carnage, yet being unable to do anything to help.

In the Soviet Union, more than 800 people are feared dead after liquid gas leaked from a pipeline and exploded just as two crowded trains were passing. Mikhail Gorbachev flew to the scene, 750 miles east of Moscow, blaming the accident on negligence. 'These catastrophes are pursuing us,' he said. Today has been declared a day of mourning in the Soviet Union.

Extraordinary issue of *The Times*. Includes a six-page Green Consumer supplement. 'Two events of great importance for the future of the environment in Britain took place within a few days of each other last September,' the first article (by Michael McCarthy) begins, 'and it is fascinating to note that while the significance of one — the conversion of Margaret Thatcher to the Green cause — has already passed into political legend, the possibly greater significance of the other — the beginning of the influence of the market — remains largely unnoticed.

'On September 12, 1988, John Elkington and Julia Hailes published *The Green Consumer Guide* and at a stroke put into the hands of every shopper in Britain a tool to channel precisely growing feelings about a whole range of concerns into individual purchasing choices . . . Into a country suddenly waking up to all things 'green', the Green Consumer was born.'

Earlier in the paper, there is a piece by Tom Burke on the growth of the Green movement in Britain. Its membership is thought to have grown from 1.8 million in 1980 to nearly four million today — and if present growth rates continue could reach six million by 1992. The annual income of the 15 top green organisations, in which *The Times* includes the National Trust, is more than £163 million a year. 'A very large portion of that is going on influencing people's perceptions,' Tom comments, 'and it makes the advertising budgets of most companies look puny.'

Drive down to Guiting Power in Gloucestershire to visit the International Centre for Conservation Education.

Next drive to Gloucester — with ICCE Director Mark Boulton to do an interview on BBC Radio Gloucester, then on to Wallsworth Hall, just outside Gloucester. 100 or so people, celebrating ICCE's fifth birthday. Evening introduced by Sir Peter Scott, as ICCE's President. He is now looking very old and frail. I speak for 30 minutes on the 'Business of Saving the World'. Followed by Mark, then WWF Chairman Sir Arthur Norman. At the dinner afterwards, spend a good deal of time talking to Lady Medawar, widow of Nobellist Sir Peter Medawar. A renowned biologist in her own right, Jean Medawar has worked with Max

Nicholson on Common Ground International, aiming to build bridges between population control experts, demographers and conservationists.

The interplay between population and environment is certainly going to be central to world politics. Isabelle goes to hear Sir Crispin Tickell, Britain's UN Ambassador, talking at the Royal Society on the Greenhouse Effect. Climate change, he says, could turn 300 million people into environmental refugees in the 21st century. As global warming causes sea levels to rise, many of those living in, for example, the delta areas of the Nile, the Ganges and the Yangtze would be forced out of their homes and livelihoods. Some islands, such as the Maldives in the Indian Ocean, would soon become uninhabitable. Bangladesh with its population of over 100 million and Egypt with its population of around 70 million would be particularly affected.

Today Julia and I are among 14 Britons added to the United Nations Environment Programme's Global 500 Roll of Honour in recognition of our environmental achievements.

Tuesday 6 June
Extraordinary heroism among the students and people resisting the Chinese Army in Peking. *The Daily Mail* points out that in a country where population pressures have forced a one-child-per-couple policy, each youngster's death tears the heart out of an entire family. There are even fears that the country could be on the brink of civil war. The army is deeply split. Some units, it is reported, have been firing on others. Vile atrocities now being reported. The students are reported to be leaderless, forlorn, lost.

More positively, Solidarity has scored a massive success in the Polish elections. The failure of many Government candidates has inflicted a devastating blow on Communism in Eastern Europe. And the process has only just begun. Where it will take us all, God only knows.

The gas explosion that wrecked the Trans-Siberia railway in the Soviet Union had the explosive power of a 10-kiloton bomb. Local people had detected the gas hours before the explosion, but no one did anything. When the gas ignited, it formed a wall of fire up to a mile and a quarter wide. The blast felled all the trees within two and a half miles.

A letter from TUC General Secretary Norman Willis in *The Times*. He stresses that the unions are pro-environment. 'Trade unionists care as passionately about the environment as anyone,' he says. 'I look forward to a closer working relationship between the trade union movement and environmentalists.' Having once sat next to him at an RSA lunch, I know he is a sincere, straightforward man, but the mainstream unions' track-record in the environmental field has been indifferent, at best.

Prince Charles is back in the headlines. Worried about global warming, he is looking at the possibility of burning straw to heat his homes. 'There is a hell of a lot of straw lying around which gets burnt each year,' he explains. 'I know people who have this equipment into which they stuff great big bales. You can heat largish houses that way.' He certainly has a number of those.

Sense of vast forces breaking loose: as they tried to bury the Ayatollah Khomeini yesterday, frenzied mourners — in a crowd estimated to be two million strong — broke open the coffin, dumping the Ayatollah's corpse on the ground.

As the earth swallowed Khomeini's mortal remains, a British judge was sentencing an Armenian orchid collector for uprooting rare plants from far-away soils. The accused 'raped' the jungles of South America and Asia to bring back rare species to Britain. He was jailed for 12 months yesterday and fined £20,000. Sentencing Henry Azadehdel, the judge said: 'I suppose that because of modern transport there must be very few plants out of the reach of man's grasp and the activity of hunting down and uprooting species of animal and plant life goes on at a fearful pace.' Further wonders of modern transport technology: Khomeini arrived at the cemetery in a refrigerated truck.

Drive down to Marlow to see Volvo Concessionaires about the environmental audit. Start work immediately by visiting a dealership just outside Reading. By the end of visit, they are calling up the suppliers of the masking paper used in their paint-spraying booths to see if it is — or could be — made of recycled paper and wondering whether some of their fire extinguishers contain ozone-destroying halon propellants.

Time magazine runs a piece called 'The Greening of Hollywood'. Partly interesting because of the growing use of the word 'green' in the States, partly because of the rapid growth in environmental issues among actors and media people there. 'It's important to raise the environment to the same level as national security,' says Robert Redford. 'If we poison the planet, what is there left to defend?' It will be interesting to see how the Green movement develops in the USA. One thing is clear: it will take a different route from the one we are travelling in Europe.

Thursday 8 June
Gaia is studying the North American Indians at school. Send her in with some of our books on Indian cultures, including 'How Can One Sell the Air?', an impassioned plea by Chief Seattle of the Duwamish people to the President in 1855. Among the extraordinary lines:

'All things are bound together.
All things connect.
What happens to the Earth
happens to the children of the Earth.
Man has not woven the web of life.
He is but one thread.
Whatever he does to the web,
he does to himself.'

Nicholas Ridley is now proposing a carbon tax to counter the Green-house Effect, but manages to make it sound as though it is little more than a ploy to boost nuclear power. Ironically, residents in Sacramento, California, have voted to shut down the Rancho Seco nuclear plant. This is the fifteenth time Americans have been asked to vote on the future of a nuclear plant, but the first time they have come down in favour of shutting an operating plant.

In the wake of the Three Mile Island disaster in 1979, which involved a similar reactor type, the Rancho Seco management set out to prove the plant's worth by keeping power prices low. They did this by cutting back on maintenance so that the plant soon began to experience failures, shut-downs and, on Boxing Day 1985, a near-disaster.

Started the day in ultra-modern Lansdowne House, Berkeley Square, with Stanhope Properties. Joint presentation by David Cadman of PMA and myself. Two of the Stanhope people say their wives have bought *The Guide* and have been making a nuisance of themselves! Then on to give a lecture at the London Business School.

Saturday 10 June
Most of the day spent in the office. One subject of conversation with Elaine in the morning and with Julia now as we pump out the text and tables for the next *Guide*: can the environment have too much publicity? Just look at *The Times* today. Among the articles: More green farms; green gardening with Susannah York; and a how-to piece on the environment-friendly dinner party, entitled: Greens for dinner? The answer is that anything can have too much publicity, but the media response to major issues is almost impossible to stage-manage.

Britain may not like it, but the European Community environment ministers have agreed to cut car exhaust emissions in small cars by two-thirds by the end of 1992. And EC Environment Commissioner Carlo Ripa di Meana says he will push for a strict EC-wide speed limit, to help cut exhaust emissions.

Nicholas Ridley, meanwhile, has dropped the hot potato of the carbon tax proposed earlier this week — saying that he has no plans to adopt such a tax here, but was simply raising the idea for international discussion. He hardly looks like keeping up with George Bush, who has declared that he wants to be remembered as the 'environmental' President. The *Guardian* reports Bush as saying to environmentalists earlier this week that: 'It's time to renew the environmental ethic and to renew US leadership on environmental issues around the world.' His big announcement is due on Monday.

A small Brazilian film production company has bought the rights to the Chico Mendes story, beating a number of Hollywood studios. Not all Brazilians are delighted, among them former colleagues of Mendes. The company normally makes slick TV mini-series and soap operas.

Monday 12 June
Saving the global environment would cost the wealthy, industrialised nations of the North 'only' £6.4 billion a year in aid to the poorer countries of the South, Professor David Pearce told a meeting in Paris.

But the limits of the developing Global Village are shown up by what has been happening in China. In a population of more than 1 billion, perhaps 800 million are peasants — and their knowledge of recent events in Tiananmen Square is limited or non-existent, for the moment at least. The failure of the students to break through to the broad Chinese masses is now increasingly clear.

Compared with the Chinese peasant who earns less than £20 a month, the American tourists prepared to pay up to £25,000 for tours of Antarctica are as rich as Croesus. Now Antarctic scientists are worried that thousands of US visitors are causing massive damage to the delicate ecosystem. 'Tourists trample grasses, lichens and mosses which can take years to grow under extreme conditions,' Dr David Drewry of the British Antarctic Survey told the *Daily Telegraph*.

Spar, back on the Green Consumer beat, has launched a new green label scheme, which combines the chain's fir tree with the phrase 'Future Friendly'. We really do need a national labelling scheme to avoid consumer confusion.

And Ark is in a bit of trouble. Chrissie Hynde, lead singer with the Pretenders pop group and a director of Ark, is threatened with court action by McDonald's unless she withdraws her call to fans and Ark members to boycott the hamburger restaurant. She is also under attack because of an alleged call for fans to fire-bomb the chain. A McDonald's in central Milton Keynes was fire-bombed on 8 June. As a vegetarian, Ms Hynde has said that her dream is to put businesses like McDonald's out of business.

Tuesday 13 June

President Bush has announced his massive rethink of US environmental policy, in the wake of the Reagan Administration's 'do-nothing decade'. 'We will make the 1990s the era for clean air,' he said. 'Ours is a rare opportunity to reverse the errors of this generation in the service of the next.' Under the new plan, coal-burning power stations will be required to cut sulphur dioxide emissions by ten million tons and nitrogen oxide by two million tons by the year 2000. America's electricity bill is expected to rise by around 2% as a result.

And car-makers are going to have to switch to cleaner fuels like methanol, to clean up the air in cities like Los Angeles, Houston and New York. A third target are the 2.7 billion pounds of toxic chemicals spewed in the air every year in the States, many of them cancer-causing. The plan is to cut emissions by between 75% and 90%. The total cost of the programme will be $9 billion–$12 billion.

The Alaskan oil spill has helped speed the greening of America. Membership applications received by the US National Wildlife Federation, for example, have jumped from 8,000 a month to 21,000. A spokesman for the Sierra Club told the *Wall Street Journal* that they have installed 100 extra telephone lines to cope with incoming calls.

Big Oil, which had thought it had cracked its environmental problems until this latest disaster, is clearly worried. 'Environmental groups just see a window of opportunity,' to score points with the public, a former Mobil Oil Vice-President for public affairs fumes to *Business Week*. 'They're professional attackers.'

Day starts with interviews with Michael McCarthy and then with Paul Vallely of *The Times* on the need for a Green Label scheme. Have to be careful not to break the confidentiality enjoined by the Department of the Environment in a letter received this morning. The DoE is now working with the DTI and wants to come and talk before putting together a report to go to Ministers early in July. Feel that we must keep the pressure up on Government or it will slide away into a half-hearted, half-cock scheme.

The papers are full of a Mintel survey, entitled *The Green Consumer* (price £750), which suggests that 12 million Britons are true Green Consumers, prepared to pay a substantial price premium for environmentally-benign products. 27% of the sample said that they avoided products which damage the environment, use too much energy, cause unnecessary waste, involve cruelty to animals or adversely affect other countries. 5% extra on a green supermarket item would be acceptable to 71% of shoppers, Mintel suggest, equivalent to more than 31.5 million people. Julia, Dorothy and Tom are quoted, all expressing surprise. But the surprise — even shock — in corporate boardrooms is likely to be rather greater.

In the evening, across to Islington with Julia for Charles Secrett's leaving party at the vilely named Slug & Lettuce pub on Islington Green. Great sense of the gathering of the clans and rousing speech from Jonathon Porritt, underscoring the work that Charles has done over the last eight years to pull FoE closer to organisations like WWF, the Green Alliance and SustainAbility. Charles is off to Brazil with his family later in the month. Not clear what he'll do, apart from learning Portuguese. Feels that Brazil is like the States 100 years ago. He'll be missed, although no one is as far away as they once would have been now that telephones, computers and faxes are starting to turn us into Global Villagers.

Wednesday 14 June
Drive down to Guildford, in brilliant sunshine but what looks like the beginnings of an LA-style haze. Filming for the 'Second Nature' video, being made by Patrick Veale of Independent Business Television, for the NCC and Shell UK. The fictionalised story centres on a teacher who takes her schoolchildren to a meadow by a river to learn about natural history, but then finds that a local firm is polluting the river — and plans to build over the meadow. The denouement happens in a radio station and we spent all day filming a series of studio-based sequences in sweltering heat.

Thursday 15 June
Voted Green for the first time this evening. Part tactical, part experimental. Certainly would not vote for them in a national election on the basis of their present manifesto. But, as the *Financial Times* put it today, the 'rise of the Greens is the one true Euro-phenomenon'. The paper also suggests that the surge in Green voting in Britain 'could be of mould-breaking proportions'. But our first-past-the-post electoral system will mean that the Greens are almost guaranteed not to win any seats in the European Parliament.

In the news: Italy plans to spend $28 million to fight evil-smelling algae polluting the coastal waters of the Adriatic, forcing bathers out of the water; the British Antarctic Survey has found traces of cadmium, lead and zinc, as well as hydrocarbons (from cars) in Antarctic snow, and traces of DDT and agricultural chemicals in the tissues of seals; and disturbing evidence from Greenland. Research by an international team led by Dr Willi Dansgaard, of the Geophysical Institute at Copenhagen University, has found that the Greenhouse Effect could trigger climatic changes much faster than previously thought. Because the processes that drive 'climatic flips' are 'non-linear', it turns out that very small changes in, for example, temperature, can have a disproportionate impact on the climate.

Julia leaves for the Canary Islands, where she is to address a conference of supermarket wholesalers. My article on 'The Greening of Advertising' is splashed across two pages of *Campaign* magazine today. 'Will the green bubble burst?,' it asks towards the end. I argue that it is more like a green froth, with an enormous number of bubbles stirred up by profound changes in our societies and in our perceptions of the world we live in.

Friday 16 June
The televised show trials of Chinese demonstrators begin. Young men paraded with cardboard signs around their necks, 'confessing' their 'crimes'. Extraordinary attempts by the Communist Party to show that things have returned to 'normal'. It lists the damage caused in recent weeks as including the destruction of 60 buses and 14,910 potted plants! Amazing that they kept such a careful inventory of the plants when the bodies of the slaughtered were dragged away uncounted.

Started the day, complicated by yet another Tube strike, with Dow. Dow has decided that plastics recycling and energy-from-plastics-waste schemes are going to be critical if the use of plastics in cars is to grow. Once again, they seem keen that we start work almost immediately.

The shape of things to come is also suggested by a piece in the *Financial Times*, which focuses on the aluminium industry's new claim that its metal is 'environment-friendly'. But the whole thing hangs on recycling — which still looks like a distant prospect for most aluminium cans.

Meanwhile, seven companies — Allied-Signal, Du Pont, Atochem, ICI, ISC Chemicals, Daikin and Montedison — join forces to test safe alteratives to ozone-depleting CFCs.

And the Japanese Government announces that it will ban the import of worked ivory — and of raw ivory that does not come directly from African producer countries. The ban by the world's largest importer of ivory will take effect immediately. The announcement, Dr Simon Lyster of WWF told the *Daily Telegraph*, 'is about as unexpected as an Englishman winning Wimbledon. Japan has rarely bowed to international pressure on a conservation issue in the past'. It's worth noting, however, that Japan has taken this decision in an attempt to avoid a total ban later this year. And Tanzania has arrested more than 400 big game poachers in response to mounting worldwide alarm about the elephant 'holocaust'.

Harvard University call to ask whether I would spend two months in Thailand in 1992, to prepare the next edition of the country's Natural Resources Profile. Apparently the last Profile, which I helped to put together in 1986, has been picked as the most successful to date in a recent review. I say that the most that I could manage would be two weeks, but still feel that I would like to keep a toe in the Third World. That's where the most critical environmental problems are.

Saturday 17 June
Pent-up emotions pour forth in Hungary, where yesterday nearly 250,000 people publicly mourned the executed leaders of the 1956 uprising for independence and democracy. Many of those taking part were not even born at the time, but the rage runs deep.

Extraordinary story in the *Guardian* about the scuttling of the German fleet in Scapa Flow 70 years ago, on 21 June 1919. Because the steel used to make the 11 battleships, five battle-cruisers, eight light cruisers and 50 destroyers was made in the pre-nuclear-test era, it is uncontaminated. As a result, it has been 'quarried' for use in shielding delicate instrumentation used to measure radiation. So some recycled pieces of the Kaiser's dreadnoughts have probably landed on the moon.

Back on Earth, it looks as though the British Greens will gain their largest vote ever anywhere. The Greens say they are gradually developing a new form of economics based on the idea of a steady-state economy in which we conserve rather than consume. Not quite the idea behind the Eagle Star's recently launched Environmental Opportunities Trust, advertised in the *Financial Times*. It aims to help investors profit from the growth in the environmental products and services industry. The paper also devotes two-thirds of a page to 'The Cost of Going Green', which refers repeatedly to *The Green Consumer Guide*.

Alongside the article, there is a piece by James Lovelock, who costs the contribution of the world's tropical forests as a planetary air-conditioner. He suggests a value of £30,000 per acre, compared with less than £100 earned by the same area land cleared for cattle ranching, before it is exhausted. So the 55 square feet of land needed to produce enough meat for one burger could provide an atmospheric cooling service of £380 a year.

Sunday 18 June
GREEN BP FELLS RAINFOREST runs the front-page banner headline in *The Sunday Times*. The Insight team notes that BP owns a majority share of Companhia de Mineracao Jacunda, which is mining casserite, the ore used to produce tin, in the Amazon basin. Along with companies like Barclays Bank, BAT and Shell, the article says that BP has been investing in projects which destroy the rainforest. The controversy comes hot on the heels of BP's 're-imaging' campaign, during which the company used

advertising slogans like 'Now We're Greener than Ever' and 'For All our Tomorrows'. Environmental specialists within BP had long warned us that this issue could explode.

In today's *Observer*, Geoffrey Lean notes that the Greens dismiss the Brundtland recipe of rapid growth in many parts of the world economy, to meet the needs of a rapidly growing population. I sympathise with the Greens, but can see no option but to go for greener growth.

Valin Pollen call to say that we have got the contract to audit Manweb, a regional electricity board in the Manchester and North Wales region.

In the evening, listen to Dr Norman Myers addressing the Business Network. Norman talks of industry's role in the transition from a 'cowboy economy' to a 'spaceship economy'. Calls on me a couple of times to speak from the audience, and then I have to sum up. Afterwards, a considerable number of people come up and ask whether SustainAbility can employ them. It's a strange paradox that we have so many offers, but can find so few people who would genuinely fit.

Write the diary shortly before midnight, as the results come in on the European elections. There seems to have been a swing to Labour, coupled with a very commendable turnout for the Greens.

Tuesday 20 June
The main news is that the Greens won more than 2.25 million votes in the UK Euro-elections. The Green Party, having gambled on fighting all 78 UK seats for the European Parliament, were second in five seats and third in nearly 50 seats. The Greens are claiming that this is the beginning, but from the sample of people I have spoken to it would seem that a very high proportion of voters voted Green tactically — and will probably switch back come the next national election. Whatever happens, however, this result will put massive pressure on the mainstream parties to get their environmental act together. 'There are three stages of political credibility,' says Sara Parkin, co-ordinator of the European Greens. 'First you are ignored, then you are ridiculed and attacked, and the next time you are taken seriously.'

At the moment, the Greens are very much in the second stage. Proportional representation would have given them 11 MEPs, instead of which they were left seat-less. Europe-wide, the Greens and their allies won a total of 39 seats in the European Parliament, compared with 20 last time. If the UK had proportional representation, the Greens would have been the third largest political group in Strasbourg.

In *The Times* Jonathon Porritt notes that June 15 1989 will be remembered as a Green Letter Day for all those who care about the environment. But he also notes that: 'Today's pale Green environmentalists often shy away from darker Green analysis, revealing in the process deep flaws in their own lacklustre reformism. To call yourself Green, yet not question the nature and the costs of economic growth, is transparently dishonest.'

What Jonathon seems unable (or unwilling) to accept is that some environmentalists might question economic growth, yet — for perfectly plausible reasons — come up with different answers to his own.

On the bus home, pass a bus-stop sporting a new Peaudouce advertisement. 'Green peace,' it says. The implicit message is that the company's '100% chlorine-free pulp' nappies are baby- and environ-ment-friendly. They are sailing much too close to the green wind.

Wednesday 21 June
The public executions start in China.

The US oil industry is launching a $250 million, five-year programme to improve its response to oil spill disasters. The UK Government, meanwhile, announces that it is to make the nuclear power stations it wants to privatise more attractive to potential investors by promising to meet the costs of waste disposal and decommissioning! The agreement would cover all existing stations. Labour accuses Energy Secretary Cecil Parkinson of effectively writing the nuclear industry a blank cheque. The fact is, he has little option.

Thursday 22 June
Strange package arrives through the post. A Malaysian bullfrog has apparently been adopted in my name at London Zoo, anonymously. The date on the certificate is 23 June, my 40th birthday. The accompanying photograph is wonderful: a great balloon of an animal. It later turns out that Lois and Tony Kingham are responsible.

Stanhope Properties say they want PMA and ourselves to go ahead with our green audit. Over to the Department of the Environment, as (they say) first person to be consulted by the DoE and DTI on the prospects for a Green Label scheme in Britain. Push hard for a Government-backed scheme and for a steady expansion of the issues and product sectors the scheme would cover. As John Beishon, director of the Consumers' Association, said recently in *The Times*, 'There has to be an agreed set of standards pretty quickly, or the whole thing will be chaos, and the whole idea of any label will be devalued.'

Consumers are being urged by the water industry to share baths and let their cars stay dirty, to save water. Six of the ten water authorities have already imposed water restrictions, in the worst water shortage since 1976.

In America, meanwhile, wind erosion has scoured more than 14 million acres of the Great Plains between November and May, the worst damage in more than 30 years. 'A truckload of topsoil costs $40 a ton,' a Soil Conservation Service official tells the *Wall Street Journal*. 'If you can see soil moving, you're losing at least 15 tons per acre. That's three times the tolerable limit. I'm sure we had fields (in Kansas) losing upwards of 50 tons per acre. That amounts to about one inch of topsoil. It takes nature about 100 years to develop an inch of topsoil.'

Also in the States, Procter & Gamble is looking for ways of recycling disposable nappies! The idea is that the plastic outer layer would be recycled to make flower pots and garbage bags, while the pulp would be used to make cardboard boxes and building insulation. The company is responding to widespread concern that the pace of waste disposal is rapidly exhausting the available landfill sites.

McDonald's, the world's biggest hamburger chain, is sending out a million leaflets to its 300-plus UK restaurants protesting that it is not involved in rainforest destruction, according to *The Times*. The 'McFact Cards', printed on recycled paper, aim to squash the rumour that beef for the company's hamburgers comes from South and Central American cattle ranches created by felling and burning rainforests.

In Italy, the Greens are taking an interesting path, turning up at Montedison's annual general meeting and quizzing chairman Raul Gardini about his company's environmental performance. The *Wall Street Journal* notes that the activists 'wore natty suits and ties or makeup and smart skirts' (quite a combination!). 'We need some entrepreneurs to espouse the environmental cause and support us,' said one activist. 'Gardini seems open to that. We chose this style because we don't want to give the impression that we're veterans of '68 who run around attacking capitalists.' Again, they want an environmentalist on the company's board.

The 'green tide' now sweeping around Europe, which President Bush has described as coming on like a freight train, will make it difficult for EEC member states to stop the proposed European Environmental Agency — discussed by EC Commissioner Carlo Ripa di Meana at a press conference in Brussels yesterday. So far, though, it doesn't look as though the Agency will be developed along the lines of the US Environmental Protection Agency. Its powers will be fairly limited, although it would at least be independent of the Commission.

Friday 23 June
40th birthday. In to work with the children, on their way to school. Gaia says that at St Paul's there has been a change in the most-favoured career

option. Once the girls wanted to be doctors or surgeons, now 'environmental specialist' heads the list!

Walking through Holland Park, pass a sleek, top-of-the-range silver-grey Mercedes, with a dead mistle thrush pinioned against its streamlined radiator grille, the bird's exquisite wings spread out almost as though by an ornithologist like Audubon. A collision between two divergent forms of beauty.

Annie, Fiona, Isabelle and Julia give me a massive birthday card, made out of photos and press headlines about our work. Annie has made a green cake, complete with marzipan continents.

Another birthday present, this time from McDonalds. Julia and I receive letters from lawyers representing the hamburger giant, threatening to take us to court. They say they have nothing to do with tropical deforestation, as we suggest in *The Green Consumer Guide*. They want a complete retraction in court within seven days or they say the roof will fall in on us. And our lawyer has just gone off on honeymoon!

Extraordinary difference in coverage of dioxins in the papers today. POISON THREAT TO BREAST-FED BABIES roars a headline in *Today*, which claims that babies are exposed to 100 times the safe level of dioxin when breast-feeding. Dioxins are produced, among other things, by chemical reactions, municipal and hospital incinerators, coal burning, cars using leaded petrol, cigarettes, bonfires and the bleaching of wood pulp for paper tissues and coffee filters. *The Times*, on the other hand, talks of dioxin being 'cleared' by a new Government report. The guinea-pigs originally used to test dioxin were much more sensitive than humans, the report says.

In the news: Britain's Green Party may yet have a say in the European Parliament, if a plan hatched by West German Green MEPs comes to pass. They are discussing the possibility of sharing their seats with British Greens. More than 10,000 fish have been killed in the River Derwent by acetic acid leaking from a Courtaulds acetate near Derby. More positively, Avon, one of the world's largest cosmetic manufacturers, says it has dropped animal testing of its products. It admitted that consumer boycotts and demonstrations by animal rights activists had influenced its decision.

Saturday 24 June
Great deal of musing in the papers about the next step for the Green Party. Will it become a pressure group or make a bid for power? Much of the debate comes down to the question of whether you are a light or dark Green. If you are the former, you may be content with green consumerism and a fairly pragmatic approach to greening the world. But if you are the

latter, you probably believe that the only way to save the world is to elect Green Governments in all the industrialised countries. Since the prospect of the second option seems so remote, the dark Greens would be foolhardy to rule out the first.

Beautiful day. A great deal of preparation to get garden and house in a fit state for the evening's party. House has been reclaimed from the builders and is beginning to look fairly civilised again. The garden is fairly hopping with rabbits, which are digging burrows everywhere they can find a secluded corner. It's becoming harder and harder to catch them and put them back into their cages in the evening.

The garden is lit with flares in the flower-beds and lanterns hung in the apple trees. Liz Knights of Gollancz brings, among other things, a three-foot green bow-tie, illustrated with *The Green Consumer Guide* logo and the figure 40.

Sunday 25 June
Up again to No. 4 in the bestseller charts.

The Thames is way down, with much of the bed showing. The *Observer* reports on the drought, quoting one Nottinghamshire farmer: 'It's much worse than 1976,' he said, 'especially for us up here who have to farm this light soil. It will need to rain every day from now on in if we are going to save half of our spring barley from ruin.' The National Trust is now thinking of closing a number of nature reserves and beauty spots to the public, for fear that their tinder-dry landscapes will be swept by fire.

Fascinating piece in *The Sunday Times* about the growing competition between the major papers to capture the green reader. Although *Today* was the only paper to actually urge its readers to vote Green in the Euro-elections, it is not alone in having identified the greening of Britain as a social trend which could help it attract new readers. The *Guardian* comes out as the favoured green paper.

The *Daily Express*, in an editorial last week, attacked the 'greening' of *Today* as 'cynical and dishonest, part of its shameless whoring after every trend that might just mean the addition of one or two more readers'. *Express* Editor Nicholas Lloyd added: 'Rupert Murdoch, *Today*'s proprietor, must be surprised to find himself owning a newspaper backing a party opposed to cutting down trees for newsprint.'

On the political front, the Chinese Communist Party has purged Zhao Ziyang, last seen in tears after failing to end the pro-democracy hunger strikes in Tiananmen Square. Closer to home, Democrat MP Simon Hughes has threatened to leave and join the Greens — giving them their first Commons spokesman — if the Democrats do not pull up their green socks.

'BP in the rainforest' story continues, with news that Brazil is considering legal action against the company. BP chairman Sir Peter Walters publishes a letter in *The Sunday Times* today, in response to last week's article. 'The subject of the environment is rightly a major concern for everyone,' he says. 'The need for society to strike the right balance between conservation and development is crucial, and it is never easy.'

Same letters column carries one from McDonald's. It concludes by stressing: 'nowhere in the world does McDonald's use of beef threaten or remotely involve the tropical rainforests.' They must be pretty sure of their facts to make the claim — we clearly have a good deal of cross-checking to do. This week, Inchcape is hammered, because of its logging operations in Borneo. *The Sunday Times* accuses the company of 'leaving half an acre crushed for every tree felled'.

Monday 26 June
Another Soviet nuclear submarine is on fire off the Norwegian coast and, on the other side of the Atlantic, hundreds of US workers are battling to clean up major oil spills off three states after what *The Times* calls 'a weekend of navigational mishaps by foreign ships threatened to cause ecological disaster'. In the worst spill, off Rhode Island, National Guards and even convicts joined Coast Guard teams struggling to contain a spill of 650,000 gallons of toxic domestic heating fuel. Local people say the oil has turned the surf orange.

Racing away on *Supermarket Guide*. Julia chases lawyers on the McDonald's front, while I call Norman Myers — who we discover had an earlier legal run-in with Big Mac. They apparently were intent on suing him for $3 million for accusing them of clearing rainforest areas in Central America, but backed off when Prince Philip asked whether they didn't have more important things to do than hounding a well-intentioned environmentalist.

Cab to Heathrow at 16.30 and fly to Gothenburg to see Volvo. Arrive at around 22.00 local time, with a large, blood-red sun hovering over fir-studded horizon. Volvos everywhere, as if one has blundered into the automotive equivalent of a wasp's nest. Into the city on the airport bus, struck by lack of litter along the motorway.

Walk around the city centre. The place is crowded with young people, many of the young men with shoulder-length hair again. The pavements are sticky under the lime trees and the blind-aid traffic signals tick like time-bombs, turning into clockwork cicadas when it is time to cross. High over the city gleams a vast neon sign advertising McDonald's!

Tuesday 27 June
Visit the Volvo factory at Torslanda. Trundle around the plant in an open six-seater electric trolley. On either side, robots duck and weave, their welding arms flashing in and out of the shining aluminium bodies, showers of sparks splashing on to the floor. Stacks of shining new exhausts, their silver shapes distorted by the metal chambers needed to house the catalytic converters increasingly used to clean up exhaust emissions, lie everywhere. Each exhaust looks like a metal anaconda encountered shortly after swallowing a small round mammal.

Volvo, which has pioneered the use of water-based paints, is under tremendous pressure to cut back on its solvent emissions and is looking for measures which will help meet the extraordinarily tough standards now being imposed. 'Grams add to grams,' says Olle Boethius, 'and every tonne of solvent is important to us.'

Impressive level of environmental achievement, although it is striking how many minor misdemeanours we spot as we walk around. Workers sanding off car bodies without using ventilation systems; PVC strips in a skip of rubbish bound for an incinerator. Overall, however, a very high level of environmental awareness — and interest in my task. They plan to appoint an environmental auditor at Group level shortly. Overhead — and glimpsed through the doors — pairs of Air Force Drakken jets howl up into the sky.

One of the facts that emerges during the day is that the average Volvo is driven 15,000 km a year in Sweden. Apparently it would take 200 trees to absorb the carbon dioxide produced annually by a single car. We discuss the possibility of Volvo's offering to plant a number of trees for every car sold, as what the Americans would call an 'emission offset'. Also a good deal of discussion about the role of business in helping to promote sustainable development. Olle, too, is convinced that the Nineties will see growing interest in the 'ethical corporation'.

Wednesday 28 June
Big detergent companies begin their counter-attack against the Arks and Ecovers of this world, accusing them of misleading housewives about the benefits of going phosphate-free. Inevitable — and a real threat to 'green' firms across the board as consumer confusion grows. Meanwhile Michael Howard, an Environment Minister, has continued the Tory attack on the Greens by calling for 'green growth'. This is a phrase that Tom Burke came up with a couple of years back — indeed, SustainAbility has always been described as the 'green growth' company. No wonder some people assume we're Tories!

Fascinating article on environmentalism in France in the *Wall Street*

Journal. Concern about growth and jobs is so high there that the environment ranks fairly low in the pecking order of priorities. One industrialist working in the north-east of the country, often described as 'France's garbage pit', notes that pollution control measures that have led to reduced air pollution have caused alarm among local people. 'They thought we were closing down,' said Michel de Guenin. 'There are still a lot of people in these communities to whom smokestacks spewing black clouds are a sign of prosperity.' France often strikes one as the European country most in need of brainwashing in relation to environmental issues.

Meanwhile researchers at University College, North Wales, have concluded that massive 'blooms' of tiny marine plankton could be sponging up enormous quantities of carbon dioxide, helping to moderate the Greenhouse Effect. The question is: can the productivity of the seas be artificially increased? It may make sense to put sewage into the North Atlantic to fertilise the plankton there rather than dumping it into our coastal waters, says Professor Peter Williams.

Thursday 29 June
Off with Julia to the Temple, to consult the oracle on the McDonald's threat. Counsel says we start 1/nil down in libel law, since juries tend to favour the plaintiff. And the recent *Private Eye* verdict, with the magazine thumped with a £600,000 fine, is a warning that this is a threat to be taken seriously.

'I wish I could wave a magic wand,' says Counsel, although it is clear that all three lawyers in the book-lined room are enjoying the case hugely. One, bald-headed and with a strange nervous tic which makes his whole body leap, hops around us like a vulture inspecting a fresh corpse. 'The problem with companies like McDonald's,' Counsel continues, 'is that they are commercial giants and have their suppliers by the short and curlies.'

As far as the lawyers are concerned, however, this is a game of poker. The real question is whether we cave in or raise the stakes. Without wishing to turn ourselves into financial martyrs, we decide that we cannot rewrite the relevant sections of *The Guide* to exonerate McDonald's without concrete evidence from them that they have adopted and implemented an acceptable policy in relation to meat from rainforest areas. We decide to write to them to that effect.

The papers are full of the news that Overseas Aid Minister Christopher Patten is to visit Brazil next week to discuss a major British aid package designed to help save some of the country's rainforests.

Energy Secretary Cecil Parkinson attracts flak when he says that market forces must decide the extent of Britain's response to the Greenhouse Effect. Labour accuses him of having 'abdicated responsibility'. Labour also announces that it is to launch an inquiry into how it can pick up some of the protest voters who pressed the Green button in the Euro-elections in the next General Election. The party's campaign director says the aim is to ensure that it becomes 'a thorough-going Red–Green party'.

David Bellamy helped launch the TSB Environmental Investor Fund at the Waldorf Hotel yesterday. Accepting that the TSB portfolio might sometimes contain companies that were not wholly 'green', he said it was a case of 'the nudge factor'. 'We have to accept there's a wrong end of industry and persuade it the consumer wants to see things change.'

Friday 30 June
'The Green Consumer is here, in seven-league boots,' says Bob Worcester Chairman of MORI, in *The Times*. I am quoted as saying that the results are 'astounding' and comment that they will help persuade those retailers and manufacturers who are not already persuaded that green consumerism is beginning to engage not only committed environmentalists, but also ordinary people in the street and in the supermarket. Jonathon Porritt says: 'These people are not just Green Consumers. They are becoming Green Citizens.' MORI finds that the number of consumers who said they had consciously selected one product over another because of its environment friendly packaging, formulation or advertising had more than doubled — from 19% of the public to more than 42% (or 16 million adults) in the space of the last year! MORI also asked senior managers to guess what the result would be. They guesstimated 27%. 'Clearly managers are not in touch with how fast these issues are moving among their own consumers,' said Worcester.

Series of meetings through the day, including one with Karen Bishop and a colleague from Channel 4. They are making a series of films on the future of transport. One is based on 'time-lapse' photography of the M40 extension, showing the process of change from green fields through construction sites to the final motorway, blurred with traffic and (presumably) fumes.

Extraordinary article in *Today*, about green dating agencies. (Where is this all going to end?) Focuses on a couple who met through a dating agency called Country Partners. 'By choosing an agency geared to environment-conscious people,' said Caroline Laws, 'you increase your chances of meeting someone who has the same interests as yourself.' It seems we are now on the way towards a selective breeding programme for Green Citizens!

JULY

Sunday 2 July

Teddy Goldsmith, writing in yesterday's *Financial Times*' Planet Earth column, argues that the Industrial Revolution triggered a 'gross diversion' from the 'Way' — the path that traditional societies followed to ensure that they did not disrupt the Cosmos.

'Modern man,' Teddy says, 'is committed to precisely that path that will most disrupt the critical order of the Cosmos; since economic development means systematically replacing the biosphere or national world with the technosphere or man-made world. This explains why the destruction wrought to the natural world in the last 40 years, during which economic development has really got under way on a global scale, is greater than all the destruction done to it since the beginning of man's tenancy of this planet.'

The obvious next question: what should we be doing about it? Teddy and his colleagues are currently working on an updated version of *A Blueprint for Survival*, their epoch-making book first published in 1972. It will be interesting to see how far their thinking has changed over the intervening years. *The Guide* is still No. 5, its thirtieth week in *The Sunday Times* Top 10. And in the political rankings, Labour (47%) has jumped ahead of the Conservatives (37%), with the Greens (7%) polling as strongly as the Democrats (4%) and SDP (3%) put together.

The Government is getting into ever-hotter water over its plans to privatise the water industry, which continues to attract widespread criticism. Ministers are in the midst of legalising thousands of previously illegal discharges of sewage and other pollutants, to make the water authorities a tastier prospect for investors. Friends of the Earth, according to Geoffrey Lean of the *Observer*, may take Nicholas Ridley to court if he directs the new National Rivers Authority to allow these temporary permits to pollute.

Even worse pollution problems reported from Venice, where hundreds of tonnes of seaweed feeding on sewage and industrial and agricultural pollutants in the lagoons are, in turn, providing food for vast swarms of gnats. 'One sees the new invaders even before reaching Venice, from the train, on that marvellous curving bridge crossing the lagoons: great sloppy pea-green tablecloths, wobbling in the water,' William Scobie reports in the *Observer*.

The tides that once cleansed the canals are now as filthy as the waterways themselves. Last year the stench got so bad, Scobie recalls, that some tourists sailed down the Grand Canal wearing surgical masks. Gnats rose in such dense clouds that the airport shut down and trains stopped — drivers and pilots couldn't see where they were going.

Back in Britain, *The Sunday Times* turns the spotlight on seaside towns like Bournemouth, which are building groynes and other sea defences from tropical hardwood from West Africa, South America and southeast Asia. 'The environmental cost is 800 trees felled for the work carried out so far at Bournemouth,' the Insight team reports. 'On average, two to three acres of tropical rainforest are damaged or destroyed to extract just one tree. Protecting Bournemouth's beaches, therefore, has so far meant damage to, or loss of, an area of rainforest equal in size to Epping Forest.' The irony is that the loss of these forests contributes to the Greenhouse Effect, which in turn will cause rising sea levels that could well overwhelm such defences.

Happier news from Revlon, the major cosmetics company, which is following Avon's lead by pulling out of animal testing. 'For a long time, cosmetic companies said there was no alternative to animal experiments,' Animal Aid director Mark Gold told the *Observer*. 'However, as the public has grown more antagonistic to the practice, companies' views have mysteriously changed. Now they have found that it was possible to find alternatives after all.'

Julia and I have always disagreed about animal rights; she thinks they are peripheral to the big ecological issues, whereas I have always felt that if we can't protect the animals in our own backyard we have little hope of doing much for those in the rainforests. Also, many of the safety tests which environmentalists insist should be carried out on chemicals like pesticides involve 'sacrificing' large numbers of animals. In the end, we decided to include animal welfare in *The Guide* and gave a fair amount of space over to 'cruelty-free' products.

Monday 3 July
Fax latest article, on disposable nappies, to *Guardian*. Jules Trocchi of Air Call comes in at 08.30 to talk about the proposed Green Consumer phone-in service. We suggest it be done jointly with WWF, since we simply haven't got the resources needed, although the idea of building up a computerised database of consumers wanting to be sent, for example, free samples of new environment-friendly products is a good one.

Day is one long succession of meetings.

A new report from ACE suggests that Britain, which produces about 585 million tonnes of carbon dioxide a year by burning fossil fuels, could cut its emissions of the greenhouse gas by almost a quarter by adopting energy efficiency measures over the next 25 years without paying any severe economic penalties — and with continued economic growth. *The Independent* calculates that the average British family of four generates 44 tonnes of carbon dioxide a year, only 13.9 tonnes of which are under their control (the rest being generated by industry, commerce and government).

In the news: California and New York City public employee pension funds call on six oil and chemical companies to follow Exxon and name an environmentalist as a board member; Brian Johnson — now up to his eyes in the rainforest issue — argues that we should use more tropical timber, not less, to ensure that Third World countries value their tropical forests; and *Today* devotes a par-for-the-course leader claiming that 'the dolphin whose headless body was found on a Welsh beach was killed by Nicholas Ridley, as surely as if the Environment Secretary had wielded the axe himself'. Dolphins should be protected, the paper says, against 'murderous fishermen'. I should think Ridley papers his bathroom with nonsense like this.

The Brand New people say they see us as a major bottleneck interrupting their ability to respond to demand for green consumer marketing, particularly in Europe. Can we scale up faster, they ask? Do we need more money? We ask Noel Botha, an MBA student, to help us put together a business plan. Julia, Annie and I work late. Finish off last sections of *Supermarket Guide* and set off for home at 21.30.

Tuesday 4 July
By train to Ipswich, to progress the Volvo Concessionaires environmental report. Where grain was once loaded into ships for export, we now unload thousands of Swedish cars. No wonder people use them: the train is an hour late starting out, because of a signal failure.

The grass along the rail verges is sun-burned to a shimmering copper bronze, interspersed by electric pink blushes of rosebay willowherb. The Americans call it 'fireweed', because of its habit of blooming where there has been a forest fire. In the fields, pulsating blood-red poppies and stark elm skeletons, now little more than pit-stops for marauding owls and fly-in diners for woodpeckers. Standing in an estuary, a grey heron. Brain switches back and forth between seeing it as a romantic focus to the waterscape and as a fish-killing robot. Brilliant sun, but the wind whips between the road bridge and power station which dominate the Volvo site.

More than 100 scientists, including two Nobel Laureates and 15 Fellows of the Royal Society — where Mrs T gave her first 'green' speech last year — have signed a declaration backing Greenpeace and arguing that nuclear power is not the answer to the Greenhouse Effect. Indeed, they say, nuclear power is 'irrelevant'. Instead, they argue, 'energy efficiency measures offer far more scope than nuclear, pound for pound, in reducing the demand for fossil fuels'. But is Mrs T listening?

More than 600 doctors at the British Medical Association's annual meeting have called on the Government to cut imports of toxic waste to Britain, which they describe as 'the dustbin of Europe'. Rechem has a plant in the area. And in the USSR environmentalists are blocking the operation of a new plant — some 300 miles east of Moscow — designed to destroy chemical weapons. An extraordinary development, difficult to conceive of even a year ago.

In *Newsweek*, French environmentalist Jacques-Yves Cousteau, just inducted in the Academie Française, is asked whether he is encouraged by the growth of Green parties in Europe? 'I hate it,' he replied. 'We need to convince all parties of the necessity of ecology, not only one party. The problem is that if you are elected as a member of one party, that means you are against all other parties. This is a big mistake. I have met with and given information to whoever has been elected — right, left or center.' Although I agree with him, there is no question that the Green parties have helped advance the environmental cause throughout Europe.

Cousteau is profoundly pessimistic. 'Logically,' he says, 'we are doomed, but then logical reasoning often fails. American computers during the Vietnam War failed to anticipate the impact of the Vietnamese bicycle (used by the Viet Cong to ferry arms and munitions). Maybe there is an environmental "bicycle" that will surprise us all.'

Wednesday 5 July
'If nuclear war is the Earth's equivalent of a heart attack,' says former UNEP director Maurice Strong in the *Wall Street Journal*, 'environmental damage is its cancer.'

Interestingly, *Today* splashes its front page with a story on the QE2, entitled 'Dustbin of the Sea'. Crewmen apparently regularly throw plastic sacks of kitchen waste, much of it non-biodegradable plastic, overboard, under cover of night. There have been complaints that bottles and champagne corks with QE2 markings have been washing up on beaches. The maximum fine for such offences is a derisory £2,000.

But the big news of the day is that Bryn Jones has been forced to resign from Ark. The storm has at last broken there, resulting in an acrimonious split. It turns out that an American millionaire, Isaac Tigrett, has taken over the helm and intends to concentrate on pushing Ark's 'environment-friendly' products.

The McDonald's saga is developing when their lawyers tell Julia that they (Big Mac's lawyers) are split on whether our words were actually defamatory. Our own lawyers jump on this and insist that this is our first 'on the record' discussion with McDonald's.

In the news: FoE say that the only green fridges are made by Amana and Indesit, who guarantee to remove and recycle the CFC coolants. AEG and Siemens have refused to do likewise, while Electrolux, Philips and Hotpoint are still pondering what to do for the best; the Co-op says 'no' to irradiated food; and the Ferruzi Group launches biodegradable plastics made from corn starch with a give-away promotion based on 750,000 biodegradable plastic Mickey Mouse watches.

Thursday 6 July
In a green version of the Trojan Horse operations, 200 West German environmentalists hidden aboard a ship yesterday invaded part of the huge Hoechst AG plant on West Germany's Main River. They were protesting against the production of CFCs at the plant.

In the news: Overseas Development Minister Christopher Patten has signed a (limited) aid package in Brazil designed to help the country slow the pace of rainforest destruction; in the House of Lords, Baroness Hooper, Under-Secretary for Energy, introduces proposals to strengthen the duties of electricity generators and suppliers to protect the environment once the industry is privatised. Environmental guidelines will have to be prepared by all licensed suppliers and generators, in consultation with the Countryside Commission, NCC and, where appropriate, the Historic Buildings and Monuments Commission; and the TSB's new Environmental Investor Fund, advised by David Bellamy, has been caught up in the uproar about Attwoods, the waste disposal company under investigation for bribery and alleged large-scale pollution, which is on the TSB approved list of green shares.

Stan Eales, our designer, comes in with some brilliant designs for the Green Shopping Day posters and leaflet.

This afternoon part of a panel for a live, 60-minute broadcast on the environment on Radio 1. Hosted by DJ Nicky Campbell. Share the platform with people from a pop band (Hue and Cry), FoE, the local Chamber of Commerce, Professor Heinz Wolff (the bioengineer and TV scientist reponsible for 'The Great Egg Race' series) and comedienne Pamela Stephenson.

The Hue and Cry chap launches forth into a harangue on hamburgers and the rainforests, quoting *The Guide* almost verbatim during the live broadcast. Afterwards a couple of McDonald's people race up and suggest a meeting in London to talk things through. I point out that they have already loosed their legal hounds on us and that we have been busy assembling information to substantiate our claims. Decide to play this as a game of poker — bluffing a bit. It all ends up with them assuring me that they want to move forward sensibly rather than going through the courts. I mention that their legal action is not only costing us thousands in legal fees, but has also dried up supplies of the book, which is now out of print.

Travel back to London with Heinz, Pamela and a couple of her people, Simon and Sue. Spend most of the trip back talking through her plans for her new Parents For Safe Food pressure group. Catch cab, with some difficulty, back to Barnes. Sheet lightning pulses along the horizon as I walk the last stretch home at 01.30.

Friday 7 July
Julia off to Hong Kong and Australia for three weeks, to build contacts with Kevin Condon and others in advance of the publication of *The Australian Green Consumer Guide*. Meanwhile, news comes through that *The Canadian Green Consumer Guide* is in trouble after the Canadian adaptor went completely off on a tangent, writing the book he always wanted to write — rather than adapting ours.

Janet Barber of WWF says our green tourism proposal has hit problems, because her Conservation Review Group is worried that SustainAbility is too successful. They want a share in the royalties of *The Green Holiday Guide*, which we consider to be a quite separate project to the one we are proposing to WWF. It looks as though we can get around the problem, however, and it seems that my previous report — on environmental auditing — is now seen as a key plank in the WWF UK platform for the next year.

Meanwhile, the articles about Ark's grounding flood in. The group has apparently shut down for three weeks for 'management restructuring'. Not surprisingly, they are being overwhelmed by calls from their 10,000-or-so members wanting to know what is going on. Asked for his reaction, Jonathon Porritt tells the *Guardian*: 'There was a quite un-green arrogance about the launch and the whole style of the organisation, with its glitz and gloss and the high-flying celebrities. Ark wasn't interested in working with anyone else, they wanted to be everything to everyone, to have the best marketing, the best campaigners, the most broad-based membership organisation.' Very much our reaction, too. But it is always sad to see an environmental organisation getting into trouble. There are too few of us in action as it is.

McDonald's lawyers have apparently called Gollancz to say that following the Cardiff meeting they want to drop the lawyer-to-lawyer meeting on Monday and instead go forward with a less combative meeting later in the week. The whole issue has apparently been pushed up the tree to their Managing Director.

In the news: two ICI workmen killed by ammonia fumes at the company's fertilizer plant in Billingham, Cleveland; a new pollution control aid package is signed between West and East Germany; and the Royal Commission on Environmental Pollution — to which I gave evidence a long time back — finally publishes its report on genetic engineering, calling for tighter controls over the deliberate release of genetically engineered organisms into the environment.

An opinion poll carried out by *The Independent* and NOP concludes that the Greens have tapped a widespread fear that drastic action is now needed to save the environment, the implication being that the potential for further Green political advances is considerable. 45% of those surveyed said they would now 'seriously consider' voting for the Greens.

Meanwhile, environmental issues are expected to top the agenda at next week's economic summit meeting in Paris. 'Restoring the environment is not a sprinter's game,' says EPA head Dr William Reilly. 'There is something of a race on by some of the economic summit participants to be leaders, to be the greenest of all on this issue. It is going to require steady, long-term commitments.' The problem with some politicians is that they want to be decked out in green laurels today, but will quickly forget about the environment when the next political bandwagon starts to roll.

Saturday 8 July
The meeting of African nations on ways to save the elephant collapsed in almost total disagreement yesterday. East African nations wanted a ban, southern African countries opposed the idea. Shuttle diplomacy will be tried to get the negotiations back on the road. According to *The Independent*, the debate behind closed doors was 'heated and acrimonious'.

Nicholas Ridley last night launched a savage assault on what he described as the 'vapid romanticism' of Green policies. He argued that Green solutions were the equivalent of going to the doctor with indigestion and being told you need your leg amputated. Both Britain and Japan apparently plan green statements at next week's summit meeting. But (hopefully) the Government will have been deeply embarrassed by the post-retirement attack on its policies by Dr Derek Ratcliffe, the NCC's chief scientist. Mr Ridley's period in office had been a deeply depressing time for conservation, Derek said. The Secretary of State, he explained, 'has insisted that when we give grant aid to other bodies, such as the RSPB, to purchase land, it is on the understanding that there are no restrictions placed on shooting, hunting and other field sports.' So, it seems, you can protect birds as long as other people can blast them out of the sky. The Government's cuts in the Council's funding, Derek concluded were unworthy of a government with claims to protect the environment.

Sunday 9 July
The Guide is at No. 7, although we are now getting calls from people who can't get it because the next printing is delayed, pending the outcome of the McDonald's saga.

The first major attempt to discredit the Green Consumer revolution has backfired on the industry that launched it, the *Observer* points out; while the SDIA, which initially dismissed *The Green Consumer Guide* as 'pseudo-scientific rubbish', is attacking the claims of rivals like Ark and Ecover, a survey shows that many other EEC countries already have phosphate-free versions of the brands sold here. (And they are made by the same companies that are saying the switch is unnecessary here.)

The Government — and particularly Energy Secretary Cecil Parkinson — will be embarrassed by a new UN study that shows that in 1987, the last year for which figures are available, the UK's carbon dioxide emissions rose 2.6% to 156 million tonnes — at a time when world emissions grew by only 1.6%. Parkinson wants to overturn a House of Lords amendment inserting strict energy conservation measures into his electricity privatisation measures. The report also says that nearly two-thirds of Britain's broadleaf trees, including oaks over 60 years old, are losing their leaves partly because of air pollution. Only Czechoslovakia and Greece show equivalent levels of damage.

Impact of the Greenhouse Effect is suggested by the plague of algae now threatening the Adriatic. *The Sunday Times* reports that a vast, glutinous mass of partly decomposed algae that hit Italian beach resorts in 1988 has reappeared in unprecedented strength, threatening marine life and the fishing and tourist industries. Scientists blame climatic changes and pollution. And Italy's Environment Minister closes a controversial Montedison chemical plant, in northern Italy, for six months because of pollution risks.

In the *Observer*, Cambridge University whale expert Dr Margaret Klinowska says that the Greenhouse Effect will almost certainly drive many species of whale and dolphin to extinction, because the richest feeding grounds will move towards the poles, which means that the productive areas will shrink.

Meanwhile the Japanese and Korean fishermen are decimating the shark populations off the Galapagos Islands, hacking off their fins before discarding the bodies. The fins are a delicacy in the East and can fetch up to £10 a pound.

Finally, hot on the heels of her call for an end to Brazilian deforestation, Mrs T has apparently ordered Brazilian mahogany for the refurbishment of No. 10's White and Blue Rooms.

Monday 10 July
Early meeting with Dorothy and Dr Fiannoula Wynn of ICI's biotechnology side, who is working on commercialising their bacterial biodegradable plastic, Biopol. ICI want help with developing their environmental 'case' for Biopol and with establishing a corporate identity for the bio-products side of their operations.

Lunch with David Baldock of the Institute for European Environmental Policy, to discuss possibility of using him and other IEEP resources in our work for companies — particularly on EEC policy and regulation fronts, and on the environmental implications of 1992. Environmentalists are currently focusing on the negative impact of the growth likely to be triggered by the single European market. But progressive unification offers opportunities, too. Discuss pricing of strategies in this field: he recalls Robin Bidwell of Environmental Resources Ltd, saying he aimed to be seen as the Red Adair, who you always called when you got into trouble. Maybe we should present ourselves as 'Green Adairs', the people you get in touch with if you want to prevent problems happening in the first place!

Then meeting with Stewart Boyle of ACE, John Winward of the Consumers' Association and others, at which we agree to put together a joint manifesto and workshop to put pressure on the DoE and DTI to take the Green Label scheme proposal more seriously.

The *Guardian* reports on Christopher Patten's visit to Brazil and focuses on Nicholas Burch, a 35-year-old Londoner who used to work with the Forestry Commission before moving to Brazil eight years ago. Burch set up his own reforestation company with his own money a couple of years back. So far, he has planted 50,000 trees: Brazil nut, rubber, mahogany, fast-growing softwood, cacao and heart of palm trees among them. Burch believes that the solutions to deforestation will come from private sector initiatives like his, although he notes that at the moment Government incentives work in such a way that you're rewarded for clearing the forest and not for conserving it. Coincidentally, I received a letter from Burch and Jeremy Holt today, announcing the establishment of their new company, Produtos da Amazonia. The idea is to make profits from rainforest products, reinvesting them back into Amazonian conservation and sustainable development.

Green Sir James Goldsmiths in the making? I hope so, although if the enterprise takes off these environmental entrepreneurs will be faced with some tough trade-offs.

Tuesday 11 July

Newspapers are full of an attack on Greens launched by Ridley yesterday at the conference in Newcastle — organised by the Association of Metropolitan Authorities — where I am due to speak today. The Green platforms in the recent Euro-elections, he claimed, were 'unscientific rubbish, based on myths, prejudices and ignorance'. He is apparently considering setting up a new statistical office to counter the 'disinformation and wild accusations' that he sees as characterising the environmental debate.

Amazingly, he says that 'the jibe that we are the dirty man of Europe is a falsehood put about to weaken our negotiating position'. Jonathon Porritt has challenged Mr Ridley to come up with examples and told *The Times*: 'This is the kind of off-the-cuff knocking copy which is Ridley's substitute for political thought. The man is essentially incompetent . . . '

Up to Newcastle by train to find there has been a bomb scare which closed the station for several hours. Arrive at the Civic Centre to find it has been closed by a NALGO strike and the AMA conference has been transferred to the nearby Polytechnic. Listen to Jonathon addressing the conference, chair workshop on green consumerism in local authority purchasing and then catch train back. Total of ten hours spent travelling for 90 minutes active work.

Meanwhile the Australians are taking the Greenhouse Effect seriously. They are launching a new £3 million network of monitoring stations in the South Pacific, concerned that rising sea levels will drown the islands of Kiribati, Tonga and Tuvalu. But the islands face an even more immediate threat: their economies are being undermined by Japanese and Taiwanese fishermen, using drift-nets up to 50 miles long, decimating stocks of tuna and other fish.

Wednesday 12 July

Another brand going green: Hovis announces that it plans to bring out a stoneground wholemeal loaf made from organic flour. The new loaf will be the same size as the traditional brown loaf, but cost 59p — 17p more. A particularly worrying example of premium pricing for green products. How many of us can afford to pay that much more for our daily bread? But maybe economies of scale will drive prices down.

The *Financial Times* reports that advertisers are being taken to task by the Advertising Standards Authority for jumping on the 'green band-wagon' with false claims. It has upheld claims against environmental benefits claimed for Austin-Rover's Metro Surf car (claimed to be 'ozone-friendly'!) and BP's Super-green petrol ('no pollution of the environment'!).

Pamela Stephenson's Parents for Safe Food announced yesterday that 'high' levels of Alar have been found in apples and apple juice sold by Marks & Spencer, Safeway, Waitrose, Tesco and Sainsbury's. Alar was also found in baby foods, including Heinz's *Pure Fruit Baby Food* and Cow & Gate's *Apple Dessert*. Actress Rula Lenska tells the *Guardian*: 'Once an apple a day kept the doctor away. Now it looks as if it will bring cancer one day.'

Meanwhile, Nicholas Ridley continues his rampage through the green china shop, announcing that he plans to dismember the Countryside Commission and the NCC. NCC Chairman (Sir) William Wilkinson was not even consulted. 'The NCC is clearly being punished for daring to comment publicly about defects in Government policy, such as those relating to forestry,' FoE comment. I cannot help but agree.

Once the office has quietened down, race through work, leaving Annie's and Fiona's desks covered with notes on things to do and follow up tomorrow, when I shall be in Chester. Write a three-page fax to Julia in Australia.

Thursday 13 July
Up at 06.30 and off to Heathrow to fly to Liverpool.

Beginning audit of the Manweb regional electricity board, which is preparing for privatisation. They see visual intrusion of their power lines as the major issue, followed by electromagnetic radiation generated by both power lines and electrical equipment. I argue that the key issue for investors is going to be the Greenhouse Effect and the likely drive in the 1990s for increased energy efficiency. Can Manweb develop an energy efficiency business? Deputy chairman Richard Gales thinks it can.

Stanley Clinton Davis, the former European Commissioner, has called Nicholas Ridley an 'environmental hooligan'. The Royal Society for Nature Conservation fears that the NCC proposals are simply the first step towards privatising the NCC's 63 national nature reserves. Significantly, meanwhile, the DoE has failed to come up with any instances of the 'disinformation and wild accusations' — purveyed by the Green Party — which Ridley complained about earlier in the week.

Someone who clearly hasn't been scanning the survey results: Environment Council chairman Dr Martin Aickin reported in *The Times* as saying 'The Nineties are heralded as the green decade, and it is fashionable to talk of the Green Consumer, although whether such a being exists is in some doubt.'

Friday 14 July
The Women's Environmental Network write to say they won't be participating in Green Shopping Day. Counsel, Heinz's PR company,

contact WWF to say that they have heard through the 'environmental grapevine' that WEN, FoE and Greenpeace are planning to launch a massive counter-attack against Green Shopping Day. It is said that they are distancing themselves from SustainAbility — and particularly from me.

Apparently my views are causing considerable offence. No details given! I am described as light Green at best. Today is Bastille Day and one cannot help but imagine a time when dark Greens will denounce light Greens and would-be Greens to some Revolutionary Council. Potential for the Green movement to tear itself apart pretty much as the Labour Party did for a while. Decide to leave any response until Monday. But it all leaves a very sour taste. I don't mind competition, even conflict, but prefer it to be out in the open. At the same time, however, sense that this clears our decks for action.

In the news: the Advertising Standards Authority has received a complaint about Panasonic's use of the word 'green' in its advertising of its mercury-free batteries.

McDonald's finally come back with a date for the meeting: 24 July. We have already lost sales of 4,000 copies of *The Guide* and could well lose another 6,000 because of the delay. But Big Mac say they are taking the challenge in our last letter to them seriously, and are pulling in information from around the world.

In the evening, to a Bastille party at Annie's. Fiona comes as a Tour de France cyclist, sporting the words 'Bastille Bikes: Tour de France, 1789'. The best I can manage is a green T-shirt and an Amis de la Terre badge.

Saturday 15 July
Timothy Hornsby, Director-General of the NCC, has accused Mr Ridley of trying to 'balkanise' the NCC. On the issue of the proposed reorganisation, he entirely agrees with the Government's aims. 'You want a more sensitive regional presence, aware of the nature of the country in Scotland, aware of the need to do balancing acts, aware of different pressures, capable of co-operating with the Countryside Commission.' Reading between the lines, it is clear that Timothy, who some environmentalists saw as a Government plant in advance of just such a reorganisation, thinks Ridley has taken leave of his senses.

Glorious morning. Elaine and I are bound for the National Centre for Organic Gardening, which we reach around noon.

The excuse for going is the second National Organic Wine Fair, organised by the Henry Doubleday Research Association (HDRA) and sponsored by Safeway. Ironically, when HDRA was founded it considered an earlier 'green revolution' the enemy. Around the world, farmers were being persuaded to grow new 'miracle' crops, which depended on large injections of artificial fertilizers and synthetic pesticides. The real answer, HDRA founder Lawrence D Hills explained to anyone who would listen, lay in organic farming and gardening.

Over the years, more and more people began to listen. We used to go down to the HDRA AGMs in east London in the early 1970s, when most of the people attending seemed to be in their Sixties. The original one-acre site near Braintree was soon outgrown, however, and HDRA bought ten acres of run-down farmland near Coventry in 1984, transforming them into the National Centre for Organic Gardening.

In the wake of their popular Channel 4 series, 'All Muck and Magic', Alan Gear, his wife Jackie and their helpers receive 500 letters a day. HDRA, which had 5,000 members when it moved, now has 15,000 and is recruiting 50 new members a day — a clear indication of the booming interest in organic gardening.

The Centre, also known as Ryton Gardens, attracted around 10,000 visitors in 1986, when it first opened to the public. This year, it looks as though it will pull in an estimated 60,000. And HDRA's turnover has also rocketed, from £100,000 to £1 million. But, Alan notes wistfully, the rate of investment in new facilities and staff means that they are still broke. 'Once again,' he says, 'we are in danger of being throttled by our own growth.'

Visit Ryton Gardens and you will find a hive of experimentation, from the lines of compost heaps to the guillotined PET lemonade bottles serving as mini-cloches. Bring a length of carpet, which the Gears use as mulching, and you get in free! Increasingly, too, the experiments are taking root overseas. HDRA has already planted more than 20,000 trees in Cape Verde, is looking at ways of greening China's semi-arid and salt-caked Yellow River Delta, and has also supplied seed for over one million trees to Ethiopia.

Now that HDRA has rolled out the green carpet for its new patron, Prince Charles, it looks set for a period of accelerated growth. If the Gears can cope with the strain, this can only be a Good Thing. They calculate that Britain's 18 million gardeners in Britain cultivate a total of one million acres, which suggests an enormous potential for a quiet revolution in our own backyards. Amazingly, although only 10% of visitors are already HDRA members, 90% say they will use some of the methods they have seen in their own gardens. They have seen the future — and it works.

Monday 17 July
The economic summit meeting in Paris yesterday heard President Bush describe 1989 as a watershed year for the environment and call for a

global crusade to save it. Mrs T argued: 'If we are to pass on the heritage safe for our children's future, we must take action now.' She called for 'higher growth (whatever that might be) compatible with a sound environment.' Said Chancellor Kohl: 'For the first time, there's a clear signal for joint responsibility from industrial countries for preservation of the world. We have no time to lose.' More than a third of the eventual 22-page communique was devoted to green issues.

Positive news, to set against the less happy news that FoE have secretly taken a decision to pull out of Green Shopping Day. Talk to Dave Gee, who is due to take over from Jonathon Porritt and he says he will try to come along to the Consumers' Association meeting in September on green labelling. But it's clear that FoE are manoeuvring to launch a counter-blast to 'the frothier end' of green consumerism. We do not expect WWF to stay with us if FoE back off, so the question is whether we should go it alone — with the support of the many other enthusiastic conservation, women's and consumer organisations around the country. After talking it through, we conclude that we all want to push on.

The Times publishes a massive piece on green consumerism and eco-labelling today. Paul Vallely and Anne McElvoy describe *The Guide*'s publication as a 'watershed . . . It has been the kind of success about which most pressure groups only dream'. Later on in the day, *The Times* call to see if I would contribute a weekly column. Say I can't, what with the *Guardian* and other commitments. Pity, though.

Another Soviet nuclear sub appears to be on fire 80 miles off the Norwegian coast. The Russians say it is just practising — or maybe it was diesel smoke from an exhaust.

Later in the week, Greenpeace founder David McTaggart sails into Leningrad aboard the new *Rainbow Warrior*, to announce the formation of Greenpeace International. The *Observer* reports that Parliamentary Deputy Professor Alexei, expected to become the first head of the Soviet branch of Greenpeace International, has told the Communist Party to green itself 'rapidly and decisively' or 'ecological dissatisfaction will be politicised outside the Party'. The main problem, he says, has been 'enormous industrial development without any ecological restriction'.

The literary journal *Novy Mir* last month quoted a local doctor in Uzbekistan as saying: 'Out of 1,000 new-born babies, 100 die before they are a year old. Deformed babies have begun to be born . . . without an anus, with shortened intestines, feeble-minded, without a limb or without a skull, just skin on the face.'

We leave the office at 22.30. Finish diary at 00.15 and try to call Julia in Sydney. She's in Melbourne but should call tomorrow morning. Australian Prime Minister Bob Hawke has just helped the Commission for the

Future to launch its Personal Action Programme for the Earth, a 24-page Green Consumer guide. They use the expression 'environmentally-friendly consumer'.

Tuesday 18 July
Fiona has talked to Chris Church of FoE, who says that the problem has more to do with the fact that FoE has an AGM a week before Green Shopping Day — at which it will almost certainly decide to be more aggressive on Green Consumer issues. And it is concerned that Heinz is linked with the US company Sunkist, which is involved in tuna fishing — and therefore with the dolphin death problem. Julia has also called and is determined that we should push on regardless. In fact, Heinz had told us of the Sunkist issue right at the beginning. We said that if Green Shopping Day was to work with their participation, they would need to discuss the issue in public.

'Just when Exxon thought it was safe to go back in the water,' a Democratic Representative tells the *Wall Street Journal*, 'they're facing a new day.' A US appeals court has ruled that companies responsible for oil spills should pay the full cost of restoring the environment to its original condition. The same ruling could apply to companies caught up in hazardous waste scandals. 'It is a major and significant decision that will probably cost industry billions of dollars,' said Erik Olson, attorney for the National Wildlife Federation, one of the organisations that brought the case against the US Interior Department. It will certainly help rather more business brains to pay attention.

The *Financial Times* reports the results of a German study on the proportion of GNP spent on environmental protection in the leading industrial nations. With the exception of the Netherlands, which spent 1.34% in 1988 compared to 1% in 1975, most other countries have slipped badly. Japan's spending has fallen precipitously from 1.6% to 0.7%. The UK's spending has dropped from 1.5% to 0.74%. Only the Netherlands, West Germany and Canada are still over the 1% mark.

Energy Minister Cecil Parkinson is slammed by the House of Commons Energy Select Committee in terms of his handling of everything to do with the Greenhouse Effect. It rejects outright the claim that there is nothing the Government can — or should — do to tackle the problem. The idea that the Greenhouse Effect should be simply left to market forces is seen as utterly wrong.

'As in the case of energy efficiency, where the total effect is the cumulation of many individuals' decisions,' the Committee says, 'so the global response to the Greenhouse Effect will be the sum of the effort of individual countries.' The MPs quote Edmund Burke, to the effect that:

'Nobody made a bigger mistake than he who did nothing because he himself could only do a little.' We quote him in relation to the potential of green consumerism, all the time!

Wednesday 19 July

Under a cloudless African sky, President Daniel arap Moi of Kenya yesterday set fire to a pyramid of poached 'white gold', or ivory. The burning of the 2,000 elephant tusks, worth £2 million, was a potent symbol of the growing determination of some African governments to control the illegal ivory trade. Since President Moi declared war on poaching, there has been a shoot-to-kill policy, with dozens of poachers killed.

The Italian Government calls an emergency cabinet committee meeting to discuss the Adriatic algae problem. A Rimini restaurateur, meanwhile, has been offering his clients plates of spaghetti covered with algae sauce. 'We've sold 100 plates of it in 48 hours,' he told *The Independent*.

French Environment Minister Brice Lalonde, in London, says he wants to see a green label scheme in operation EEC-wide before 1992. 'I do not want to see 1992 bringing in a free flow in dirty products, but in clean ones,' said Lalonde, previously a Greenpeace and Les Amis de la Terre activist. In September, he takes up the presidency of the council of European environment ministers for six months. CBI Director-General John Banham told a conference yesterday that 'the Green Consumer rightly demands packaging — particularly plastics packaging — that can be safely and efficiently disposed of. At the same time we cannot ignore filthy streets, or the readiness of the public to scatter litter all over our parks, even when an empty litter bin is less than a few feet away.'

Did interviews today with *Country Living* and the *Evening Standard*. *Fortune* magazine also in pursuit. Talk to Janet Barber about proposed Green Label meeting in September. Race to get off fax to WWF and then later talk the Heinz saga through with Jane Kaufman. WWF have talked to Greenpeace chairman (Lord) Peter Melchett, who says there is no anti-Green Shopping Day campaign in Greenpeace, although it turns out that WEN are planning a 'No Shopping Day' for the same day. If it stirs controversy, so much the better. Also turns out, quite fortuitously, that 28 September will be the day after the anniversary of Mrs T's first major green speech.

In Canada, the Duchess of York 'adopts' a Beluga whale, calling it Coquine Blanche (White Mischief). In Britain, the Democrats launch 'Campaign Earth', in an attempt to recapture a bit of green credibility.

Full-ish moon hangs low in the sky as I get back home around 23.00. Feed the rabbits in the dark. Yesterday's news now lines their cages.

Thursday 20 July
So tired that fail to wake up with the alarm and arrive late at the office for what proved to be an extraordinary meeting with a consultant representing Littlewoods, a major family-owned company that wants to put considerable sums into the environmental movement over a period of 20 years! It wants to start with an environmental audit and then to move on to practical projects. One of these could be a series of Littlewoods Lectures on the Environment. Exciting prospect, but so many of these initial contacts fall away once the commercial implications of 'going green' sink in.

One man it would be interesting to hear would be Joe Hazelwood, the captain of the *Exxon Valdez*, now branded as America's Environmental Enemy No. 1. A profile in *Time* suggests that Hazelwood was not solely to blame for the disaster. Since 24 March, however, he has been a man under siege, with journalists surrounding his home and anonymous death threats.

Hot, sticky day. Work with Daren (Howarth) on *The Universal Green Office Guide*; do a 40-minute phone interview with *Fortune*; several other companies ring during the day to ask for environmental audits, including Addis.

Sir Geoffrey Howe, in a speech to the Radical Society last night, looked forward to a Europe of free enterprise and 'green growth' in the 1990s; and Transport Secretary Paul Channon says Britain's traffic could double over the next 40 years, ironically at a lunch celebrating the work of the Campaign for Lead Free Air (CLEAR). CLEAR are organising a 'Day of Adjustment' for 28 September, which will coincide with Green Shopping Day. We see strong links between the two, but will CLEAR?

Friday 21 July
20 years ago, at 03.52 on 21 July 1969, Neil Armstrong stepped on to the moon. Nearly one-fifth of the world's population had abandoned work or fought off sleep to watch the extraordinary event on TV or listen to the radio. 'I'm at the foot of the ladder,' the Man on the Moon said. 'The surface seems to be very finely grained. I am going to step off the LM (Lunar Module) now. That's one small step for man, a giant leap for mankind.' To mark the anniversary, President Bush announces Mars mission.

For those condemned to tread through the drifts of litter that line Britain's streets, some welcome news in the form of an announcement from Nicholas Ridley and Virginia Bottomley that litter louts face penalties of up to £1,000. 'A litter-strewn environment can no longer be tolerated,' said Mrs T. But Mr Ridley is now under enormous political pressure from Tories who feel he will lose them the next election, because of his failure to 'go green' and sell the poll tax effectively to a highly suspicious electorate.

Michael Heseltine is now ramping up his campaign for the leadership of the Conservative Party, saying in a major speech yesterday that the Government has left a vacuum where its environmental policies ought to be. Pointing to the environmental agenda, he noted that 'the agenda is a long and familiar one. What is new is the level of public concern. Such is the head of steam that for every one of the items on the agenda, solutions will have to be found'.

In Australia, Prime Minister Bob Hawke has launched a major policy statement on the environment — appointing Sir Ninian Stephen, until recently the country's Governor-General, as an international Ambassador for the Environment. The cornerstone of the new policy is a £147 million anti-erosion, tree-planting programme. A total of one billion trees will be planted over the next decade and a 'Save the Bush' campaign started.

Saturday 22 July
Scorching, humid day. In France, the region of Aquitaine (or Gironde) — where we are going in August — is ablaze with forest fires. The huge area affected has raised the spectre of 1949, when forest fires claimed 84 lives. The fire service suspect that some of the fires have been deliberately lit — or relit.

This is also the season for burning the rainforest. As I walked through Covent Garden a couple of days back, I noticed that The Body Shop is using its shop windows for a campaign to stop the burning — apparently the Oxford branch alone has collected more than 6,800 signatures on a petition to President Sarney.

Mr Ridley is dubbed 'this environmental Genghis Khan' by Labour MP Ron Davies. Labour will be making a concerted drive to capture the Green vote. Council of Green Party, whose membership has almost doubled — from 7,500 to 14,000 — meets this weekend in Birmingham to plan next moves. They will be aware that they are vulnerable on the questions of economic growth and defence. One Council member told *The Independent* that it was 'absolute rubbish' to suggest, as the Party's critics have, that the Greens want to take us all back to candles. 'Obviously there would be growth in certain sectors,' she said, 'especially recycling.'

Ironically, exactly what I have been saying since the early 1980s, particularly in the UK response to the World Conservation Strategy, which was published in 1983. And the likely doubling of the world's population over the next 40-50 years means, like it or not, that growth will also be needed on an even broader front. We have to ensure that it is greener growth than it would be if developers and industry were left to their own devices.

Over a snatched supper of tuna (!) sandwiches, switch in to Abel Gance's 1927 silent marathon epic on the life of Napoleon. At one stage he stands apart from a family group, pondering whether to opt for a quiet family life or to plunge back into the political mêlée. I think I know how the poor man felt. Driven.

Sunday 23 July
Another Florida-worthy day.

Fascinating piece by Norman MacRae in *The Sunday Times* on 'the rocky ride to capitalism'. Communism, he says, is dying. 'After mis-celebrating 1789, Europe faces familiar lessons for a startlingly similar 1989. A Bourbonism called Communism is dying, and the task for civilised men is to smooth the exit of the corrupt and elite 5% who are generally the sole beneficiaries of either planned socialist economies or absolute monarchies.'

The massive wave of industrial dissent in the USSR leads him to talk of the 'Soviet Disunion'. *Perestroika* is under attack from critics who claim it is out of control. Communism has all too clearly failed to deliver the goods. By the 1980s, after 65 years of Communism, a Soviet citizen was even less likely to own a motor car than was the average black African.

Of course, many Greens would approve of the approach of consci-ously holding down car ownership, although that wasn't what the Russians had been consciously trying to do. The *Observer* notes that three years ago the West German Green Party published a programme called 'Reconstruction of the Industrial Society' — and was laughed at for its pains. Now the Social Democrats (SDP), who could form the next Government, have produced a report called 'Ecological Reconstruc-tion of the Industrial Society'! Among the things it proposes, a tax on industrial 'environment-sinners'.

The concept of environmental sin is an interesting one. If the pressures continue to build, as one environmental problem stacks upon another, we could be building up a fierce sense of guilt in many people. Although the Catholic Church is built on guilt, this trend could be very dangerous. Have a mental image of prairies of dry grass set alight by a spark. Perhaps a green version of Islamic fundamentalism sweeping around the world? From whence the Green Messiah?

Monday 24 July

A Green Letter Day for Chris Patten: he is appointed Secretary of State for the Environment in Mrs Thatcher's biggest Cabinet reshuffle yet. Nicholas Ridley goes to Trade & Industry.

Across late morning in LA-style weather to Speedbird House, Hatton Cross, under the flight-lanes into Heathrow, for a meeting with British Airways. They are looking for a Head of the Environment and are prepared to offer around £50,000. According to the ad in yesterday's *Sunday Times*, BA is looking for a candidate with an appreciation of 'how environmental issues can complement instead of clash with business aims'.

Off to the palatial/modern offices of Barlow Lyde & Gilbert, the lawyers representing McDonald's. They have pulled out all the stops: apart from the President of the UK business, there are five other people, including Shelby Yastrow (Senior Vice President, McDonald's Corporation), Sid Nicholson (Chief Personnel Officer) and Ray Cesca (Director/Atlantic, International Purchasing). Our side is made up of Liz, Gollancz's lawyer John Rubinstein, our lawyer Stephen Ronaldson and myself.

As we settle down around the boardroom table, high above the Cityscape, I consciously lighten the tone with a little humour and thank them for squeezing out the time to see us. It turns out that Cesca, an energetic, friendly corporate version of Barry Manilow, had broken off from a family holiday in the States to make the meeting and flies back this evening on Concorde. He does the main presentation — and it looks very much as though McDonald's are in the clear on the rainforest issue. He has just come back from Brazil, where he visited many of the key areas. He had previously lived out there for some years.

Yastrow, also an American, says that McDonald's considers itself a 'citizen of the globe'. He says the rainforest issue has been much more of a problem for them in Europe than in the States — and that they are now 'spending money like drunken sailors' attempting to address it. It's quite clear that we are dealing with a clash of two different cultures here, for all Cesca asks how he could live with himself if he were really involved in felling rainforests and stripping away his daughter's future? Interestingly, several times, different people mention children challenging them in their homes and elsewhere.

Take them to task for failing to produce a coherent statement of their position and policy on rainforests. Yastrow says they have just finished a policy statement and it will be faxed to me. It is quite clear that they do not now intend to take this to court, indeed our lawyers feel the McDonald's case is not water-tight, particularly in relation to their operations in Costa Rica.

I refuse point-blank to retract what we have written in 'open court', but agree to rewrite some short offending passages of *The Green Consumer Guide* to reflect the fact that McDonald's have not been causing rainforest destruction. I also suggest that we could help communicate the fact that they now have a policy to a wider public. It looks as though that may be the route we go.

Wednesday 26 July
Start day with Spillers in New Malden. They say they want an audit. Not the sort of company I would choose to work with, given that a good deal of their business centres on pets — and on the slaughterhouses and animal products processing needed to keep the nation's pets fed.

The task of greening some of the company's employees would be considerable. 'Try asking a guy who is pitchforking offal all day to think of Total Quality Management or the environment,' suggests Guy Hutchinson, who is driving the company's efforts to 'go green'. Most people only see the can in the supermarket, with a pretty cat's face adorning it. You don't have to go far behind, however, whether the company is Spillers or Pedigree Petfoods, to find it's a fairly grim business of 'muck and bullets'.

Mike Bowtell says we have won the BT environmental audit contract and he wants the process to start in the autumn. He says the aim is to ensure that BT, if not a green forerunner, 'is at least a better-catcher-upperer'.

Catch cab, after a fair amount of walking, but London congeals by the time we get half way down Oxford Street. A smoking red line of buses stretches off into the haze where Marble Arch should be. Get out and walk all the way back to Holland Park. The number of filthy, smoking exhausts has to be seen to be believed. Arrive back at the office around 19.00, face streaked with soot. There is concern that the continuing hot weather and growing volumes of exhaust emissions will produce LA-style smogs. FoE will recommend a new survey of air pollution later this week.

In Alaska, meanwhile, there is concern that Exxon may be on the verge of abandoning the clean-up on 15 September, in the hope that rough weather will do much of the rest of the work as winter sets in. 'This is what we have feared all along,' Erik Olson of the National Wildlife Federation told *The Independent*. 'We suspected it was Exxon's plan to declare victory, pull out early — Vietnam style — and then say Mother Nature will take care of the rest.'

In the UK, the CBI is at last drawing up a plan to help business 'go green' and produce more environment-friendly products. And a development that suggests that the pressure will continue to build: twelve British

Greens plan to demand 'their seats' in the European Parliament. Their action will help to push the drive for proportional representation in Britain, at least for Euro-elections.

Thursday 27 July
To Bangor with CEGB Environment Development Advisory Panel. We drive out to the edge of Snowdonia to see the Dinorwig pumped storage hydro-electric plant, dug deep into the heart of a mountain. The entrance tunnel is in the midst of a derelict slate mine of massive proportions. Once inside, we don yellow plastic helmets and hum through endless tunnels in an electric bus, passing scenes which could come straight from a James Bond or Indiana Jones film. 12 miles of tunnels now honeycomb the mountain, half of them full of water.

Friday 28 July
At the final EDAP meeting, we review the joint environmental policy statement prepared by National Power, PowerGen and the National Grid Company. It represents a strong charter for the environment. It remains to be seen whether the privatised electricity supply industry can implement it effectively.

Race back to London in the afternoon, arriving in Barnes around 19.30, only to find an urgent message from Annie. Heinz have pulled out of Green Shopping Day and have already sent out a press release to the press list we had given them for other purposes with a message which seems calculated to damage us. Kiss the children hello — and goodbye — and drive to Holland Park. Draft a counter-release, which Fiona and Annie then pack up and post.

Point out that Heinz (1) wanted its imprint over everything and (2) therefore wanted to ensure that there was no chance that Green Shopping Day would be controversial. We believe that green consumerism has enormous potential power to wake up individual consumers and business, but it is guaranteed to be controversial!

Once again, though, WWF have been, to put it politely, faint-hearted. Presumably one must simply put it down to their being panicked by the thought of losing other potential sponsors. The problem for them may be that we decide to approach sponsors direct, to simplify the whole process, an outcome which WWF's Corporate Department have been concerned about for some time. In future green consumer campaigns, we will almost certainly aim to develop the promotional platform ourselves, rather than trying to work with other campaigning groups from the outset.

Better news from Gollancz. McDonald's have accepted the limited changes to *The Green Consumer Guide* and the printing presses will apparently be rolling shortly with the new impression.

Saturday 29 July
Up very early and off down to Somerset for a wedding. Stop off at the Iron Age hill fortresses of Hod Hill and Hambledon Hill.

We decide to climb Hod Hill, the smaller of the two hills. We work our way to the top, through clouds of butterflies. The fort, actually a Roman fort built within an earlier Iron Age one, is well known for its wild orchids and butterflies like the Common Blue, Meadow Brown and Marsh Fritillary. The sheer height of these places has ensured that they have (largely) escaped the plough, fertilizers and pesticides. But, although I have rarely encountered another living soul there, there are signs of visitor pressure in the form of erosion.

Sunday 30 July
One call, from the *Yorkshire Post* which has received a copy of the Heinz press release. Fax them a copy of ours. They say that a key factor in success is your ability to handle problems and failures, but I really could do without all this at the present juncture!

Things are also hotting up in Greenhouse Effect research. *The Sunday Times* reports that research involving NERC scientists suggests that as the climate heats up the oceans will become less efficient in absorbing greenhouse gases from the earth's atmosphere. The implication is that the doubling of carbon dioxide expected to take place in the next 50-100 years could happen within the next 30. The work has shown that phytoplankton are almost wholly responsible for the removal of carbon dioxide in the spring, but that the growth of these organisms is significantly hit if the seawater warms up.

You don't need to be a clairvoyant to predict political and social turbulence if global warming accelerates, or is seen to be on the verge of speeding up.

The *Observer* reports that some members of the Animal Liberation Front, who have been responsible for the fire-bombing of stores selling fur products and of laboratories involved in animal research, plan to widen their range of targets. Among the names the new grouping is toying with is Green Front. A new anarchist newsletter, *Business as Usual*, says: 'Real freedom in our lives cannot be achieved without the massive escalation of attacks on the capitalist system of repression.'

AUGUST

Tuesday 1 August

WWF make it clear that they are not happy that we sent out a press release without consulting them — although Heinz did exactly the same to us. We feel we were 'bushwacked'. In the event, the press coverage is surprisingly positive, very much taking our side on the issue. And a number of other companies are showing considerable interest in taking over where Heinz left off.

Both the Tories and Labour announced yesterday that they are going after young Green voters in the build-up to the next election. An analysis presented to the Labour Party last week concluded that Green Party voters were, in *The Times'* words, 'predominantly youthful, middle-class, well informed, southern, formerly Alliance supporting and disproportionately female'. Meanwhile, British Greens have been given a voice in the European Parliament's Green group, even though they have no elected members.

Signs of future trends? The first green supermarket, De Groene Winkel (the Green Shop), opens in Holland, with the groceries costing up to 30% more than similar items sold in mainstream stores; and US supermarkets are waiting for deliveries of Rainforest Crunch, a new ice-cream made entirely from fruits, nuts and oils grown in the Amazonian rainforests. 'The idea is to offer a positive alternative for the people who have to make a living in the Amazon,' anthropologist-turned-entrepreneur Jason Clay tells the *Daily Telegraph*. As long as their environmental performance is monitored as closely as any other company's, such ventures are very much to be welcomed — indeed encouraged.

News also breaks that US 'Stealth' bomber, which has cost £14 billion to develop, uses chemicals sprayed into the plane's exhaust to hide its tell-tale condensation trail. It is estimated that each plane will carry around a ton of ozone-destroying chloro-sulphonic and fluoro-sulphonic acids. It looks as if the defence 'business' is going to be one of the key environmental targets of the 1990s.

Wednesday 2 August

Today carries a large piece on Green Shopping Day, but we have managed to steer them away from the Heinz story. *The Times*, on the other hand, are hot on the trail as are the *Financial Times* and World In Action.

Spend a couple of hours with David Cadman on the Stanhope report.

Thursday 3rd August
Following yesterday's piece in *Today*, we are splashed across the front page of *The Times* this morning, with the story headlined HEINZ DROPS BACKING FOR GREEN SHOPPING DAY. Fairly balanced piece, from our point of view, but not difficult to imagine that Heinz will not have been pleased.

Julia, Annie and I start the day with WWF in Godalming, meeting George Medley, Jenny Barlow and Kate Brooks. WWF agree to cover our irrecoverable costs and George suggests he convenes a meeting of the leading environmental groups to talk through philosophies and approaches.

Constantly having to duck in and out of meeting and take calls. Among them, one from John Aspery of Heinz. We had suggested a meeting between ourselves, WWF, Counsel and Heinz, simply to get matters sorted out before we disband that relationship. John seems willing to move in that direction. Meanwhile FoE send out a press release saying that green consumerism is OK, they are not against Green Shopping Day and will not be launching an anti-Green Shopping Day campaign — but that they had been planning an anti-Heinz campaign on the tuna issue.

Part of the problem has been that green consumerism is now beginning to send out real shock-waves, both in business and in the environmental movement. It's all rather like trying to go through the sound barrier in a Spitfire. You've got to have a plane built for the job. In the case of the Heinz link-up, we had to communicate through WWF, who communicated through Counsel, who passed on what they thought appropriate to Heinz. It was like a game of Chinese whispers.

Environment Secretary Chris Patten announces a pre-privatisation 'green dowry' worth about £500 million, on top of the write-off of £5.5 billion of debt, to sweeten the water industry's privatisation. Anne Taylor, Labour's spokesperson on water, calls the move 'a desperate bid to make the water sale work'.

And Peaudouce have announced a new development on the disposable nappy front, introducing a biodegradable plastic backing sheet. FoE are considering registering their name to protect it against unauthorised use, as in a current series of ads for Appletise. And Next launches fifteen cotton products based on chemical-free 'green cotton'.

McDonald's have now accepted the rewording for *The Green Capitalists*, which is pretty strong stuff. Great relief. By the early evening, feeling drained.

Friday 4 August
Car picks me up at 08.00. Across to a studio in St John's Wood, built into a converted church, to film five short items to appear on Claire Rayner's 'A Problem Shared' programme on Sky TV. First time I have used an autocue: seems to go well.

The Times today carries a Barry Fantoni cartoon showing two women commenting on a *Times* headline reading GREEN SHOPPING DAY — HEINZ PULL OUT. The caption: They probably offered 57 excuses.

Forest fires continue to rage across the South of France and in South American countries like Bolivia and Brazil. In São Paolo, the Director of the Brazilian Government's space research centre, which analyses satellite images of the forests daily, says the intensity of the burning this year is as bad as last year. He tells *The Independent*: 'We do know that burning in the Amazon is still gigantic. It's time they showed us a wealthy farmer in handcuffs.'

In Rome, meanwhile, the Italian Government proposes emergency aid of £360 million for businesses crippled by the slimy algae that have fouled the Adriatic.

Another fast and furious day; endless telephone calls from journalists. Finally finish at 22.30.

Saturday 5 August
A good deal of attention in the weekend's press devoted to Nikolai Vorontsov, the Soviet Union's newly-installed environment chief. He apparently hopes to tackle the country's dire ecological problems by imposing a new environmental code, with the same force as the criminal and civil codes. Several months ago, several miles of a river in the Ukraine caught fire when a worker tossed in a cigarette butt. The pace of *glasnost* threatens to overwhelm the Soviets with dire news about their environment. I don't know them well enough to know whether such pressure will trigger action or deep despond.

Elaine and I drive down to Gloucestershire for my brother, Gray's, marriage to Christina Wiens-Perez. Delightful service with some 150 people in the flower-bedecked 12th-century church. Shades of 1992 with the bi-lingual service sheet. Some 50 of Christina's family and friends have come from Spain, along with relations from Germany and Poland.

Sunday 6 August
Hania, aged ten, is christened, at her own insistence. Gaia, who was christened when she was around one, has always known she can provoke Hania in a crisis by calling her a 'pagan'.

174

Attend morning service in Great Rissington, where our local vicar, David Bush, holds sway. But when, later in the morning, we all go on to the church in Little Rissington for the christening, Hania looks resplendent in her bridesmaid's dress again — but at times seems in a daze. Only later do we realise that H has been deeply hung over, having sampled various glasses at the reception last night.

Although any belief in God was wiped from my brain by a childhood in Northern Ireland and Cyprus, history at school and the sociology of religion at university, am still fascinated by religion as a mode of communication and social control. Listening to David Bush's sermon, on the subject of the Transfiguration, it struck me that all his images of 'glory' were taken from Nature: a sunrise, the opening of a flower, birds in flight. Yet, because Christians have always seen this world as little more than a stepping-stone to Heaven, Earth has generally been given short shrift. Maybe the position will change, indeed a number of world religions now aspire to 'go green'.

One of the challenges that faces us is to come up with late 20th century versions of the Parables and Commandments — codes by which ordinary people can live. 'And it came to pass that a man, walking beside the waters of the river, did cast in his cigarette and, verily, the waters leaped into flame unto the horizon. It is a sign, the people said.'

Monday 7 August
Up at 06.00 to catch train to Liverpool. Prodip Guha, the Littlewoods Director of Marketing, is deeply interested in Third World issues. His office is on the 11th floor of the company's tower block, overlooking Liverpool's docks. Spectacular scene, although the dock strike is only just winding down today. He asks me if we will work for them for five years. Given the time-scale of the issues, the idea is attractive — but we would have to be *very* sure of the company.

As the train streaks back towards Euston, the landscape is blurred with fires as farmers burn off their stubble. Fleeting images of hedges in flames and herds of cows almost invisible in roiling clouds of smoke. The whole business is completely out of hand. How can we complain about what the Brazilians are doing?

Julia on the six o'clock news, commenting on Friends of the Earth's recycling programme. David Bellamy speaks out for McDonald's and is promptly picketed by the Green Party while involved in an anti-litter campaign in Derbyshire. 'I will advertise for McDonald's and say how hard they're working for the environment,' Bellamy told *Today*. 'And all the money will go to conservation, not the bloody Green Party.' Confess I sympathise with both sides on this one!

Tuesday 8 August

At last, the Green Label idea is on the political agenda. 'It is clear that the Green Consumer is on the warpath,' junior Environment Minister Virginia Bottomley said yesterday, launching a discussion document entitled 'Environmental Labelling'.

By using the word 'warpath', *The Independent* noted in an editorial today, 'she conjured a vision of North American Indians wending their way in single file through the woods, shopping baskets in their hands. They are pitted against a lethal enemy: the so-called cowboys, unscrupulous manufacturers who are prepared to slap "environmentally-friendly" labels on products which are destroying the planet'.

Next month, Britain will press its EEC partners to introduce a Community-wide green labelling scheme (something the Commission is already looking into). If the EEC fails to respond in time, Britain could go ahead with its own scheme. We argue that Britain should press ahead whatever happens.

On a related front, the Green Alliance has managed to pull together an unlikely consortium of interests (FoE, National Federation of Women's Institutes, Pesticides Trust, Transport and General Workers' Union and the British Agrochemicals Association) to attack the Government on pesticides testing. The current system of control is condemned. BAA director John Page emphasised the need to reassure consumers. Overworked and underpaid, Government pesticide inspectors operate in 'Victorian slum conditions', he said.

The Greenhouse Effect is in the news again. A recently cancelled long-term monitoring programme of Channel fish had shown species such as the red mullet, the marbled electric ray and the triggerfish displacing cold water species. This, some biologists believe, could well be concrete early evidence of the impact of the Greenhouse Effect. They argue that the programme, or Russell Cycle, which had been carried out every week for 60 years, should be restored.

And the Building Research Establishment says that Britain's need for central heating could be cut by almost half by the year 2050 as a result of global warming. But the demand for air-conditioning during the summer months would grow.

The Canadian Green Consumer Guide has been delayed, along with Green Consumer Week. The author the Canadian publishers had recruited failed to deliver the goods and law suits are now flying between him and the publishers. The internationalisation of our Green Consumer initiative is going to be quite a challenge for us.

Thursday 10 August
Miss World turns green? In a bid to revive the flagging fortunes of the annual beauty show, the focus this year will be on the environment! In addition to being encouraged to wear cruelty-free cosmetics, the girls wishing to follow in current queen Linda Petursdottir's footsteps will be asked about the environmental problems facing their countries.

In the wake of the Soviet-registered toxic waste tanker *Khudozhnik Saryan* being refused permission to unload its cargo at Tilbury for onward transport to Rechem's incineration plant at Pontypool, Gwent, Liverpool refuses to handle toxic waste cargoes; some shore crews involved in the Alaskan oil clean-up have refused to use an untried dispersant, because of health and safety fears; and the House of Lords says in a new report that nitrate in groundwater controls could ruin many crop farms; people in Cornwall have been warned not to eat shellfish as a four-mile orange tide of algae spreads along the coastline between St Michael's Mount and Newlyn.

Rain sluices down. Walk through Holland Park under tiny umbrella belonging to Hania, and get soaked. *Today* carries another Green Shopping Day cartoon. The *Financial Times* reports that the spending power of European Community consumers will increase by more than 50% in the next five years to a level almost as great as in the USA. And the paper also describes the 'eco-tax' currently being proposed by West Germany by the Social Democrats — spurred on by the country's Greens. The idea is to raise energy taxes by more than 30%, to conserve fossil fuels and cut polluting emissions. And WWF confirm that they will not be supporting Green Shopping Day in the wake of the Heinz debacle.

Saturday 12 August
A Dutch group calling itself 'The Seething Spuds' has claimed responsibility for destroying 400 genetically manipulated potato plants in a protest aimed at an Agriculture Ministry research project.

And in Canada the Loblaw retail chain, which controls around 27% of the country's food market, has trademarked the names 'G.R.E.E.N.', 'environmentally-friendly', 'body-friendly' and 'ozone-friendly'. The company, which has already bought 50,000 copies of *The Canadian Green Consumer Guide* for promotional purposes, expects the environment and health to be the dominant consumer issues of the 1990s.

Sunday 13 August
The papers are full of the Greenpeace campaign against toxic waste shipments, although much of the coverage is critical. Simon Jenkins, writing in *The Sunday Times*, says 'the Greens' handling of the PCB issue

has broken new heights of crass barminess'. Meanwhile, the first shipment of Canadian PCBs is due in Rotterdam today, bound for Rechem's plant in Pontypool, South Wales. Chris Patten is expected to support the incineration here of the PCBs. If only the UK incineration industry had been developed in a professional way! We need it — but it's far from a credible option at the moment.

Giving the environment such a high profile is going to have profound consequences, Brian Walden points out in *The Sunday Times*: 'I doubt if those in positions of power in industrial societies fully grasp the extent of the changes that are coming. A useful analogy might be with the attitude of the pre-war governing classes towards welfare. They knew it mattered, but never would they have believed the number of concerns it would cover, the amount of money it would consume, and the millions of welfare-providers it would employ within a generation.' Dawning sense of how political all this is going to be!

Monday 14 August
The skies opened last night, with crashing thunder and lightning. This morning the pavements are covered in soil swept from raised beds or lawns where the sun has baked the grass into a frazzle. Mercifully the office is fairly dry, even though I had left the skylights open to the elements.

The news of the protests against the PCB cargoes wiped £24 million off the value of Rechem's shares yesterday — they fell from 729p to 635p when trading opened. Sir Hugh Rossi, chairman of the all-party Commons environment committee, has attacked the ban imposed by ports like Liverpool. 'There is absolutely no justification for it,' he told the *Financial Times*. 'We are being carried forward on a wave of hysteria. I think the port authorities have been extremely weak-kneed by allowing themselves to be bullied in this way.' But an interesting example of the way environmental issues will affect stock markets in the coming decades.

Meanwhile *Today* lays into Labour environment spokesman Dr Jack Cunningham and Paul McCartney. Cunningham is taken to task for his consultancies with Albright & Wilson, British Nuclear Fuels and Dow Chemical, while McCartney is pilloried for having unsuccessfully courted business sponsors for his £15 million world tour — before turning to FoE and saying that, as a green gesture, he would pay for the tour himself because commercial sponsorship was un-green. One of the viler aspects of the tabloids picking up on the environment seems to be that we are now on a seesaw where they build up green reputations and then — just a few days later — try to shred them.

Wednesday 16 August
Environment Secretary Chris Patten welcomes a report prepared by Professor David Pearce, his special adviser on environmental economics. The report calls for new taxes to discourage pollution by industry and by individuals. 'It is very close to my own thinking,' Patten tells *The Independent*. 'I am taking it very seriously.' The acceptance of Green economics would mean a radical change in the way that we calculate 'growth' and GNP. The national accounts would need to be changed to embrace both the growth in man-made products and services and the costs of any environmental damage caused as a result. One report has suggested that the failure to take environmental costs into account in Japan has led to economic growth in recent decades being overstated by some 40%. The greening of economics is a critical challenge. At the moment we have a massive 'language gap' between economists and environmentalists.

Fly to Norway ready for tomorrow's conference. Supper with Haagen Sund and conference organiser Eystein Husebye. The Norwegian edition of *The Green Capitalists* looks excellent.

Friday 18 August
Back to London and into office at 06.45 to finish off TSB article. Then back home, pick up family and drive to Dover. Enormous pressure of traffic on M25, giving real sense of growing pressures generally in the South-East. Hovercraft roars across to Calais, then drive to Boulogne and catch the motor-rail for Brive-La-Gaillard.

Read fascinating article in *Wall Street Journal*, on architect Paolo Soleri — who had been building a city, designed to blend architecture and ecology, in Arizona for the last 19 years. Elaine and I visited Arcosanti, north of Phoenix, in 1973 in the build-up to the first OPEC oil crisis. Even then I wondered, in an article published in the *Architectural Association Quarterly*, whether Arcosanti would ever be more than a glorious set of ruins, an ecological folly.

Soleri's writings and drawings represent one of the most exciting influences on my thinking about cities, although his concept of beehive-style cities like Novanoah, floating on the sea, or Arcodiga, a massive dam honeycombed with living spaces and all the other necessities of urban life, is simultaneously exciting and unattractive. But it's not a bad idea to try living in Utopia before trying to thrust it down other people's throats.

In fact the disjunction between the man's drawings and what he was building in the desert was stark. The construction site was more like a hippy encampment, with raccoons and skunks wandering under the huge trestle tables at which we ate supper under the stars — to the drone of cicadas. The cast concrete apses were also home to black widow spiders, one of which had laid the cook low the week before we arrived, and rattlesnakes. At Arcosanti's peak, it housed only 200 people, now apparently down to 60.

Soleri himself seems to have turned inwards since his wife, who we met, died in 1983. Now a 'hale 70-year-old', Soleri apparently pads around in shorts and sandals preaching his gospel: that the American dream of single family homes and automobiles in every garage promises environmental disaster. He is distressed that American-style consumerism has engaged the rest of the world. But like other visionaries who surfaced in the 1960s and 1970s, he has had an important impact on the minds of the generation that will take power in the 1990s.

Saturday 19 August
Breakfast in Brive. Then drive west to see the Lascaux Caves. Discovered in 1940 by four young boys, the caves were promptly dubbed 'The Sistine Chapel of the Perigord'. The walls of the original caves are covered in an unbelievably beautiful fresco of bison, bulls, horses, deer, ibex and other animals.

Unfortunately, in spite of precautions such as weak lighting and air-conditioning, visitor pressure produced two forms of damage in the caves: the so-called 'green disease' (excess growth of moss and algae, fuelled by the carbon dioxide in visitors' breath) and 'white disease' (less visible, but more serious and resulting from a deposit of white calcite). The amount of carbon dioxide produced by visitors was such that you apparently couldn't light a match by the end of a day.

The solution was to build a facsimile of the caves in an open-cast quarry some 200 yards from the original caves. The new caves were built out of ferro-cement, laid on a metallic framework. A mortar was used to reproduce the limestone surfaces and Monique Peytral then copied the original paintings, using the same materials as the original artists.

It was extremely hot as we went down into Lascaux II, but rain was spitting and thunder rumbling in the distance. My initial fear was that the Lascaux II would turn out to be a French version of Disneyland. But once we were through the airlock, the experience was extraordinarily uplifting.

Next, to Le Roque St-Christophe, an extensive area of cliff-dwellings which reminded me strongly of some of the Indian cliff dwellings we saw in Arizona during the early 1970s — and on which Soleri modelled some of his ideas. For half a mile, the rock rises above the Vezere Valley. Traces of art and tools show that it was occupied 20,000 years ago. La Roque was an astounding stronghold, used against everyone from the Vikings to the English — who were the only people to take it, by siege. The fortress was destroyed during the Wars of Religion.

As we stand on the deserted ledges of the troglodytic city, lightning streaks across rolling purple-black storm clouds. In the days of the Vikings, the city's defenders used horns and acoustically sited caves or cliffs to send amplified horn-blasts at the speed of sound down the valleys.

Then on, via Bergerac, to Haux, near Langoiran on the Garonne. Met by Madame Claverie-Brett, an attractive and extremely elegant French sculptress who owns the Chateau de Haut Sage. Ringed with pine trees and cypresses, the chateau stands on a prominence, surrounding a beautiful swimming pool. Lightning still streaks across the horizon as we explore the high-vaulted rooms of the wing in which we shall be staying. The main living room has a massive fireplace, with large fire-dogs and contains great sections of tree trunk. The children are sleeping in beds which have been set into the structure of the old stables.

Sunday 20 August
Awake to the cooing of doves. Drive in to Langoiran, to see the Garonne in spate after last night's rain. The water is covered with mysterious mounds of bird feathers, as though part of it has flowed through a poultry slaughterhouse. Many of the buildings are made from a coarse yellow sandstone, which is hollowed out by the wind and rain — and appears to have structural properties somewhere between Cotswold stone and Weetabix.

The doves and pigeons at the chateau make a lovely sound, and flit from the roofs down to the pool-side to drink and bathe. Their main purpose in life soon becomes clear, however, when Madame offers us some pigeons for supper. Gaia and Hania say they have seen her making off to the kitchen with birds tucked under each arm. 'Merci, mais non,' we say weakly. 'Nous sommes vegetariens.' I suspect that won't help the pigeons much.

In Britain, an ecological disaster has hit the Mersey estuary — which is currently the focus of a high profile clean-up campaign — as a Shell oil pipeline ruptures.

Monday 21 August
George Adamson, the 83-year-old British wildlife conservationist, was killed by bandits in remote eastern Kenya yesterday. Nine years ago his wife, Joy Adamson, was murdered while studying leopards at the Shaba game reserve. *Born Free, Living Free* and *Forever Free*, the bestselling books about the Adamsons' work with Elsa and other lions, made them

household names when I was young. Another martyr for the cause of conservation.

In the afternoon, we drive through the endless pine forests of Les Landes, reclaimed from marshland and heaths, to the Ecomusee (or Eco-Museum) of Marqueze, just outside Sabres. It is a complete reconstruction of a *quartier* — a typical rural community as it would have been 50-100 years ago. A small green train trundles through the woods, like a time-capsule taking us back to the time when the village was humming with life. A *mélange* of thatched barns, water mills, charcoal-burning and resin-collecting. The children like the chicken coop on stilts, to keep out foxes, and I am taken by the orchard of old varieties of apples, pears, cherries and peaches, no longer grown commercially and therefore increasingly rare.

Thursday 24 August

Gaia finishes Ben Elton's novel *Stark*. Pressures me to read it so we can discuss it. The heroes of the book are hippies, who are once again all the rage — certainly among Gaia's friends.

Nature, meanwhile, has published an incredible environmental engineering plan, which would involve putting giant aluminium mirrors weighing 45,000,000 tonnes into orbit around the Earth to cut incoming sunshine and offset the Greenhouse Effect. The cost of the 20-year project, estimates Professor Walter Seifritz of the Paul Scherer Institute, based near Villingen, Switzerland, would be about 6% of the world's present GNP — about equivalent to its current military expenditure. Another suggestion which is being advanced is to reflect sunshine by painting roofs white and covering the oceans with white polystyrene chips!

We spend much of the day on the Atlantic shore of Aquitaine, near Arcachon. Visit the Dune du Pilot, 2.7km long, 500m wide and 114m high, Europe's highest. The seaward side sports the ruins of a German fortification from WWII, while the landward side slopes right into the pine forest, with the vast expanses of sand punctuated by the skeletons of dead pines.

The beaches are stunning, but human pressures are everywhere. Mirage fighters thunder in through the heat haze, while the sand dunes are densely strewn with the most extraordinarily diverse range of plastic products. We collect some and put them in the bin as we return at the end of the day, but the task of cleaning up the beaches would be a Herculean one.

Not all the rubbish comes from sun-bathers or from nearby rivers. A fair amount is dumped at sea. A couple of days back Cunard finally confessed that the QE2's crew had been throwing sacks of rubbish overboard. 'We accept that there was an infringement,' said Cunard spokesman Eric Flounders. 'It happened because the crew took a short cut.' Thousands of other ships are doing the same. The QE2 alone generates five tonnes of rubbish a day.

Many sun-bathers lie naked, apparently perfectly happy in the midst of the refuse. Further south, much of the coastline is under the control of the Army — it may be a good thing in conservation terms!

This part of France is the product of an extraordinary process of environmental engineering. Once these lands were classed as 'wasteland', with insect-infested swamps and endless sand-dunes. From 1788, the engineer Bremontier began fixing the ever-mobile dunes with *madriers* (or wooden beams), and then planting them with *pin maritime* (maritime or umbrella pine), *ajonc* (gorse) and *genet* (broom). The pine forests now cover nearly one million hectares.

The pines are cut after 15-20 years for pit props and paper production. If left for 30-40 years, they can be tapped for resin. Everywhere you look, the pine trunks are bleeding from wounds inflicted by *gemmeurs*, or resin-collectors. Whereas the resin was once collected in tins, it now runs down into plastic sachets.

In Britain, Audi overtakes Volvo, becoming the first car manufacturer to offer catalytic converters as *standard* equipment on all models at no extra cost.

Saturday 26 August
A pottering day.

Meanwhile, the man who first predicted the Greenhouse Effect could warm the planet more than 20 years ago now says the trend should be encouraged! 'Limiting carbon fuel consumption will be not only useless, but even dangerous,' Mikhail Budyko says. While the Americans worry that the Greenhouse Effect will turn their 'breadbasket' into a dustbowl, Budyko predicts that Africa could once again be under forests. 'Paradise can return,' he predicts.

But it is worth noting that two countries are particularly likely to benefit from global warming: Canada and the Soviet Union. England's climate, he believes, will remain unchanged.

Time magazine carries a profile of David McTaggart of Greenpeace. The organisation which started out as a 'hippy navy' now has some three million members world-wide and 700 staff members. 'I really don't have any morals,' McTaggart is quoted as saying. 'You've got to be prepared to keep the No. 1 thing in mind: you're fighting to get your children into the 21st century, and to hell with the rules.'

In Britain, the *Guardian* reports, the rat population has apparently grown by 20% in 12 months because of the weather, litter and inadequate pest control. Weil's Disease, a potentially fatal illness spread by rats' urine, is increasing, particularly among anglers and other water sports enthusiasts.

Sunday 27 August
Rain storm. Drive the back country roads around Langoiran, walking around graveyards and churches. The Langoiran war memorial includes half a dozen dead deportees during WWII. How can anyone forgive such savagery? Yet read *The Cardinal of the Kremlin*, Tom Clancy's novel, and interested that it ends on a note of reconciliation between the Soviet Union and the USA. Very much the mood of the times.

Meanwhile, in Italy, a Mont Blanc glacier has begun to reveal a macabre secret that it has held for 23 years. *The Sunday Times* reports that the glacier has begun to give up debris of an Air India plane that crashed on the mountain in bad weather in January 1966, killing all 117 aboard. 116 bodies are still inside the fuselage, trapped in a slow-moving 'river' of ice. But it may be another decade before the bodies can be freed and buried. It's a strange thought that many of our greatest cities may one day go under ice, as the planet moves into the grips of the next Ice Age. Is the Greenhouse Effect postponing or accelerating that 'evil' day?

Monday 28 August
Bright sun but high winds as Gaia, Hania and I wade into the Atlantic surf. Fierce undertow. A seagull flaps furiously into the wind, but gets nowhere. And, as a yellow plastic sunflower-oil bottle rolls down the beach in the wind, I find it difficult to ignore the crust of plastic that lies around the broken ruins of part of Hitler's 'Atlantic Wall'. How can we change people's hearts and minds to the extent that they simply will not put up with this sort of mess?

Reading *The Inner Limits of Mankind*, by Ervin Laszlo, a renowned concert pianist in the 1940s who later turned his hand to science and philosophy. A science advisor to UNESCO and member of the Club of Rome, whose 1972 report *The Limits to Growth* shook the complacency of the Modern Age, Laszlo looks forward to a New Age which 'will be as different from the Modern Age as the Modern Age was from the Middle Ages'. To save the world, he says in *The Inner Limits of Mankind*, we have to change ourselves and the way we think. He sees the salvation of planet Earth in the emergence of a new type of individual, globally oriented, spiritually enlightened and environmentally aware. The book starts with a commentary by the late Aurelio Peccei, a founder of the Club of Rome who I had the great good fortune to meet in Versailles in 1984. Peccei notes that while there are undoubtedly outer limits imposed on us by the carrying capacity of our environment, 'the question of inner limits emerges as more important than that of outer ones'.

Laszlo notes that: 'We contemplate changing almost anything on this earth but ourselves.' This is a key issue for the 1990s — but I think a large number of people are *already* changing.

Given that 99% of the species that ever lived on this planet are now extinct, there is no reason to expect that our own species will last for ever — but its tenancy on Earth can certainly be extended. We must come up with positive visions of the future to which people can aspire. He suggests that we aim for *Sustainability, Development, Equity* — not quite as ringing as *Liberté, Egalité, Fraternité* emblazoned on so many of the public buildings here in France, but a good first stab!

Laszlo's use of the word 'heresies' rings worrying bells in Aquitaine, where religious wars raged for centuries. Further south, the Albigensian Crusade saw the Vatican crush one of the most glorious civilisations, built up by the Cathars, as 'heretical'. Whole towns were put to the sword, whether or not they espoused the right faith, on the basis that 'God will know his own'. The Revolution also saw heretics hounded and destroyed. The Girondins — revolutionaries who believed in a federal rather than a centralised future for France — were sent to the guillotine here.

If human history is anything to go by, there is a real danger that the Green movement will fritter away much of its growing strength on the extinction of heretical versions of the 'truth', rather than concentrating on the task in hand. In Britain, the Greens are now showing 6% of the 'vote' in opinion polls, down from 8% last month.

Tuesday 29 August
North into Medoc country, to Chateau Margaux and Fort Medoc, conceived 300 years ago in 1689 and built for Louis XIV. The gate still sports the carved royal sun of Le Roi Soleil. We have a picnic on ramparts pock-marked by voles and overlooking the broad, red-brown Gironde. Watch a water-snake hunting in the star-shaped moat. Then across to Atlantic coast, driving down through the forests of Le Porge. Devastated by fires, with fleets of cranes and trucks growling through charred ash-scapes as any salvageable timber is felled and shipped out.

Thursday 31 August
Call office. I use the telephone in Madame's sitting room. The walls are painted with heads, planets and other oddities. Her sculptures are all hips, breasts and copulations. On the dinner table the candelabra are made

from Nautilus shells, beautiful but they would have been much better off left attached to their owners at sea. Strong flavour of Dali to the house and its slightly eccentric elegant furnishings.

Annie reports that most of the news is bad. SustainAbility has turned down £20,000 from Peaudouce, because even non-chlorine-bleached disposable nappies can hardly be described as green products. Alucan are not going to sponsor Green Shopping Day.

Appropriately, perhaps, on the day that Sir Peter Scott's death from a heart attack is reported, just two weeks before his 80th birthday, we visit Le Teich Ornithological Park — on the shores of the Bassin d'Arcachon. Occupying part of the estuary of the Eyre and covering 120 hectares, the reserve is on one of the most important bird migration routes in Europe. Outside the aviary, in the wilder areas, we see little more than coots, cormorants, gulls, swans, a smattering of ducks and what may have been a Marsh Harrier. But many of the more than 260 species seen at Le Teich have flown via Slimbridge, where the birds should be wearing black wing-bands today.

On his last, fatal journey to the South Pole, Captain Robert Falcon Scott wrote to his wife, Sir Peter's mother: 'Make the boy interested in natural history. It is better than games.' He excelled in both, founding WWF (with Max Nicholson and Guy Mountford) and the Wildfowl Trust, and winning a bronze medal for Britain in single-handed sailing at the 1936 Olympics — in addition to becoming national gliding champion in 1963. Sir David Attenborough describes Sir Peter as 'the patron saint of conservation'.

Apart from the fact that the launch of WWF in 1961 induced me to campaign to get all the boys at my prep school to give up their pocket money for a week to raise funds for WWF (and there is still a message of thanks from Prince Philip in an album somewhere), Sir Peter's course cut mine not only on 5 June this year but also when he sat on the selection panel which awarded me a Churchill Fellowship in 1981.

NORTH SEA IN GRIP OF KILLER RED SLIME, a *Today* headline screams. The paper claims that the pollution of the North Sea means that it is at risk from the same algal slime that has invaded the Adriatic coast. Professor Rutger Rosenberg says that submarines are finding evidence that the sea is sickening. 'We found brittle starfish had arched themselves up to reach what oxygen remained,' he told a pollution conference in Gothenburg, Sweden. 'When we returned a week later, all were dead. It was a chilling sight.'

Also in the news: Shell looks like being the first company to be prosecuted by the new National Rivers Authority, following the Mersey spill; seals, polar bears and some whales are at risk of extinction because of PCB pollution, according to Professor Joseph Cummins, a geneticist at the University of Western Ontario, Canada; and Greenpeace is drawing up plans for a campaign against solvents used, for example, in the dry cleaning industry.

SEPTEMBER

Friday 1 September
Although Elaine and I have been together for 21 years, today is our 16th wedding anniversary. Also the 50th anniversary of the German invasion of Poland. WWII was under way, ending six years later and leaving more than 50 million dead. The papers and magazines like *Time* are full of accounts of the ways in which the war created the political realities which shaped the world in which we now live.

Now the inconceivable seems to be happening in Poland. A Solidarity-led, non-Communist Government is preparing to take power — the first in half a century in Eastern Europe. Amazingly, the move seems to have the tacit endorsement of Mikhail Gorbachev. The political map of Europe could be completely reworked. What an extraordinary year!

A terrible microcosmic reality for the children: Andrea calls to say she let the rabbits out for a run on Wednesday night and one has been taken by a cat or fox. It happens to be their favourite, Buff. Emotional crisis.

In the afternoon, I go riding — on a beautiful white mare — with G and H in the woods of La Brède. We ride through dappled sunlight, oaks and bracken, the horses periodically stepping on water mint and releasing a haze of perfume. At times, we stir clouds of dust and horse flies buzz in our wake. But it is not hard to see why people fall in love with horses and riding.

Monday 4 September
Back home. Striking, as I read Ben Elton's *Stark*, to see the front page of *The Times* today. FEARS THAT PLANKTON COULD SPEED UP GLOBAL WARMING its main headline reads. Reporting on work carried out by Dr John Woods, Director of Marine and Atmospheric Sciences at NERC and Britain's most senior Government marine scientist, the paper suggests that not only will marine plankton not 'mop up' excess carbon dioxide from the atmosphere, but the process of global warming could well slow the rate at which they absorb the gas.

No existing models of the Greenhouse Effect take plankton's role into account. The geological record now seems to suggest that this process of accelerated warming happened at the end of previous ice ages. The implications may be that the currently accepted time-scales for global warming are too long.

The Independent also publishes photographs showing the massive deformation of plant life in the radioactive zone around the Chernobyl nuclear plant. Taken by Vladimir Shevchenko, Head of the Laboratory of Ecological Genetics at Moscow's Vavilov Institute of General Genetics, the photographs show baby oaks with misshapen leaves up to eight inches long, raspberries and strawberries with pale leaves because of chlorophyll loss and firs whose foliage has bushed out and turned black in the wake of the accident. Some trees are growing to giant size. Pine needles can be ten times heavier than normal and other trees are sprouting outsize leaves.

Very difficult meeting with Heinz, Counsel and WWF today, at which Heinz offered a very much lower sum than we had asked for. We refuse to decide on our position at the meeting; Julia has been taking legal soundings. Rebecca (Bolt) started today and things are beginning to hum on the consultancy side. BT have sent through the contract for the environmental audit project we shall be doing for them.

In the evening, Mike Temple comes across from Bovis — part of the P & O Group — to see whether we would be prepared to tender for an environmental audit and strategy process for them. Other contenders would be David Bellamy Associates and Travers Morgan. We agree to submit a proposal by next Monday.

Julia runs me home around 21.30 in the catalytic-converter-equipped Volvo 480 Volvo Concessionaires have loaned us for the build-up to Green Shopping Day. We shall be using it to promote the idea that motorists ought to 'join the drive for cleaner motoring' by buying a 'cat-car'.

Prince Charles has announced his plans for a 100,000-strong volunteer community army designed to give everyone aged between 16 and 25 the opportunity to spend short periods in full-time voluntary work.

Wednesday 6 September
Day starts with early meeting. Later, near-despair in the office when the Land and Food Company ring to say their site for a new development is falling through, therefore no public flotation, therefore no need for publicity, therefore no interest in providing food for the Green Shopping Day launch. We also hear that *The Times* supplement for the day is being jeopardised by the shenanigans of the major supermarkets, who are all refusing to have their ads appear on any page facing an ad placed by a competitor.

Write to Janet Barber today to say that we cannot accept the £10,000 grant WWF have now offered for our 'towards sustainable tourism' project, because our attempts to work alongside WWF have almost uniformly brought political (Green Shopping Day) or logistical (environmental labelling proposal stalled; environmental auditing report delayed) problems. We will have to fund it ourselves.

The TUC Congress sees one trade union leader, Bill Brett, brandishing a hamburger and describing it as 'the most popular suicide pill in history'. TUC General Secretary Norman Willis said: 'We are borrowing perilously from future generations. We shall not be able to sustain development unless action is taken now.' The Congress backed prison sentences for directors of polluting companies and called for 'environment strikes'.

In Ireland, Merrell Dow, the US pharmaceutical giant, is forced to drop plans for a £52m new plant because of widespread opposition from East Cork farmers and environmentalists. In the UK, the British Union for the Abolition of Vivisection (BUAV) announces plans to launch a boycott against French-owned L'Oreal, the world's largest cosmetics firm, because of its continuing commitment to animal testing.

In Madrid, a Green Patrol of 300 police in green helmets and riding green motorbikes will crack down on such environmental sins as littering and faulty car exhausts. And Ford announces that it will start UK production of catalyst-equipped Fiestas, Escorts and Sierras from November. Indian Prime Minister Rajiv Gandhi proposes to the Non-Aligned Movement summit in Belgrade the setting up of a global environment fund. A UN conference in Nairobi hears that the loss of the ozone layer could devastate the world's food supply — since many plants grow smaller leaves when exposed to increased ultraviolet radiation.

Thursday 7 September
Mrs T tells a conference of the Inter-Parliamentary Union that 'green growth' is not only campatible with environmental concern, but necessary to pay for higher standards of environmental protection. The phrase, coined by Tom Burke and first used to describe SustainAbility, 'the green growth company', is now popping up everywhere.

In the news: Exxon appoints a marine scientist, John Steele (President of the US Woods Hole Oceanographic Institute) to its board, following intense pressure from several influential New York City pension funds; British Coal signs a 'green pact' with the NCC, pledging to protect nature and wildlife during opencast mining; Shell plans to raise a new offshore gas platform to be built in the North Sea by a metre, to cope with anticipated sea rises caused by the Greenhouse Effect; and following Wednesday's election, Dutch PM Lubbers has narrowly held on to power. Half the country lies below sea-level and green issues are almost monopolising the political debate.

Friday 8 September
Julia and I meet with David Gee, Campaigns Director and Director-designate at FoE. A getting-to-know-you session. It seems we have a fair amount in common, including an interest in 'green growth' and environmental auditing. He asks whether SustainAbility might be interested in auditing companies that approach FoE offering sponsorship. We say that the pressure is already so intense that we would have difficulty coping, but offer to help think through what sort of auditing would be required.

Try to finish the *Guardian* piece, but have to jump in a taxi home to collect the car and drive down to Chipping Norton, where I am due to speak to the North Oxfordshire Green Party.

The evening is chaired by Marcus Colchester of Survival International. The mood is very positive and a surprising number of people come up afterwards to thank us for doing what we are doing. A reassuring evening, because it underscores the fact that most people are relatively uncompli-cated: they simply want their environment saved. The newspapers today are full of the 'news' that fundamentalist Greens plan to mount a concerted campaign at their party conference later this month to push the Party further to the left. The politicking in their field is much more obvious if you live in London and media-watch than if you live in Chipping Norton!

Saturday 9 September
In the Bordeaux area, they are talking about the earliest harvest this century, after the long, hot summer. Not since 1893, when the picking began on 15 August, has Bordeaux started its harvest so early. Here at least, the Greenhouse Effect may be bearing welcome fruit — with many experts predicting an excellent vintage.

The Times reports that the exodus of 'names' from Lloyd's of London continues, with 1,750 resigning this year, as the wealthy individuals who back the £11 billion insurance market grow increasingly concerned about the insurability of such problems as environmental pollution and asbestosis. The insurance market has a lot to learn in this field.

Tuesday 12 September
Up at 06.30 with Helen and off to Euston, then on to Chester with Caroline Cecil of Valin Pollen to start the Manweb audit. Caroline is clearly rattled that we have not brought detailed questionnaires to use on

those we are meeting, including the deputy chairman, Richard Gales. We insist that flexibility and 'following our nose' is important at this stage, but we will obviously have to accelerate the process of developing the audit framework. People want to *see* structure. Tiring day.

Thousands of East German refugees are streaming through Czechoslovakia and Hungary into West Germany. West Germany has promised the refugees special dispensation for their cars, including Trabants and Wartburgs, which are unbelievably polluting by present-day West German standards. The real problem, though, will come when the East Germans — and other East Europeans — enjoy car ownership levels equal to our own.

In New York, meanwhile, the populist Soviet politician Boris Yeltsin has been predicting a new Russian revolution that will drive Gorbachev from office. Asked how long the Soviet leader has before frustrated expectations blow the lid off, he said: 'Not more than a year and probably about six months. That's all he has got.'

Paddy Ashdown, leader of the Democrats, has ruled out an electoral pact with the Green Party. The decision is easily understandable. He warned of what he called the 'narrow Calvinism' of the Greens, arguing that an extreme fringe 'tend to treat human beings as just another pollutant — an evil, a curse, inevitably sinful in their actions and, therefore, if beyond redemption, then of course a proper subject for control'.

Dr John Houghton, Director-General of the Meteorological Office — who I met at Mrs T's reception earlier in the year — is quoted in *The Times* today, predicting that the Greenhouse Effect will bring wetter winters in Britain. 'Global warming,' he said, 'is probably the most important scientific (problem) facing mankind.'

Wednesday 13 September
Earthscan is publishing David Pearce's report on environmental economics under the title *Blueprint for a Green Economy*. It contacted major parties to see how many copies they wanted. 'Labour HQ? Fifty copies, please,' reports the *Guardian*. 'Conservative Central Office? Errh. Just one, thank you.'

Lunch at the Royal Society of Arts. Asked to join RSA Environment Committee, which seems to be all Lords, Attenboroughs and Prince Philips, but said would only come on board if there were a number of younger members. RSA has played an extremely important role in promoting debate and action at the interface between industry and the environment, but seems slightly adrift at the moment. Nothing that can't be fixed, though.

Later start work on the BT audit process. The sheer size of what we have taken on is only just beginning to hit home. Sketch out elements of Spillers proposal. ITDG chairman Dennis Stevenson, also chairman of the Tate Gallery, agrees to speak at Green Shopping Day launch.

Papers full of a *Marketing* survey of marketing people, which found that 92% think that the Green movement is not a passing fad. On the other hand, 89% condemn what they see as industry's superficial response. Tesco, The Body Shop and Sainsbury's come out well, while Procter & Gamble, Unilever and ICI come at the bottom of the league. I am fairly sure, however, that we will see many of these companies moving well beyond their initial superficial greening.

Thursday 14 September
Meeting with HD Plastics in the morning, talking about recycled plastic refuse bags, which they sell to supermarkets and local authorities. They want a combination of product endorsement and consultancy. We say we don't endorse products and also suggest that they might like to think a bit further before asking for any consultancy work. Also Reed International ring during the day, interested in consultancy. Littlewoods confirm that we have won the audit contract with them.

In the news: 79 beagle pups on their way by ferry to Sweden, for use in experiments by a drug firm, suffocate when the ventilation in their lorry fails during the 24-hour crossing. Interesting, given that the pups would presumably have been 'sacrificed' on the altar of science before long, that the drug company said 'the kennel management and the driver of the truck are heartbroken' and a spokesman for the kennels said 'I am absolutely gutted by it'. People's brains are peculiar organs.

Anita Roddick and 250 helpers delivered one million letters to the Brazilian Embassy, protesting against the burning of Amazonia. The Body Shop are negotiating with the Kayapo Indians to supply ingredients for a 'Rainforest' range planned for 1990.

Saturday 16 September
Gaia, Hania and I drive in to Holland Park. With Annie, Fiona, Julia and Rebecca, we pack up Green Shopping Day action packs and prepare them for posting.

The children love the work and the atmosphere in the office. By the end of the day we have got over 1,000 action packs ready for posting on Monday.

Grim whole-page-plus story in *The Times* today about the fires in France. Initial focus on two pilots, fighting the fires by water-bombing them at little more than tree-top level. Just when one fire was almost extinguished, their wing-tip clipped a tree and they spun in. Both pilots were killed instantly — and the fuel spewing from the wreckage restarted the blaze. The *pompiers* who fight the fires, particularly in the south, believe that many are started by contract arsonists, working for developers who want to build housing tracts and office complexes.

Just the sort of people who leave the Earth in their Star Arks in Ben Elton's novel *Stark*, which I finish this evening. At the end, the world's most powerful industrialists have gone and left the consumers to their fate. 'Strangely there was little bitterness, or anger, it was all too hot and hopeless for that. People knew they were all to blame, not one single person was without guilt.'

And then, on page 451, the lines Gaia had quoted to me in France, when she finished the book. '"If only," people sighed, "if only we had *done* something. Acted when we still had time, even just ten years ago," they said, "back in the late eighties, the early nineties when there was still time."'

Sunday 17 September
The Green Party announces that it plans to cut the UK population to 30-40 million — by persuading people not to have more than two children. The cuts, it says, would be achieved over more than a generation. Elaine and my mother both react by saying they agree, although neither particularly looks forward to such policies being imposed by some of the more strident Greens! Both feel like 'rats in a cage', increasingly aware of population pressures, traffic, noise, pollution, litter and so on.

Watch the Green Consumer Video, featuring John Craven, which North-South have put together with Julia's help. A useful treatment, but it remains to be seen whether WWF can get it out to a suitably wide audience.

Meanwhile, a new Harris poll shows that the Green Party's non-environmental policies are pretty much unknown to most of those who voted for it in the Euro-elections: only 12% knew it wants to pull us out of the European Community — and the same proportion is aware that the Greens oppose economic growth.

Press still brimming over with green stories. Patten announces that he is shelving Ridley's plans for privatising the NCC. Officials now admit that the plans were devised by Ridley to weaken the NCC, which he profoundly disliked.

NATO'S MEAN MACHINE GOES GREEN, reads a headline in the *Observer*. West Germany endures some 3,000 Nato Military exercises each year, but this year — in the wake of Gorbachev's overtures — the Germans are more worried about wildlife and the environment than they are about the

Russians. On the British side, some 200 environmental officers have been appointed to keep damage to a minimum and the largest British exercise is called White Rhino, after the endangered species.

An extraordinary day in that it has been 'ordinary'. No work; we drive across to Chiswick to look at some furniture for the children's rooms, pop into the office to pick up some action packs to deliver to a family in East Sheen and go for a walk in Richmond Park. This evening, the TV ads for the serialisation of *The Supermarket Guide* by *Today* begin, fronted by Richard Briers — perhaps best known for 'The Good Life' series.

Late evening: rattle off a review of a book on the rental value of land, called *Costing the Earth*, for the RSA. Not the most riveting book I have read, but environmental economics is going to be at the heart of any concerted push towards sustainability.

Monday 18 September
We hit the front page of *Today*, with a picture of Richard Briers holding *The Supermarket Guide*, with several pages inside. The coverage is generally fairly tacky, with much play made of 'supermarket wars' and so on. More to come. But this early coverage is already spurring a good deal more media interest. Start day with Julia and Helen at BT talking to Chris Earnshaw, responsible for the BT Network — with 206,000 employees. BT is Brobdingnagian.

Numerous requests for copies of the audits report. Still not a squeak from WWF. They could hardly impede us more if they tried. Further conversation with Ray Mathews of Heinz today.

Off the East Coast of the USA, meanwhile, two oil tankers have collided, setting the sea alight and causing a 20-mile oil slick. The prompt action of the emergency service, however, seems to have prevented the accident turning into an ecological disaster. Isabelle goes across to a presentation by NERC researchers who have just returned from a three-year circumnavigation of the Earth, carrying out work that promises to help us understand both long-established phenomena like El Niño, the enormous changes in temperatures of the Pacific Ocean which have long disrupted the South American fisheries — and weather patterns — as well as emerging problems like the Greenhouse Effect.

Yesterday, preaching in Canterbury Cathedral during the Canterbury Festival of Faith and the Environment, the Archbishop of Canterbury, Dr Robert Runcie, said that mankind was in danger of becoming the 'endangering species'. He noted that the growing public interest in ecology and the environment could genuinely be called 'religious', but he went slightly off the rails in claiming that the movement is based on belief in a creator of the universe. I would say that the overwhelming bulk of the movement to date has been made up of agnostics or atheists — indeed environmentalism has in some senses been an alternative religion.

The Times caught the right note in an editorial today, pointing out that the Judaeo-Christian tradition, with its ethos of subduing the Earth, 'is one of the main reasons the planet got itself into its present ecological mess in the first place'. (Ditto the Communist 'religion': the *Wall Street Journal* carries an article on the 'biological Chernobyl' at the Soviet Sverdlovsk Biological Warfare Facility ten years ago, in 1979. An accidental release of anthrax spores, presumably being studied as biological weapons, is thought to have killed hundreds of Soviet citizens.)

Although longer term a green religion could pose a threat to Christianity, for the moment the Green movement and Christians have common interests and can presumably make common cause.

Tuesday 19 September
On the front page of *Today* again, with a four-page supplement inside. An interview with Richard North of *The Independent*, one of the best environmental correspondents around. He gets behind stories — and can see the longer term trajectories, having been an active environmentalist for years.

Another, Michael McCarthy, has a major piece in *The Times* today, in which he raises the question whether the green bubble will burst? He quotes Michael Heseltine extensively, to the effect that we are not seeing a sea-change in attitudes. Instead, Heseltine argues, environmental concern stems from prosperity — and will disappear come the next major recession or slump. Others, not surprisingly, disagree. 'You can be prosperous or poor,' says Stanley Clinton Davis, 'but if you're ill, you're ill. Society is seen increasingly as very ill indeed, environmentally.'

Robin Grove-White, also quoted by McCarthy, *does* believe we are seeing a sea-change. And James Cornford, of the Institute for Public Policy Research, the left-wing think-tank set up last year to be a 'candid friend' to the Labour Party, agrees. He sees young people being captured by green ideas in very much the same way as the Thirties young were seized by socialism and the Sixties generation by rock'n'roll and alternative lifestyles.

He suggests that young people coming to political consciousness now will take environmental issues seriously as part of their picture of the world, in a way that the older generation do not and that's going to be reflected in the policies of the future. As a political reality in the long-term that's going to be very important.

Rikki Stein comes in, a contact from Earthlife days. He is thinking of getting a five-continent music festival off the ground for 1991, linking rainforest regions. Sounds over-ambitious, but interesting. While we are talking, Liz Knights brings in the first copies of *The Supermarket Shopping Guide*, this time on 100% recycled paper. They look great.

More on the greenhouse. West Germany announces that last year it released 798 million tonnes of carbon dioxide into the atmosphere, compared with 740 million tonnes in 1986. 28.7% came from industry, 24.2% from households and 21.8% from transport.

Wednesday 20 September

In the news: A petition with 3 million signatures, 450,000 from Britain, was handed to UN Secretary General Perez de Cuellar in New York yesterday, calling for a special session of the UN General Assembly to halt the destruction of the tropical rainforests. UK Energy Secretary John Wakeham told the World Energy Conference in Montreal yesterday that energy efficiency is the most cost-effective response to the Greenhouse Effect — in direct contrast to his predecessor, Cecil Parkinson, who favoured nuclear power. And the Chunnel is in trouble, with environmental improvements included at the Government's insistence driving the forecast costs from £1.2 billion to at least £3 billion. [The estimated cost has since more than doubled again.]

Across to the Consumers' Association with Julia and Dorothy, for the workshop on eco-labelling chaired by CA Head of Policy John Winward. Among those represented: CEED, the Co-op, the DoE and DTI, FoE, Procter & Gamble, Varta and WWF. Fascinating interplay, with strong push towards a Government-backed (and initially, at least, Government-funded) scheme, focusing on key issues and on products that relate to them. Some comment that Julia and I at times argued different corners, but clear that we — at least — are not toeing any Party line.

Thursday 21 September

Julia speaks to Green Party Conference in Wolverhampton. Is heckled to begin with, but does a creditable job. Hear a report on the green consumerism debate on BBC Radio as I come back from WWF's offices in Beauchamp Place in a cab.

The WWF meeting was to discuss Procter & Gamble's new *Ariel Ultra*, a concentrated washing powder which uses 30% less chemicals to achieve any given wash. It is also phosphate-free, a major development.

In Brussels yesterday, the European Commission decided to prosecute Britain for its failure to meet water purity standards. Chris Patten, who had tried to head the Commission off at the pass, described the decision as 'astonishing, inexplicable and unfair'. Many environmentalists would disagree. The Government's furious response can perhaps be explained by the fact that the decision could place a large question-mark over the impending privatisation of the water industry.

Ray Mathews of Heinz calls to say that they have agreed to pay towards Green Shopping Day, which will be a great help. Later in the afternoon, the BBC come in to ask me if I would appear on a 30-minute, face-to-face interview to be screened at the end of the year. The idea is that they are going to do 30 people who have been significant in the 1980s and give them a reasonable amount of air-time to expand on their thinking. Others being filmed include Anita Roddick, Arthur Scargill, David Owen and Ian Botham! [Later, the idea founders because no one can get their brains around the fact that a real environmentalist can work within a limited company quite as well as within a charity!]

Elsewhere, Hurricane Hugo has been laying waste to the Virgin Islands, precipitating looting and general mayhem, and is now bound for Florida. Richard Anthes, a meteorologist who heads the university consortium that operates the National Centre for Atmospheric Research in Boulder, Colorado, says that more hurricanes will result from the Greenhouse Effect. 'We can say with some confidence that the frequency of category four and category five hurricanes (the most severe) will increase,' he says, 'but we can't say by how much.'

Friday 22 September
A massive IRA bomb explosion at the Royal Marines School of Music at Walmer, near Deal, in Kent, has killed at least nine bandsmen.

Drive in to the office. The papers are full of the Green Party conference — and Julia's speech features in most of the articles. But the papers spend more time talking about the number of copies of *The Green Consumer Guide* sold than they do about the way in which green consumerism works. It's interesting that *The Supermarket Guide* has already sold 75,000 copies — and Gollancz is printing another 35,000 copies. *The Green Consumer Guide*, launched two weeks earlier last year, sold a total of 95,000 by Christmas.

David Icke, the BBC presenter who is also prospective Green parliamentary candidate for the Isle of Wight, was just one of a number of speakers to attack the supermarkets. 'Providing environmentally-friendly products is a very laudable thing,' he said, 'but to rely on green consumerism is like trying to stop a tank with a pop gun.' I suspect you could even stop a tank if you could get enough bubble gum under its tracks! And Jonathon Porritt made a stirring speech in which he called for the Party to streamline its organisation and procedures. He warned: 'It is only by remaining resolutely free of the sterile left-right debate that the Green Party can rebut the final accusation which is now being flung at it:

that you are all a bunch of crypto-Fascists, just waiting to seize the reins of power, issue compulsory hair shirts, close down the chocolate factories and confiscate people's wickedly self-indulgent deep freezers.' He said that having listened to the Party's three speakers, it was difficult to work out exactly where they stood on the question of economic growth. One seemed to believe in not much growth, one in not quite growth and one in no growth at all.

The Greens drop their population targets and denied that they believe that families should be limited to one child. They back a boycott of Nestlé instant coffee, to pressure the company to change its policy of giving free baby milk powder to hospitals in developing countries. They also called for a programme of local energy audits to help householders and industrialists to boost their energy efficiency and pick the cleanest fuels. Also today: The CBI launches its action plan for a cleaner environment. Robin Paul, chairman of the CBI's environmental committee, said: 'We must now help set the agenda and help business come to grips with the plethora of complex issues which collectively make up the environmental debate.'

Then on to Hertford, arriving half an hour late at Addis, around 10.30. Traffic in North London appalling. Addis, who make a great deal of plastic-ware, want an environmental audit. We agree to put together a proposal. It is very clear that companies like this are now coming under tremendous pressure from supermarkets, who want assurance that a growing range of products are environment-friendly. They admit that they hardly know where to start.

In the afternoon, I go on to the first meeting of a new committee formed by the DTI to develop a national strategy for recycling. Around 40 people, drawn from government, industry, trade associations, environmental groups and consultancies. The DoE says that landfill costs are due to rise at least three- or four-fold in the wake of impending legislation, which should help recycling. DTI is clearly taking green issues much more seriously, although there is a good deal of cynicism around the room about the prospects for success.

Home by 18.00. Put up a very large tent on the lawn. Gaia is having a sleep-over party with six or seven girls. Build a barbecue pit and grill fresh sardines — and, later, marshmallows. The stars shine clearly in the sky, while the dazzling beams of jetliners swing through the sky like gigantic fireflies.

Saturday 23 September
The Independent runs Richard North's piece, with an enormous cartoon of a wolf in sheep's clothing—in fact a fleece of vines and other greenery. Half way through he says: 'Everyone always knew that he (me) would be a

success. He was wearing proper business suits when most of the eco-freaks hadn't found their way to the Oxfam shop for their first tweed jacket.'

A bit over-the-top, although (and this I didn't tell Richard) I wore a suit to anti-Vietnam War demonstrations in the late Sixties, for the simple reason that I thought it would count for more if people saw some conventional-looking figures in amongst the Hippies and Trotskyists. My hair was a little long to be totally convincing, though.

Richard ends on SustainAbility's growing desire to use our increasingly high public profile to pull Third World environmental issues up in front of Britons. They are 'bubbling under' — to use the old Top 20 term — in the news at the moment. For example, Commonwealth Finance Ministers yesterday warned that, while sustainable growth would require much higher standards of environmental protection, aid agencies should not impose tough new environmental conditions on Third World borrowers.

The Zimbabwe Government has also announced that five southern countries — Botswana, Malawi, Zambia, Mozambique and Zimbabwe — plan to form an ivory-selling cartel to defy international efforts to impose a ban on elephant products. They feel that they are adequately protecting elephants and are being 'patronised' by Western conservationists.

Thought this was bad news, until I bumped into Mike Kock, who works as a wildlife vet in the Zimbabwe national parks and natural resources department. He had recently been on an elephant cull and found it a gruelling, grim experience, but said that elephant numbers were increasing at 5% a year in Zimbabwe — and all the animal was used, not just the ivory.

Interesting article in *The Economist*, noting that Christopher Patten has reason to thank Nicholas Ridley for his 'rigorous intellectual approach to the environment'. He developed three principles that will be the core of Tory environmental policy: first, cleaning up costs money (so we must be prepared to pay); second, the state is not good at regulating public-sector bodies like the water authorities (so privatise them and then regulate to ensure they clean up); and, third, market forces can be harnessed to the cause. David Pearce's report was commissioned by Ridley — and looks set to become a fund of new ideas for the Government. But Patten will face a number of problems that can be laid at Ridley's door as much as anyone's, including the state of Britain's water.

Another iconoclast has been work in Cardiff. Speaking at the annual Friends of the Earth conference yesterday, Professor James Lovelock told his audience not to worry about radiation and PCBs. I would love to have seen their reaction. He also said that environmentalists must learn to love the multinational chemical corporations — who alone could come up with the replacements to CFCs now needed to save the ozone layer. He also attacked much of today's big science. Science's greatest triumph, he said, 'was the discovery of DNA and the genetic code; its greatest shame was blood-up-to-the-elbows vivisection.'

Sunday 24 September
Awake to green overload. The Sunday papers are awash with green stories — the heap of cuttings from *The Sunday Times, Observer, Mail on Sunday* and *Sunday Correspondent* alone begin to rival a healthy compost heap in size. The *Observer* runs as 12-page supplement on the environment, with our work extensively covered — and including my article on how consumers can help buy a better world. Chris Patten concludes that 'Green Consumers can move things forward far more rapidly than any number of Acts of Parliament or European Community directives'.

The Green Consumer Guide (up to No. 7 this week) and *The Supermarket Guide* are mentioned time and again in all the papers. Green Shopping Day, too. The Co-op, for example, takes a full-page ad in the *Mail on Sunday* built around Green Shopping Day. The *Observer's* editorial begins: 'The first anniversary of Mrs Thatcher's green conversion, which falls this week, will be marked by a Green Shopping Day — an event that may offer some satisfaction to Alderman Roberts' daughter.'

The *Sunday Correspondent* runs a seven-page article by Lewis Chester on green consumerism. Overall the piece strongly endorses green consumerism. 'Elkington has not merely captured an idea whose time has come,' it says, 'but one that has long been waiting for expression.'

'It may be true that green consumerism does not do much more than mitigate the effects of basically unsound environmental choices,' Chester argues later on, 'but this in itself is a considerable advance.' And he notes that opportunities for green rip-offs 'certainly exist, but do not appear strong. Not as strong as the dark Greens' opportunity to make inroads into previously uncharted areas of support.'

Exactly our view. Indeed, Sara Parkin, interviewed on TV today by Brian Walden, was harried on the question of whether the Greens would use coercion to drive through their programmes. She continuously said they wouldn't, suggesting that they would rely on information and persuasion — including information designed to help consumers choose supermarket products on the basis of their environmental performance. Clearly, Mrs Parkin and I continue to have diametrically opposed views! The Greens are currently polling 7% of the 'vote', versus 42% for

Labour, 39% for the Tories, 6% for the Democrats, 4% for the Nationalists and 3% for the SDP.

In the evening, drive down to Selsdon Park Hotel, near Sanderstead in Surrey, for the DoE workshop focusing on 'awareness raising and public participation'. Probably still the only person arriving in a car fitted with a catalytic converter.

Monday 25 September

A lot of familiar faces at the workshop, but many new ones too — there are representatives from 26 countries. The workshop is one of four building up to the 1990 Bergen conference on the follow-up to the Brundtland Report. The event is chaired by Peter Morgan, previously a Director of IBM (where I came across him on the sustainable development front) and now Director-General of the Institute of Directors.

Environment Minister David Trippier gives an uninspiring talk, although he did exert himself to the extent of wearing a blue tie striped with green. My presentation was made to the consumer workshop, chaired by Consumers' Association chairman John Beishon. Almost all of my recommendations went forward in the final topic report — on top of which John added a strong endorsement of Green Shopping Day.

Today is the start of National Unleaded Week, organised by CLEAR. Rolls-Royce warns that motorists using mixer pumps, supplying both leaded and unleaded fuel, risk destroying their catalytic converters — since as much as two litres of leaded fuel can be left in a pump when a green motorist starts to fill up. BP agrees that anyone with a catalyser should use unleaded-only pumps — but no one thought to mention the fact until now.

Thursday, which is both Green Shopping Day and CLEAR's Adjustment Day, will see the AA carrying out an expected 15,000 free car conversions, to enable them to run on unleaded. Nine environmental organisations (including Greenpeace, FoE and WWF) launch *Roads to Ruin*, a joint attack on the Government's plans to spend £12 million on roads.

Tuesday 26 September

On Barnes Pond a motionless heron sits atop a 'No Fishing' sign, while the fish breach in the waters — which are way down and must be fairly oxygenless because of the lack of rain.

The phone never stops ringing. All lines shine red — and the fax bleats continuously on top of the electronic trill. Local groups, press and companies wanting help. Good deal of interest in the difference of opinion between us and the Greens on green consumerism. At the Friends of the Earth annual conference over the weekend, Jonathon Porritt warned that: 'Green consumerism is a target for exploitation. There's a lot of green froth on top, but murkiness lurks underneath. The belief in the boardroom is that we can be bought off.'

ICI in trouble again. The company is closing a chemical plant in southern Taiwan — because of pollution concerns — only a few weeks after the company announced plans for a new £190 million project on the island. Local fishermen claimed that a sub-contractor was dumping waste acid near the coast, instead of taking it 20 miles out to sea. ICI says that the acid dilutes quickly in seawater, but environmental pressures are building rapidly in Taiwan in advance of a general election on 2 December.

Growing interest in the States in the Valdez Principles, a ten-point voluntary code designed to persuade business to move towards the sustainable use of natural resources, coupled with the appointment of environmental directors and the introduction of annual environmental audits. 'Any company that ignores environmental precautions or fails to act responsibly as a steward of our biosphere will be the focus of shareholder action,' said Joan Bavaria, head of Ceres (Coalition for Environmentally Responsible Economies), which drafted the Principles. It looks as though the Valdez Principles could have a real impact in North America.

Across this morning to BT to see Ian Drewer, Head of Risk Management. Fascinating meeting. The approach of talking to people responsible for other activities that cut across BT's operations (such as quality assurance, energy efficiency, health and safety) is beginning to pay real dividends. But it is clear that the clash between the old civil service-style culture and newer ideas and people are producing a 'noisy environment' in which to try and communicate new big ideas.

Wednesday 27 September
Yesterday Fiona went along to the launch of *Ground Truth — a Report of the First Green Year*. Compiled by Media Natura and a number of other environmental groups it reviews Mrs T's first year. 'Mrs Thatcher seemed to promise much but has failed to deliver results,' said Chris Rose of Media Natura. 'Where progress has been made it is almost invariably, and grudgingly, at the behest of the European Commission or other international agencies.' True, indeed, it's a real embarrassment to be a Briton in Europe these days.

Today, Julia went to the launch by FoE of a discussion paper, *Beyond Green Consumerism* by Sandy Irvine. The press try to drive a wedge between FoE and SustainAbility, but Jonathon Porritt makes it clear that he supports what we are doing — but is worried about the way some parts of industry are responding. So FoE have come up with the idea of a 'Green Con of the Year' award to spotlight companies that are making unjustified claims or overcharging for environment-friendly products.

Meeting with *Marketing Week*, who want to put together a report on the extent to which marketing people have got their brains around the green issue. They also are interested in the idea of an environmental audit.

Among other signs of tensions in the Green movement, the latest news from the British Trust of Conservation Volunteers (BTCV). Activists have seized power in the BTCV, and have tried to dismiss the Trust's director, Ian Branton. Under his direction BTCV's income has grown from £500,000 a year in 1980 to more than £9 million, while staff numbers have grown from 20 to more than 150. Some of the organisation's 14,500 paid-up members apparently believe that, as a result, that its very success has led to a chasm between the management and membership. Mr Branton's supporters feel that his resignation could lead to a financial crisis.

In the news: a full-page ad in *The Times* for Sainsbury's new 'Greencare' range of household cleaners ('In the battle to save the world, the home front will be of vital importance'); and Peter Fend, a satellite remote sensing expert with New York-based Ocean Earth claims that the Chernobyl disaster was caused by land subsidence and faulty civil engineering, not by unauthorised experiments — if he is right there must be suspicions about a string of reactors built along the same fault line along the Pribyat river.

Julia spinning around in a blur of interviews. The new book and Green Shopping Day feature several times on the national TV news. Annie, Fiona, Isabelle and Rebecca working madly to get things ready for tomorrow. Most of them are still working in the office at midnight.

Among other things, I speak to a conference organised by the International Petroleum Industry Environmental Conservation Association (IPIECA) conference at the Kensington Park Hotel. Senior managers from companies like Arco, BP, Exxon and Shell. Seem to have struck the right note on the scale of the environmental challenge. As I leave some of the delegates are talking about how they can ship me across to the States.

Appear on the BBC's 'Late Show'. The five panellists sit in front of a trio of screens showing burned-out rainforest, and our feet are on a large 'ozone-friendly' label image on the floor. Monitors boom out Mrs T's stentorian voice, pumping out her Tory Party green speech from late last year. A 15-minute film sequence includes Dorothy and Julia. The other panellists include David Icke of the Green Party and advertisers Tim Delaney and Maurice Gluck. The time shoots by. A good airing of the issues — and an extraordinary plug for the book.

Thursday 28 September

Appear on Sky TV news just before 09.00. Then by cab back to the office, to pick up papers, then on to The Brewery in Chiswell Street, EC1, for the Green Shopping Day launch. The driver has the radio tuned to LBC and the Green Shopping Day story comes on continuously. FoE are sounding supportive, with obvious reservations on consumerism generally, but the Women's Environmental Network are snapping at every ankle in sight.

The launch goes very well. Several hundred people — including people like Dennis Waterman, Rula Lenska and Pamela Stephenson — turn up and the setting is spectacular. The atmosphere is tremendously exciting and the unusual mix of people occasions much comment. There are displays by Alucan, Universal Office Supplies, Victor Gollancz and Wella. The food has been supplied by the Alan and Jackie Gear of the National Centre for Organic Gardening and the organic wines by Venceremos.

The panel is made up of myself, Julia, Dorothy, Dennis Stevenson (chairman of ITDG — founded by Fritz Schumacher) and (no relation) Pamela Stephenson (of Parents for Safe Food). Fair number of TV crews and a mass of other media people. The strategy of using the launch to open out the debate to embrace, for example, Third World issues goes down well.

At the same time, a number of people ask whether FoE and SustainAbility have colluded to stir up press interest by pretending to have a public brawl! In a way, it's a bit like the Salman Rushdie/*Satanic Verses* saga, with us in place of Rushdie and the Greens in place of the Muslims. Will *The Supermarket Shopping Guide* benefit from all the publicity — and will we end up in hiding like Rushdie? After today, I don't think so — although David Goode of the Greater London Ecology Unit mentions he was advised not to use me for a conference because I was 'out of favour' with the environment movement. He thought the whole thing ridiculous.

James Erlichman of the *Guardian*, meanwhile, is clearly developing a fairly critical profile. He grilled me on how I felt I could square commenting on products and at the same time working as a consultant for companies like Procter & Gamble. Unfortunately, Elaine overheard the conversation and came down on him like a tonne of bricks. He later described her to Fiona as 'a dervish'. They talk — and to some extent make up — later.

Elaine, knowing how we have operated on a financial knife-edge for so long, is incensed that anyone should think that we are 'get-rich-quick' artists. But Erlichman is of the Ralph Nader school: the idea that one might be able to keep a degree of objectivity and independence when working with companies is completely foreign to him.

Saturday 30 September

The ozone hole has reappeared over Antarctica. Government announces that electricity privatisation will be delayed by six months, which may relax pressure on the Manweb environmental audit. Labour Party sends a copy of the September edition of *Labour Research*, which recommends *The Green Consumer Guide* as 'a useful source for "green bargaining"'.

Peter Knight, writing in the *Financial Times*, recalls that the late, vile Aristotle Onassis surrounded the bar on his yacht, *Christina*, with stools made from the penises of sperm whales slaughtered by his whaling fleet. *The Independent* reports that environmentalists are incensed by plans to establish crocodile ranches in Brazil, using Nile crocs imported from Africa. The beast grows to more than 15 feet and kills more Africans than any other wild animal. The proposed sale of 115 animals raises the prospect of escapees causing havoc throughout Amazonia.

James Erlichman's profile appears in the *Guardian*. 'Cool, detached, charming, but elusive — that's how other environmentalists sum up John Elkington, organiser of yesterday's Green Shopping Day and prolific publicist for the cause,' it begins. 'Most ecology folk still wear cardigans and green cords — Mr Elkington's perfect pin-stripes must keep the benzene fumes pouring out of the dry cleaner near his home in Barnes, south London.'

SustainAbility's 'business deals . . . make purists in the movement squirm', Erlichman says. 'Deeper Greens say green consumerism is largely tokenism or hype. Middle-class mums may salve their consciences packing their trolleys with "greener" detergents, but gestures will not save the planet.' The piece ends by saying: 'His detractors do not doubt his commitment to the environment. He has been in the field for nearly 20 years, named his elder daughter Gaia before anyone knew the eco-term, and has produced several books which have been genuine pacemakers. One dark Green informant said: "Either he is very sophisticated in the game he is playing with big companies, or he is supping with the devil. Probably a bit of both."'

Call Erlichman to say thank you — given his starting point, he managed to write a reasonably balanced piece.

In Tokyo yesterday, Yoko Ono launched a world environment drive to celebrate her husband John Lennon's 50th birthday. His assassination in

1980 marked a watershed for the Beatles generation. Gaia — then around three — still remembers Elaine weeping in the following days.

The Dutch Defence Minister, Jan Van Houwelingen, as part of proposals to restore Holland's environment, announces plans to cut the environmental impact of Dutch Army manoeuvres by 25% over the next ten years.

OCTOBER

Sunday 1 October
Reporting from Peking, Louise Branson notes in the *Observer* that one old Chinese saying holds that: 'What is false will turn into the truth after being repeated a thousand times.' The Chinese authorities are trying to wipe out the memory of the Tiananmen Square massacre with circus performances, fireworks and dancing in celebration of the 40th birthday of state Communism in China. Next weekend marks the fortieth anniversary of the Communist state's foundation in East Germany. Not a happy anniversary.

At a time when Moscow is talking of a ban on chemical weapons, Russia's secret work on genetic weapons is reported in *The Sunday Times*. 'The poisons are designed to have a very specific effect for a defined time,' writes defence correspondent James Adams. 'Soldiers in a tank regiment could be made to have violent diarrhoea to prevent them fighting. Infantrymen could be made to weep uncontrollably so that they could neither fire their weapons nor obey orders.'

Even worse is the likely proliferation of genetic weapons in the Third World. I remember talking to science-fiction writer Frank Herbert about the threat of genetic weapons, some years before the publication of his book *The White Plague*. In the book, a molecular biologist driven insane by an IRA outrage, develops a lethal pathogen that seeks out and attaches itself to the human chromosome in such a way that it kills only females. The cost of assembling a lab to make such weapons is falling all the time. After the book was published, Herbert looked into the second-hand bio-equipment market. He found a surplus $6,000 centrifuge that went for $17.95.

Tuesday 3 October
Today pastes Procter & Gamble this morning, with a front-page article slamming the company for its reliance on animal testing when producing *Ariel Ultra* — the mainstream UK detergent industry's first green washing powder. P&G will retort that they are required by law to carry out such tests, have cut animal testing by 80% in recent years, spend £2 million a year on developing and applying alternative test methods, and have recently won an award in the States for their efforts in this field. But the sensitivity of animal testing can only grow.

The paper apparently got hold of a copy of P&G's product impact assessment from one of the organisations attending the WWF briefing the other day. The danger is that this fact will dissuade companies like P&G from opening up their thought-processes to environmentalists, although that seems unlikely.

In the afternoon, David Smith of PA Consulting Services comes in and we spend some time talking through how the two companies can develop in a complementary way. At the moment it looks as though PA could well develop a service which competes directly with our own, which in the current market wouldn't matter — but we are looking for ways of ensuring that our three-legged stool (with Brand New) develops in a balanced way.

A letter from Sandy Irvine in yesterday's *Guardian* talked of the five 'Rs' of green consumerism: Refusal (Do I really need to buy this item?), Reduction, Re-use, Repair and Recycling. The list has been around for a while, but deserves a wider airing.

Wednesday 4 October
Safeway runs a large-format ad in *The Times*, trumpeting its ★★★★★ rating in *The Green Consumer's Supermarket Shopping Guide*. The ad includes a picture of the front cover of the book. We are delighted by this response, because it shows that they are taking this area seriously. And a certain amount of external praise can help enthuse people in such companies.

Other papers review a new booklet from the Institute of Economic Affairs, the right-wing think-tank. It claims that life under a government run by the Green Party or according to the policies advanced by environmentalists would be an 'ecological hell'. Chris Patten, meanwhile, rejects plans to build a new country town at Foxley Wood in north-east Hampshire.

In Australia, the Cabinet is due to reconsider plans for a mine adjacent to Kakadu National park in the Northern territory, made famous by the film 'Crocodile Dundee'. The mine could produce an estimated $7-8 billion of gold, platinum and other minerals. The country's so-called Greenies are fighting hard against the proposal, describing the area as one of Australia's crown jewels. By contrast, in 1986 the then Resources Minister called it 'clapped-out buffalo country'. It's amazing what Hollywood (or the Australian equivalent) can do for a wilderness.

Rechem International, the chemical incineration firm, and Torfaen Borough Council in Gwent, South Wales, reach an out-of-court settlement ending one of the most bitter environmental rows of recent years. The agreement forbids the Council from publishing environmental monitoring results from the area around Rechem's Pontypool incinerator, results which the firm says are unscientific. I'm not sure that the decision resolves my doubts.

Time magazine talks of a combination of carrot and stick in its 'Endangered Earth' column. The carrot is a new annual $360,000 cash award — to be split among six 'grassroots heroes', each from a different region of the world. The idea, backed by San Francisco's Goldman Environmental Foundation, is to give conservationists the kind of prestige afforded scientists by the Nobel Prize.

And the stick? Austrian Foreign Minister Alois Mock, in a speech before the UN General Assembly, has called for a UN environmental police force to protect the 'global commons'. 'Just as we have become accustomed to the Blue Helmets (of the UN security forces) in peacekeeping operations,' he says, 'we hope that in the foreseeable future UN Green Helmets may engage in the protection of the environment.'

Heated disagreement with Julia on the WWF audits report: she rightly says that WWF have let us down badly by sitting on the report, which we could readily sell for £80 a copy. I agree, but feel that pulling the report back would be tantamount to an open declaration of war against WWF. It's all part of the (sometimes painful) process of beginning to plough our own furrow.

Thursday 5 October

At the Labour Party conference yesterday, one speaker attacked what she called 'the fraud of eco-capitalism', but lost the motion. Environment spokesman Dr Jack Cunningham in effect argued for 'green growth', by saying that economic growth can be combined with increased environmental and energy efficiency standards. Green capitalism is not a fraud — but it will be the result of a very difficult balancing act. He also said that environmental concerns demand 'intervention and planning interference in the market — something we know this Prime Minister can never stomach'.

Cunningham is savaged today in *Today*, however. The paper launches an attack on Albright & Wilson's pollution record. He is a consultant to the chemical company. The *Daily Mail* reports that he is to be moved sideways to pacify green voters, because of his support for the Sellafield nuclear plant (which is sited within his Copeland constituency) and his work for Dow and Albright & Wilson.

Peter Knight comes in to talk through *The Green Business Guide*. Both Julia and I feel the three-way approach to writing the book will work well, although it will be a fair old challenge. I fax the proposed environmental mission statement to Stanhope Properties and proposed Manweb report structure to Valin Pollen. Australia's Channel 9 TV programme spends most of the afternoon filming Julia and I and activities in the office. In the evening, work on my CIA speech for tomorrow.

Exactly five years after the famine in Ethiopia, officials of the World Food Programme say that one and a half million people in Eritrea and Tigre are once again facing starvation. It will be interesting to see how the public, said to be suffering from 'donor fatigue' after Live Aid and Band Aid will respond.

Friday 6 October
Driving the cat-car, I trail a darkly smoking X-registered Ford through the tunnel to Heathrow. Internationalisation of UK shows in German and Japanese announcements on Super Shuttle to Edinburgh. Arrive at Caledonian Hotel with minutes to spare and have to start speaking immediately. Arranged by the Chemical Industries Association, the conference focuses on detergents and surfactants. Dr John Adsetts of Albright & Wilson is the other speaker. He previously worked for ICI on nitrate fertilisers and biotechnology. We turn out to inhabit the same universe and the discussion is very positive, although many of the questions turn on the issue of how the industry can 'get our message across'. I say that it will have to get involved in the broader environmental debate, not just in the controversy about detergents and surfactants.

Call Tessa Tennant. Merlin are considering a livelier investment, the new Disney development in France. Say I would approve, because 'edutainment' has considerable potential for getting some of the right messages across to ordinary people.

The bottles of Ark and Sainsbury's detergent I carry in my case resulted in my being stopped both on the way up and back by the security people.

In the news: the latest issue of the UNEP *Environmental Data Report* (1987-89) shows a continuing deterioration in most indicators of international environmental quality. The news may be grim, but at least having it in statistical form makes it more credible to politicians — and their advisors. The Bow Group, a Tory research organisation which numbers more than 100 MPs among its members, publishes a report — *The Green Conservative* — calling for a radical new 'green agenda' for the Conservative Party. If it fails to embrace the agenda, the report argues, Thatcherism will become a 'spent force'. It suggests that traditional Tory virtues, including efficiency, thrift, order, patriotism, continuity, self-help and market freedom within limits can all be harnessed to the cause.

Sunday 8 October
Our 40th week in the Top 10 with *The Green Consumer Guide*, now at
No. 5. *The Supermarket Shopping Guide* comes in at No. 6 — and John
Button at No. 9, with *How to be Green*. In a Harris Poll published in the
Observer, the Greens hold on to 5% of the 'vote', while Labour (49%)
streaks ahead of the Tories (38%).

Last night we had dinner with Earth Day organiser Denis Hayes, who is
going on to a number of other countries, including Hungary — where the
Communist Party has turned its back on more than 40 years of Marxism-
Leninism by voting to turn itself into a socialist party committed to
parliamentary democracy. Extraordinary times indeed. 'People whose
hands are tainted with blood, who have participated or assisted in acts of
murder and imprisonment of Hungarians, cannot be members (of the
new party),' said Prime Minister Miklos Nemeth. As *The Sunday Times*
noted: 'That rules out an awful lot of people.' East Germany tries to
maintain business as usual, 'celebrating' 40 years of Communism this
weekend — as the exodus of East Germans to the West via Hungary
continues apace. A clear case of *political* fraud.

On TV, Christopher Patten says that while the break-up of the NCC
into regional bodies for England, Wales and Scotland will go ahead, the
NCC would not be required — as Ridley had wanted — to sell its nature
reserves to the private sector. Confirms that he is thinking about the use of
tax subsidies and penalties to encourage 'green growth'. Good news, so
far as it goes.

The USA and USSR agree to destroy the last stocks of smallpox virus,
held in high-security phials at centres in Atlanta, Georgia, and Georgia in
the Soviet Union. The aim is to prevent it being used as a biological
weapon. This will be a real test of the extent to which the superpowers
trust one another. But the decision will probably be made easier by the
fact that both sides have decided that smallpox would make a pretty lousy
biological weapon. In Australia, Prime Minister Bob Hawke has deferred
for 12 months any decision on the controversial plan to mine gold,
platinum and palladium near the Kakadu National Park.

Monday 9 October
Spend morning with Julia at the SDIA conference, just off Savile Row. My
speech is entitled 'Who Washes Greenest?' Quite clear that green
consumerism has lit a fuse under the detergent industry — and they are
still wondering where the next charge will detonate. Other speakers
include John O'Keeffe, Managing Director of Procter & Gamble; Dr
Arthur Walker, also of P&G but speaking for SDIA; Phil Gilbert of
Unilever Research; and Professor Brian Moss of Liverpool University.

Moss notes that as the public's concern about the environment grows, the total number of lakes, streams and other waterways defined as 'eutrophic' will also inevitably grow. He concludes that the best way of controlling eutrophication — or the artificial enrichment of bodies of water — is to install phosphate stripping equipment at sewage works, rather than going for phosphate-free detergents. But the range of phosphate-free products continues to grow: we receive a big box of Tesco's 'Phosphate-Free' washing powder today.

Julia is invited by Jonathon Porritt to go on the judging panel for the 'Green Con of the Year' awards.

Sellafield is in the news again, with a FoE report claiming that radioactive contamination is up to 13 times the recommended limits in some nearby areas. The nuclear processing plant was also in the spotlight in Saturday's *Daily Telegraph*. The paper reported that on Friday Mr Justice Gatehouse, a High Court judge, heard a case brought by Mrs Christine Merlin claiming that radioactivity had resulted in two of her dogs dying from cancer and goslings being hatched with abnormalities. Some, she said, had been born with 'heads on the wrong way round and wings in peculiar positions'.

The Government announced yesterday that it will carry out the first national survey of the economic viability of organic farming. A new Greenpeace report, *The Hidden Ozone Depleters*, says cleaning chemicals like methyl chloroform and carbon tetrachloride, should be banned — because they also attack the ozone layer. The case brought against Shell by the National Rivers Authority, following the Mersey oil spill, is adjourned until 6 November — so that it can go to Liverpool Crown Court, where unlimited fines can be imposed. In Lausanne, Switzerland, a 10-day session of the Convention on International Trade in Endangered Species (CITES) focuses on the destruction of Africa's elephants — and spotlights the failure of countries like Argentina, Spain, Japan and Thailand to comply with CITES regulations on other species.

Wednesday 11 October
At the Tory Party conference, Christopher Patten announces that he will have a 'Green' White Paper ready in time for next October's conference. The Government's green policy was not a passing fashion, he said: 'It's here to stay and so is our response. We're not driven by the latest opinion poll.' He continued: 'What we need is not "no" growth, but "green" growth. We need growth that doesn't sacrifice tomorrow in order to consume mindlessly today.' His speech marks a dramatic break with Ridleyism. 'The market is not enough,' he stressed, 'and I do not think we Tories have ever believed that the market is enough.' A distinct improvement.

And on a Japanese note, a couple of days back Rebecca went to the launch of Richard Branson's new adventure. He plans to make the first crossing of the Pacific by hot air balloon with Per Lindstrand. The flight, in a balloon which will be 41 feet higher than Nelson's column, will start in southern Japan and — hopefully — end some 5,400 miles later in California. Part of the purpose of the expedition will be to raise awareness in Japan of environmental problems in the Pacific basin region. The balloon's envelope will be emblazoned with — among other things — a large green banner headline: SAVE OUR PLANET.

Japanese and UK scientists plan to use the flight to check levels of freon gases (CFCs) in the jetstream. Rebecca asked whether emissions from the balloon's propane burners would cause atmospheric pollution, but was assured that they would not. Branson emphasised Japan's role in the world economy and its concern over the Greenhouse Effect. 'We believe that if our challenge will help to raise the profile of the issues facing all of us on the planet then we will have achieved the double bonus of a world record and a slightly safer planet in the future.'

In the evening, attend gala evening at the RSA organised by the Caroline Walker Trust, with a lecture on food and the environment by Jonathon Porritt. At one point, he describes the pursuit of economic growth as a means for providing environmental quality as equivalent to treating a case of food poisoning by prescribing a carton of botulism-ridden hazelnut yoghurt. The future we must aim for, he says, must be based on sustainability, diversity, self-reliance and equity. During the evening, Enoch Powell's views on Jonathon are quoted: 'I am a fellow traveller with Jonathon Porritt,' Powell is alleged to have said, 'but I like to get off one or two stops before the train crashes.'

The 1989 Caroline Walker Awards go to the Baby Milk Action Coalition (on whose behalf Jane Asher calls for a boycott of Nescafé and other Nestlé products); the *Daily Mail* (for its coverage of food and health issues); Professor Richard Lacey (the Leeds University food micro-biologist who has campaigned against contamination by salmonella and listeria); and Tesco (for its 'Healther Eating' campaign). James Erlichman also gets an award for his writing for the *Guardian*.

Friday 13 October
Friday 13th lives up to its reputation as Wall Street suffers the second biggest share collapse on record. The Dow Jones index lost 190 points, or 7% of its value. The immediate fear was that there would be a re-run of the crash of two years ago, with the worst fall ever on 19 October 1987.

Friends of the Earth announces a new campaign against energy-guzzling fridges. US regulations introduced in 1987 will make around 90% of today's fridges obsolete from 1992. As a result, the US could save energy equivalent to the power output of 21 large power stations. A typical UK fridge uses 270 kilowatt hours a year, whereas the best fridges available in Europe use only 80 kWh a year. FoE suggests a compromise target here of 170 kWh by 1993, a level reached by only one in ten of our fridges today. Clearly, there is a great deal to be done in the energy efficiency front if we are to genuinely green the 'white goods' sector.

Monday 16 October
Start day at a meeting on sustainable development organised by the International Chamber of Commerce. Walk to IBM South Bank via the shanty town of cardboard boxes under the Waterloo Bridge approach roads. Contrast with the world of IBM could hardly be more stark.

Then up to Wakefield for Industrial Society meeting in Huddersfield. Bump into Virginia Bottomley getting off the train and accept a lift in her car. Apart from the two of us, the platform comprises speakers from ICI, Lin-Pak and the Industrial Society. Back to London in Virginia's car.

Tuesday 17 October
A global ban on all trade in ivory was agreed yesterday by a key CITES committee, after more than a week of wrangling. The delegates voted by 76 to 11, with four abstentions, to add the African elephant to Appendix I of CITES — which bans all trade.

The resolution will go to the plenary session later in the week, where acceptance seems likely. However, five African nations say they plan to take a 'reservation' on the African elephant, which would allow them to continue trading legally. The key question now is whether consumer nations will continue to buy ivory.

The Consumers' Association publishes results of a survey showing that most consumers take 'environment-friendly' labels stuck on products by manufacturers or retailers as official. We must keep up the pressure for a uniform labelling scheme.

In the afternoon, across to Shell UK. They want SustainAbility to help them audit the environmental aspects of a refurbishment programme designed to revamp the image of their petrol stations and shops over the next three to four years. Say I will prepare a proposal.

After supper start nailing down creaky boards upstairs, in advance of the carpet-layers coming tomorrow. Manage to put a couple of nails through a central heating hot water pipe in the study. Dirty water sprays everywhere and the kitchen ceiling groans under the weight of gallons of water. By the time I come to type up the diary for the last couple of days, around midnight, my fingers are covered in blisters and dotted with splinters. And Elaine is at her wits' end.

Wednesday 18 October

Main news on the radio as we wake up: San Francisco has been rocked by an earthquake. A section of Route 880 through Oakland has collapsed, crushing cars and their occupants 'as flat as license plates', as one rescue worker put it. Geologists say that the quake has released only part of the energy in the San Andreas fault. The 'Big One' could still hit California within the next few decades.

On to Motofair '89 at Earl's Court, to do a filmed interview for Richard Keefe and Veronique Sieffert of North-South Productions. The cab passes through Whitehall, where I spot an aerosolled graffito in lime green: Virginia. Terse and to the point, although it's not quite clear what the writing on the wall actually meant. A Bottomley fan?

North-South are making a 'Fragile Earth' TV programme on the greening of capitalism, with the potential for greening the car industry one of the main story-lines. We spend much of the time at the Volvo stand, with the filming taking place on the second floor of the stand. Rest of show is a mélange of polished boots and bonnets and pouting bimboids. Volvo's, by contrast, features a number of environmental themes — and a video built around David Attenborough and the Royal Society for Nature Conservation.

In Kuala Lumpur, meanwhile, this year's Commonwealth conference is under way. Friday's session, due to debate environmental issues — some say to deflect attention from South African sanctions — now looks likely to be controversial. The developing countries present seem set to challenge Britain to practice what it preaches — particularly in relation to its policies on energy efficiency and the Greenhouse Effect.

'It is the developed countries that have caused the pollution of the world atmosphere,' Malaysian Prime Minister Datuk Seri Dr Mahathir Mohamed told *The Times*. 'On the other hand, it is the developing countries that have been asked to stop cutting down trees and stop growing oil palm and rubber trees, in order to preserve the environment.' More positively, the Scott Paper Company says it is pulling out of an environmentally controversial £400 million eucalyptus planting (and rainforest-destroying) project in Irian Jaya — formerly Dutch New Guinea.

In the news: Uniroyal withdraws Alar from sale. Pamela Stephenson welcomes the news, but says she is concerned that the Government itself did not take action. Britain abstained yesterday in the CITES vote on whether Hong Kong's huge stocks of ivory should be exempted from the ban on ivory trading. But the vote went the way the conservationists had hoped. The 670 tons of ivory held in the colony will now be frozen when the ban comes into force in January.

And — only 11 days after East Germany's 40th anniversary, Erich Honecker, the man behind the Berlin Wall, resigns as the country's President, following the social and political upheavals which ensued in the wake of President Gorbachev's visit. Unfortunately, Egon Krenz, the man who is replacing Honecker, seems a younger version of the outgoing President — and, as the man who ran the secret police, is if anything more hardline than Honecker and deeply unpopular.

Thursday 19 October
Speak at Forum Communications conference. Dr Elizabeth Nelson is in the chair and says that there have been no questions from the large audience. My talk triggers a fair few, as does that of David Robey, Tesco's Corporate Marketing Director. He notes that — such is the pace of events in the environmental field — Tesco's launch of its 'Tesco Cares' programme in January seems 'millions of light-years away'.

Friday 20 October
Into the office by 07.45. At 08.30 we start our first SustainAbility staff meeting. Events are moving so fast that, even though we all work in an open plan office, people are wanting more information on our various projects.

Lunch with John Baker (new Chief Executive of National Power), Frank Ledger and Dr Peter Chester (now Director, Environment, at National Power). Baker has just joined Business in the Environment, set up by Business in the Community and chaired by IBM Chief Executive Tony Cleaver. A key objective: sustainable development.

At the lunch I warn that the 1990s will see a resurgence of eco-terrorism and a variety of non-rational, quasi-spiritual responses to the big environmental issues like the Greenhouse Effect. We have got used to Greenpeace-style actions, like yesterday's in Brussels: they plugged the city's two main sewer outfalls, protesting the pollution caused by the capital of Europe. But perhaps more suggestive of the pressures of the Nineties was the news from Cape Canaveral, Florida.

The Galileo probe, launched on Wednesday by NASA on a six-year journey to Jupiter, has left a swirl of controversy in its wake. Anti-nuclear activists had feared that an accident might spray Galileo's plutonium fuel from the skies. NASA has now confirmed that a computer virus has infected one of its networks, throwing up anti-nuclear messages on computer screens at NASA centres. One of these is: Worms Against Nuclear Killers. Interesting acronym. Computer 'worms' work their way through computer and telecommunication networks by looking for — and getting — passwords.

Last night Professor Deepak Lal condemned what he called 'eco-imperialists', during the 20th Wincott Lecture in London. He argued against sustainable development, which he described as 'immoral'. The concern about the Greenhouse Effect was hysterical, he said. Countries like the USA might suffer as a result of global warming, but the trend could well prove beneficial to countries like his own, India. Not the last time these views will be heard.

By contrast, a new book from Stephen Schneider, a senior climatologist at the US National Center for Atmospheric Research, stresses that: 'We cannot continue to use the atmosphere as a sewer without expecting substantial and potentially irreversible global environmental disruption.' In *Global Warming: Are We Entering the Greenhouse Century?*, he explains that a rise of two or three degrees in average temperatures *doubles* the chances of heat waves in large US cities — and of droughts in the American grain belt.

Saturday 21 October
Storms through the night. Spend most of the day in the office, working on *The Young Green Consumer's Guide* with Julia. As we sit in the studio, great showers of ash keys rattle against the glass roof. Looking up, one sees individual ash keys rotoring off against the rain clouds.

When I get back, help Elaine catch one of the rabbits, Muffin. Beautiful, gruff but allows herself to be won over. The rapport between people and animals can seem wonderfully close — but is it all on our side of the fence? Horrid piece in yesterday's *Times*, by Michael McCarthy. Spain, he reported, faces prosecution in the European Court next month over the use of baby chimpanzees by beach photographers. The animals are captured in the wild, with their mothers and other members of the troupe usually killed in the process.

'They are drugged, dressed in children's clothes and often have their teeth broken off to prevent them biting, before being killed as they reach adulthood,' McCarthy says. The complaint against Spain was brought by WWF, who estimate that eight chimps die for every one that ends up on the beach.

Japan, meanwhile, has done a U-turn on the ivory ban. Worried about international criticism, Japan — which accounts for 40% of world consumption of ivory — has joined the world trading ban. And Antarctic experts at the biennial Antarctica Treaty meeting in Paris decided on Friday to reconvene next year to consider declaring Antarctica a global nature reserve.

The USA, Britain and New Zealand support opening up the continent to 'regulated mining'. Environmentalists welcomed the decision. Said WWF's Cassandra Phillips: 'Antarctica gives us a permanent, unpolluted baseline against which to measure what else is going on in the world.'

Sunday 22 October
Unbelievably, rescue workers pull a survivor out of the earthquake-shattered ruins of Interstate 880, nearly four days after he was trapped in a concrete tomb. Latest figures suggest that the overall death toll may have been around 150, not the 250-300 originally feared.

During the week, Britain was — as usual — in a minority of one at the Commonwealth Conference in Malaysia as ministers met at the Langkawi Island resort. Alone out of 47 countries represented on a panel of foreign ministers, Britain refused to support the idea of a new fund for environmental protection and sustainable development.

India had pressed for a Planet Protection Fund, with all Commonwealth countries devoting 0.1% of the GDP to a new fund, which would have meant Britain paying £300 million a year. The eventual Langkawi Declaration simply 'takes account' of the proposals. A lost opportunity.

The week also saw Gro Harlem Brundtland resign as Prime Minister of Norway, to be succeeded by Jan Syse, leader of a coalition of conservative parties.

Back in the office with Julia, working on *The Young Green Consumer's Guide*. Massive black storm clouds, but little rain. Around the country, 13 people killed in storms, worst since 1987 hurricane.

Chris Patten, meanwhile, looks set to be caught up in a storm as FoE discover he plans to relax the time-scale over which Britain's water authorities will have to clean up their drinking water. The concessions are illegal under EC law. The water industry is sitting on something of an environmental time-bomb.

Captain Jacques Yves Cousteau under fire, with the impending publication of a less-than-flattering biography by Richard Munson, *Cousteau, the Captain and His World*. Cousteau is accused, for example, of stage-managing a fight between two giant octopuses for a film — by having divers throw the animals together in such a way that they had no option but to fight. 'We are going to destroy millions of childhood dreams with this book,' a spokesman for the publishers told *The Sunday Times*, with apparent relish. We shall see.

Monday 23 October
News breaks about Prince Charles's impending documentary on the environment, to be shown next May during One World Week. In the

programme, he says: 'It has become apparent to me that we need to develop a new vision of the Earth and of the role we human beings have as stewards of the Earth.' A coherent, credible, attractive vision of a green future is exactly what we need — and we shouldn't leave it to the Green Party to supply it.

One such is profiled in today's *Wall Street Journal*. American architect William McDonough designs buildings that have opening windows, tacked-down (not glued) carpets and avoid mahogany. He is now working on a project in Poland, the proposed Warsaw Trade Centre. If his plans are used, much of the steel and aluminium would be recycled from Warsaw's abundant rubble, while the lights which will make the building's spire glow would be solar-powered.

McDonough thinks of the new centre as the 'Eiffel Tower of Warsaw'. In the States, he and colleagues planted 1,000 acorns to more than compensate for oak used to build a Madison Avenue clothing shop. In Poland, if he has his way, a ten-square-mile forest would be planted somewhere in the country, with the centre's developer footing the $150,000 bill. The intending developer is a Polish American, Sasha Muniak. 'In Poland,' he says, 'there aren't too many people worried about the environment. They're more worried about bread on the table.'

St Ivel meeting in the morning, to discuss green packaging for their yoghurts — particularly a new brand which they intend to launch with organic fruit. Tell them there is no such thing as green packaging. If they want short-term impact, they should go the cardboard route. If they want a longer-term strategy, then they might combine the continued use of plastics with support for plastics recycling and an environmental sponsorship programme.

The Severn Tidal Power Group publishes proposals for a ten-mile barrage which could supply more than 6% of Britain's electricity. The project is now being presented as an answer to global warming. Among those already expressing alarm, the RSPB. If built, it is said, the barrage would become the second man-made structure — after the Great Wall of China — to be visible from space.

Meanwhile, the drought has reduced the flow in many rivers, and thus the dilution of pollutants, with the result that the Drax power station in Yorkshire — which supplies around 10% of Britain's electricity and is run by National Power — has apparently been showering sewage bacteria over nearby villages. Low water levels in the Ouse have resulted in a silting up of 12 cooling towers at Drax and the resulting fallout could cause sickness and diarrhoea.

One wonders whether National Power will turn up on the TSB's Environmental Investor Fund, chaired by David Bellamy. They have invested in Shell, even in the wake of the Mersey spill. 'There is no such thing as a green company,' Bellamy is reported as saying. TSB, in my view, are riding for a fall. In the early days of a new field like this, we should adopt the Caesar's wife principle. TSB has not.

Tuesday 24 October
The news breaks today that the Overseas Development Administration will press the International Tropical Timber Organisation next week to adopt a labelling system to show which tropical timbers have been felled as part of sustainable forestry programmes.

In the news: On the 33rd anniversary of the bloody uprising against Communist rule, the birth of the new, democratic Hungarian Republic was declared yesterday. We must get in touch with environmentalists in Hungary — and other East European countries. A Phillips chemical plant in Pasadena, Texas, was still burning last night after a series of explosions ripped through it 'like an atom bomb', creating a firebomb visible 15 miles away. 22 people reported missing.

Invited today to nominate potential candidates for the new Volvo Environment Prize, funded by the company to the tune of 20 million Swedish kronor. To be awarded annually, the award — the first prize will be worth more than one million Swedish kronor — will go to an individual who has carried out outstanding work in the field of environmental science or technology. Difficult. My mind immediately turns to people like James Lovelock and Lynn Margulis, who were responsible for the Gaia hypothesis, and Joe Farman, of the British Antarctic Survey.

Wednesday 25 October
Brilliantly flushed sky as the sun rises. Driving to Heathrow, the skyscrapers along the M4 shine gold — and straddling the motorway is some strange combination of cloud and rainbow. Fly to Brussels, arriving at the Hilton International at around 10.30. Seat in 'No Smoking' area, but the seating directly behind is smoking — and occupied by several Egyptians, smoking the heaviest, darkest tobacco. People like that should be asked to sit on the wings.

Speaking to a two-day conference on the European food and drinks market, organised by the Leatherhead Food Research Association. My speech is titled: 'Greens on the Menu: Environmental Pressures on New Product Development.'

There's a strong sense that Britain is ahead in a number of key areas of green consumerism. I take away the message that SustainAbility really does need to internationalise its operations, although there is a danger that 1992 could seduce us into thinking that the main opportunities will be in Europe. Some will, of course, but we should also be looking hard at Scandinavia, North America, Australia and Japan. One of the speakers notes that in the recent Wall Street crashlet, the Tokyo Stock Exchange went its own way for the first time. Japan really is coming into its own — and its political and cultural influence will inevitably grow as a result.

The Henley Centre for Forecasting publishes a survey which suggests that British consumers are now willing to pay 6% extra for 'ozone-friendly' aerosols or 'cruelty-free' cosmetics. One way or another, the idea that the consumer counts is taking hold at last.

On the way back to Zaventem airport, the taxi follows a car sporting a rear window sticker saying: 'L'eau est pollue . . . buvez du vin.'

Thursday 26 October
I chair a business roundtable at Brown's Hotel, Dover Street, organised by *Superstore Management International*. Those around the table include director-level people from Gardenstore, Payless, Texas and Sainsbury's Homebase. The proceedings were taped and we were continuously photographed, with the results to appear as an eight-page section in the magazine.

This evening I spoke to some 30 senior people from European business, including such companies as Henkel, General Motors and Ciba-Geigy. Organised by the European Research Council on Public Affairs. During the evening, Southern Electric — another regional electricity board — ask whether we would be interested in doing an environmental audit for them. They didn't know of our Manweb work. The Conference Board ask if I would consider organising an environmental programme for them.

During the dinner, Alan Watson, the broadcaster, announces that Nigel Lawson has resigned as Chancellor and that Mrs T's Cabinet is 'unravelling'. The news is fed in as the evening proceeds. Peter Smith, who was Chairman of Earthlife and runs a public affairs consultancy, City and Corporate Counsel, mentions that he saw something on us in the *International Herald Tribune*. The *Tribune* are co-organising next week's Rome conference with J Walter Thompson.

Friday 27 October
The Government in turmoil. John Major takes over as Chancellor. Among other moves: Virginia Bottomley leaves the DoE to become Minister of State for Health.

Couple of BBC people come in during the afternoon, to talk about the possibility of carrying out an audit of the BBC in the build-up to One World Week next year. They report that the Geldof spectacular planned for 1992 has folded. Pity: it would have been a tremendous opportunity to bring Global Villagers face-to-face with environmental problems — letting them watch the rainforests burn down in 'real time', for example.

In the news: The Highland Regional Council approves a scheme to expand skiing in the Cairngorms on to a site of special scientific interest — Lurcher's Gulley. The plan has been opposed by the NCC, the Countryside Commission and 14 other groups, who have joined together in a Save the Cairngorms campaign. The decision now goes up to Malcolm Rifkind, as Secretary of State for Scotland.

Extraordinary problem facing the Greens in Spain. The *Wall Street Journal* reports that a number of ersatz green parties have been set up to attract votes away from the genuine Greens. One group, the Green Ecologists (which also sports a logo very much like the sunflower used by the Green Parties proper), took nearly half of the 400,000 votes accounted for by the Green parties in the recent Euro-elections. Surveys suggest that as many as 700,000 Spaniards would vote Green, given another opportunity, but the confusion now prevailing cannot be helping.

Saturday 28 October
Harrowing, horrible description by John Pilger in the *Guardian* of a flight into Pnomh Penh. The year: 1979.

'My aircraft flew low, following the unravelling of the Mekong River west from Vietnam. Once over Cambodia, there appeared to be no one, no movement, not even an animal, as if the great population of Asia had stopped at the border.'

From April 17, 1975, which the Khmer Rouge dubbed 'Year Zero', anyone who owned a typewriter, telephone, fridge, even spectacles, became automatically suspect — and many were brutally clubbed or hacked to death in the 'killing fields'. Also buried there are Britons, Americans, Australians. As many as 1.5 million people were killed, one-fifth of the population.

'Year Zero' Pilger reminds us, was the dawn of an age in which there would be no families, no sentiment, no expression of love or grief, no schools, no books, no learning, no holidays, no music: only work and death.

One extraordinary image sticks in my mind. In 1979, Pilger saw roadside trees that had been lacerated with small knives and hoes, as if they had been attacked by a swarm of primeval insects. The Khmer Rouge had declared the trees 'guilty' of hiding the invading Vietnamese and had sentenced these 'colonial creations' (the French had planted many of the trees) to death.

At the back of my mind, there has always been an uneasy feeling that if our environmental problems continue to grow, we will see a similar Year Zero — on a much larger scale. Our comfortable modern world gutted, its stunned populations turned out into a countryside stripped of its romantic gloss.

In the 1970s, I wrote a piece for *The Ecologist* noting that when the crash came the survivors would be those who could kick off the old ways, breaking through the motorway barriers and driving out on the incoming lanes — instead of the jammed outward lanes.

The threat of complete collapse has receded, to my mind at least, but the collapse will come at some stage. The question is how long we can postpone it.

Sunday 29 October
In the news: The *Observer* reports that plans to develop a series of pressurised water reactors are under imminent threat. Nuclear reactors at Hinkley Point, Somerset, and Wylfa, Anglesey, and one at Sizewell apparently face the prospect of being scrapped. I wonder: wouldn't be surprised if we are using many of these aging reactors many years from now. Not an attractive proposition.

Interesting twist in the Rechem saga. 'Another Re-Chem mystery for Hercule Poirot,' reports John Sweeney in the *Observer*. 'Re-Chem fans will recall The Case of The Caldecotts' Vanishing Ducks, when ten of the family's 11 ducks vanished after PCB — the chemical which Re-Chem incinerates — was found in their eggs.' The latest development is that an air filter on Re-Chem's land has registered PCB levels ten times higher than average. The company claims that the filter 'had apparently been tampered with by party or parties unknown.'

The Bank of Credit and Commerce International's new GreenCard 'affinity' card is announced in *The Sunday Times* today. Each time a GreenCard holder spends £100 or more, BCCI will donate 30p to an environmental fund. BCCI also offers, inter alia, an RSPB card. Said I would need more information on BCCI before deciding whether to join the fund's panel — but am basically worried about the whole concept of encouraging people to use plastic money and credit. 'Trustees of the fund,' *The Sunday Times* says, possibly with tongue in cheek, 'include such well-known environmentalists as Anne Diamond and Derek Nimmo.'

Monday 30 October

At least eight people died in the weekends storms, which gusted to hurricane force in places. These storms are doing a great deal to convince people that we are moving into a greenhouse world.

Spend most of the day at the Royal Society of Arts, for the second in the RSA's series of 'Future Countryside' seminars. I chair the energy working group. The word 'sustainability' is used continuously, with the most interesting definition and comments coming from Paul Ekins, of the Right Livelihood Foundation. Sara Parkin is among those taking part — and, despite the fact that I have delivered her into the lap of the industrialist (see 1 June), even pours me a cup of tea.

Soviet heavy industry has a long way to go before it is sustainable. According to a report in *The Times*, it discharged about 40 million tonnes of poisonous chemicals into the atmosphere last year. And according to a new Government report, of 158 environmental clean-up projects ordered at the beginning of 1989, only ten have begun.

Fax of an article from Australia. It reports that Penguin has already taken orders for 70,000 copies of the Australian version of *The Green Consumer Guide* — 'a first edition record by Australian standards'.

Bryn Jones launches his Landbank Trust, set up to create 'environmental partnerships' with companies. Its first link is with Dychem, apparently a manufacturer of industrial cleaning products.

In the evening, Julia, Annie, Rebecca and I go across to the Institute of Contemporary Arts in the Mall, for the launch of a new environmental law group, CIEL (or Centre for International Environmental Law). CIEL, based at King's College, London, will use legal action to protect the environment. Despite my initial scepticism, I think it could play an important role.

Thought we would double the audience, but there is a long queue on the stairs up to the Nash Room. Lots of people we know.

Tuesday 31 October

The latest crop of Right Livelihood Awards — for which Paul Ekins is Research Director — will be announced on 4 December. The Honorary Award goes to the Seikatsu Club Consumers' Cooperative of Japan, a housewives' organisation which has created an alternative economy based on principles of cooperation, human contact and ecological sustainability. The Club, which aims to achieve 'Political Reform from the Kitchen', has grown exponentially since being founded in 1965. Some 170,000 families now belong, comprising some 500,000 people. Where the Club cannot source acceptable products, it makes it own. Among other things, it runs a couple of organic dairies. And as a symbolic gesture, it buys oranges from families afflicted with Minamata disease, caused by mercury pollution.

A different form of reward continues to pull top members of Her Majesty's Inspectorate of Pollution out into the private sector. The Government cannot but be embarrassed by the defection — announced today — of HMIP's Mike Thayer, who was appointed head of the Inspectorate's new Western Region on 1 October. Resigning his £31,000-a-year job, Thayer is going to British Steel. GREEN COP QUITS FOR DOUBLE PAY is the way *Today* sums up the news. The news will not have reassured environmental campaigners, who believe that HMIP is already too weak to police industry effectively.

Internationally, hundreds of Hong Kong ivory carvers are protesting that they will be driven into extinction by the ivory ban. Although they said that they supported elephant conservation, they also warned that 1,200 traders will go out of business in Hong Kong, and more than 2,000 carvers face unemployment.

NOVEMBER

Wednesday 1 November

Horror of horrors. An inventor is seeking sponsors for a vast solar-powered space clock, the first 'truly global advertising symbol', to orbit the Earth once every 103 minutes. The minute hand would be five miles long and, at a height of 560 miles, the clock would seem twice as large as the moon.

In to Holland Park for 08.30 meeting with Jane Bickerstaffe, previously Director of the Industry Committee on Packaging and the Environment (INCPEN). We are talking about organising a seminar next year on ways of boosting the environmental performance of the plastics industry. Then a Norwegian, Endre Sjovold, comes in to talk through the prospects for working together. He is helping Norway's rapidly expanding — and increasingly controversial — fish farming industry to work with environmentalists.

Finish the Shell UK proposal and then fly to Rome for the 'Lifestyle 2000' conference, organised by the *International Herald Tribune* and J Walter Thompson.

Once airborne, read the Dutch National Environmental Policy Plan, which precipitated the fall of Ruud Lubbers's Government earlier in the year. Equally significant, his continued support for the Plan did not stop him being re-elected. The aim is to slash pollution in Holland by 70% between now and the year 2010.

Given that it was produced by the Dutch Ministries of Economic Affairs, Agriculture and Fisheries, Transport and Public Works, and Housing, Physical Planning and Environment, the Plan is a mind-boggingly radical document. Farmers will have to cut their use of pesticides by 50% — and companies will need to cut their sulphur emissions, which cause acid rain, by 80%.

As the plane comes in to land, am skimming through a *Time* magazine supplement on Italy which points out that the country is the world's largest museum. It contains over 40% of humanity's artistic valuables, according to UNESCO. But it is also highly industrialised and criss-crossed with fume-hazed *autostradas*. This summer's Adriatic algal bloom underscored the sheer volume of sewage, industrial pollutants and fertilizers now pouring into the Adriatic.

Italy's population density — at 120 inhabitants per square kilometre —

is nearly double the continental average of 67. And tens of millions of tourists flood in every year. The natural and cultural heritage they come to see is under constant attack. For example, air pollution caused by traffic fumes, domestic heating systems and industry is corroding monuments, *palazzi* and churches.

Thursday 2 November

The conference kicks off with Anthony Sampson, author of such books as *The New Europeans* and *The Anatomy of Britain*. Born in 1926, he observes that we are living through an amazing and unique time. The apparent end of the Cold War is leading to the 'unfreezing of frontiers', which could help produce a huge burst of cultural energy across the continent. An expanded Europe, he says, could well become an exporter of lifestyles. He also forecasts another period of student unrest, but — surprisingly — says he doesn't expect to see more terrorist gangs along Baader-Meinhof lines. I disagree.

He does expect a third oil crisis, however. Professor Umberto Colombo disagrees. Colombo, who is chairman of ENEA (the Italian National Agency for Atomic and Alternative Energy Sources), is perhaps best known in the environmental movement as a Council member of the Club of Rome. A techno-optimist, he points out that we are 'investing resources' through the development of new technologies such as super-conductivity and biotechnology. Despite the futuristic tone of his speech, though, his intellectual centre of gravity seems to be very much in the 1960s and 1970s.

This matters, given that the centre of gravity of the world's exploding population is changing fairly rapidly. Bo Ekman, who has been a senior Vice President of Volvo and is now CEO of the Holengroup, makes this clear. Born in 1937, he notes that during his expected lifetime — 85 years for male Swedes — world population will have grown from around two billion to eight billion. From now on, the overwhelming bulk of the new population will be born in the developing countries. The typical global citizen is now a teenager living in the Third World.

Valery Giscard d'Estaing, now president of the LDR Group in the European Parliament, disappoints. He does his best to inspire, concluding: 'What we can propose is the adventure of building a new world'. But he fails to communicate any real vision of the way that European politics can rise to the extraordinary challenges of the 1990s.

Otto Schilly, who I would have been fascinated to hear respond to Sampson's comment about the Baader-Meinhof group (whose defence lawyer Schilly was, in the days before Baader and Meinhof committed suicide), is replaced by 66-year-old Dr Wilhelm Knabe, also a co-founder of West Germany's Green Party. They should have gone for Porritt, Parkin or Burke.

Knabe is old enough to have seen other sides of Europe, walking through the fire-bombed ruins of Dresden. The year I was born — 1949 — Knabe was already replanting trees in Saxony to make good post-war over-cutting. Not surprisingly, he is against weaponry, arguing that there is no bigger waste of intelligence, resources and energy than the world armaments industry. But, once again, he fails to spell out any vision of how we can begin to switch some of the $600 billion world arms budget into activities which provide genuine environmental security.

There is no question, though, that Knabe has fought a lifelong, uphill battle to ensure that the truth about acid rain and other similar issues was not sat upon by the West German Government. 'I was a trout swimming against the current of the stream,' he concludes. 'I hope you will do the same.' He attends one of the two tutorials I run in the afternoon, on industry's response to the environmental challenge. Asks to be sent more information on what we are doing. If the mood of the tutorials is anything to go by, the tide is now going in this trout's direction. None of the business people there question the urgency of the environmental challenge — their questions are about means rather than ends.

The pace of events is illustrated by the latest edition of *Which?*. Remembering the blank response we got from the Consumers' Association a couple of years back, it is rewarding to see that they are introducing a 'Green Guide' panel into their product test reports, aimed at Green Consumers.

In the evening, turn down a dinner invitation in favour of a two-hour solitary wander around Rome. The air is deliciously warm and the historic sites beautifully lit. Without a map, I find my way to the Piazza Colonna, the Piazza Venezia, the Imperial Fora and the Coliseum. Caught in the beams of the headlights of a passing police car, a cat's eyes flash silver in the Piazza del Campidoglio, designed by Michelangelo. Wonder whether its feline genes go back to Roman times? To the south-west, the Tarpeian Rock, from which traitors were flung.

Inevitably, one's imagination focuses on Rome's period of ascendancy. It is easy, for example, to forget the period around the 12th century when disputes between the Pope and the Holy Roman Emperor yet again triggered civil war. Many of the old imperial structures were turned into fortifications. The Forum, once the heart of the Empire, became a rudimentary sewage farm. Many of its statues and columns were fed into lime kilns to make chalk.

Circumnavigate the Coliseum. So late that the only other people there are several courting couples and a number of bag ladies. One arch contains literally scores of plastic bags, purpose unknown. The place's blood-soaked history is all-too-easy to recall — indeed sense — once you are away from the speeding traffic on the Via dei Fori Imperiali. When the Coliseum was inaugurated in 80 AD by Titus, Vespasian's son, the spectacle lasted for 100 days. After the racing and gladiators, men were pitched against wild animals. 5,000 animals died.

Christians were amongst those condemned to fight against wild animals and armed men in the Coliseum. A real jolt as I see a simple, tall cross framed in the eastern entrance tunnel — presumably in memory of those early martyrs.

Throat slightly sore as I walk back to the hotel. Traffic fumes. Across the algae-infested Adriatic, in Athens, the Government has just ordered emergency measures to combat heavy air pollution, after hundreds of people have turned up at hospitals with respiratory problems. Private cars have been banned from the city centre for 24 hours, schools have been closed and industrial fuel consumption cut by 50%. More positively, in the UK young people are being invited to take part in a national network for monitoring the quality of the country's air. The campaign is backed by Watch, the junior environmental club run by the Royal Society for Nature Conservation, the Science Museum and Volvo.

Friday 3 November
Breakfast with *Reader's Digest*, for an article on the greening of Europe. Next, interview with an Italian newspaper. Late in to session with Dr Gilbert Rapaille, a University of California professor who applies Jungian psychology to entire cultures. Companies, he suggests, increasingly need to operate on a 'glocal' basis, doing business globally — but taking account of local cultures. Interestingly, he predicts that these will become increasingly diverse.

Later, Professor Charles Handy gives one of the best lectures of the entire conference, on the future of work. He says that many of his students at London Business School are extremely responsive to our ideas. He predicts that by the year 2000, 80% of Europeans will be using brain skills, compared with 40% today, rather than manual skills. And at a time when talent will be in short supply, it will tend to go to 'preferred corporations' — which are seen to be ethical, successful and forward-thinking.

What sort of Europe will we end up with, wonders Larry Hasson, chairman of RISC US. If the worst came to the worst, we could end up with 'British pasta, German humour, Swiss bullfighting and the Italian army'. Individuals may now be more autonomous, which he sees as a positive trend, but there are worrying trends, too. The recent Euro-elections not only saw the rise of the Greens, but also of the extreme Right. Religions are bouncing back, too, particularly in Eastern Europe. Ecology groups, the extreme right and the churches, he points out, are all saying 'Protect our culture'.

We need to understand our history, he says. 'A people without memory is a people without history — and a people without history is a people without a future.' By no means coincidentally, the newspapers are full of the Poles' demands that the Russians own up to the 1940 Katyn massacre of some 15,000 Polish officers. A thousand candles flicker around a stone memorial in Warsaw. And the Swedes are pushing the Soviet Union to tell them what happened to Raoul Wallenberg, who — through sheer gall — rescued tens of thousands of Eastern European Jews from the gas chambers.

This evening to Le Grand Hotel, for the final dinner — and Peter Ustinov. Among the other guests is Gore Vidal, whose latest book, *Hollywood*, has just been published in Britain. Tinseltown, he says, has given cinema-goers 'another reality parallel to the one they've lived in'. When Peter Ustinov begins to speak, it is clear that he can see the new reality that is emerging in the midst of the world on which so many of the conference speakers remain focused. But the future, he says, remains unpredictable because it will be driven by individuals.

He quotes Ronald Reagan, the first Hollywood President, as saying that the only thing that would unite humanity would be an invasion of extra-terrestrials — but points out that global environmental problems could have something of the same effect. Ustinov, who among many other things is a roving ambassador for UNICEF, recently spent three hours with Mikhail Gorbachev. While he is cautious with his praise, he says Gorbachev is that rarity among great men — intelligent, forceful *and* a good listener.

But will we — and our planet — make it, even so? In *The Times* today, explorer Robert Swan recalls his recent 1989 Icewalk expedition to the North Pole. 'One day,' he says, 'we walked 20 miles, only to discover that the ice had been moving against us and we had travelled seven miles backwards. The ice-cap should never have been behaving like that. It was melting, and what we were experiencing was the power and revenge of nature.'

In September, *New Scientist* reported that the US Pentagon is hoarding sonar readings collected by submarines in the Arctic which would help scientists understand the ways in which the Greenhouse Effect is already causing the polar ice-caps to melt. Peter Wadhams, a scientist at the Scott Polar Research Institute announced that his own data show that ice in the Arctic has thinned substantially over the last decade.

Meanwhile, NERC reports that oceans may be absorbing only 30% of man-made carbon dioxide, rather than the 50% predicted by existing models. It looks as though the pace of environmental destruction may accelerate, however fast we push ahead.

In Sofia, a 35-nation European conference on the environment breaks up without agreement because of the intransigence of President Ceausescu of Romania. Despite pressure from Bulgaria and the Soviet Union, Romania still refuses to accept that individuals and environmental organisations should be allowed to voice their concerns about ecological issues.

Saturday 4 November

The taxi's windscreen wipers tick back and forth in the rain. The driver holds a steady 140 kph past *autostrada* signs insisting on 100 kph. The dull tangerine townscape shades into a landscape of quarry-pocked hills and cat's-cradle power-lines as we speed to the airport.

Work through the first chapters of the US edition of *The Green Consumer Guide* on the flight. One extraordinary fact: the waste plastic now floating around in the world's oceans and seas weighs more than the fish we catch each year.

One Mediterranean denizen, the small-snouted seahorse, has just turned up off Devon — and scientists are taking its appearance there as proof positive that the greenhouse is taking hold. 'I know one seahorse does not make a greenhouse summer,' as marine biologist Professor Alan Southward puts it. 'But I do think it is additional evidence that we may be seeing global warming coming in.'

And what about London's weather? The city has had more sunshine this year — 1,770 hours — than at any time since records began 60 years ago, in 1929.

In Antarctica, British scientists have found that this year's thinning of the ozone layer is even worse than in 1987, the worst year to date. The fear is that the ultraviolet radiation now streaming through the hole will damage Antarctic food chains, particularly those based on marine phytoplankton.

Once home, find a foot-deep stack of mail and eight newspapers. Nice review of *The Green Capitalists* in *The Times*. 'Suddenly the virtues of recycling and environmental protection have caught on for consumers and producers alike,' says Anna Bramwell. 'For this John Elkington and his colleagues must share much of the credit, and *The Green Capitalists* briefly and readably outlines a wide range of case studies where continuous pressure on large companies and governments, combined with specific and practical suggestions for solutions, have helped control some problems and head off others.'

The *Guardian* runs my piece on environmental auditing, which asks whether the privatised water and power industries will wake up to the need for auditing? Christopher Patten launched the Government's £5 billion water privatisation programme yesterday, claiming that the prospectus is 'a far-sighted work that is good for consumers and the rivers and seas around our coasts'. The water industry won't be able to get away with such sweeping claims for long. It will have to produce audited environmental performance results.

Monday 6 November
Much colder. Breath steaming out at bus-stop. Wear gloves as I walk in to office. Gordon Davidson of the US Social Investment Forum comes in, to talk about the Valdez Principles and environmental auditing. Companies are being invited to adopt the Principles, the tenth of which requires an annual environmental audit — with the results made public.

Meanwhile a new US report says that we are losing a staggering 100 species a day. The World Resources Institute, UNEP and IUCN are joining forces to launch a three-year campaign to find ways of slowing the process of species extinction. Launched on Monday, the report pinpoints 26 'hot spots', where species are being lost at a particularly worrying rate. They include California and Florida, the Cape province of South Africa, the Amazon, the Canary Islands, the dry forests of Central America and the tropical rainforests of Africa, Asia and north-east Australia.

Later in the morning, a couple of people from Novo Nordisk, the Danish biotechnology company, come in. They want us to help con-sumers understand the benefits of enzymes in laundry detergents. In West Germany, they say, products containing enzymes — which can boost energy efficiency — are advertised as green. Here, by contrast, green products advertise the fact that they do not contain enzymes. We decide to go across to Denmark early in the New Year to talk to some of their key health and environmental people.

Tuesday 7 November
In Brazil, the Government has threatened to bomb the jungle air strips used by an estimated 42,000 illegal gold miners, or *garimpeiros*. Some 450 light planes are being used to ferry the diggers and their gold in and

out of the Yanomami Indian reservation in Roraima state. The miners are threatening to stage sit-ins at the air strips. 'If they send the army,' said one of their leaders, 'we will fight back and Roraima will become a second Vietnam.'

Closer to home, some people may be worrying about what they had for breakfast. A ban has been imposed on milk from nearly 300 farms throughout the south-west, after lead-contaminated feed killed cattle. While being shipped from India to Rotterdam, the feed was apparently contaminated by lead sulphate. Milk which may have been contaminated has been on sale for at least a week.

Positive-ish news from Hungary, where the newly named republic has decided to scrap controversial plans to build a multi-billion dollar hydroelectric dam project on the Danube. 'Our dream has come true,' campaigners from the Danube Group told *Time*.

Wednesday 8 November
Wait ages for a bus in the drizzle and so arrive late at a BT meeting in Cloth Fair. With Guy Dauncey, interview the company's head of Building Management. We find that he has begun to set up BT's first 'environmental quality circle'. Both the BT people chain smoke and an hour-and-a-half later Guy and I emerge fumigated into the rain.

Dr John Adsetts of Albright & Wilson comes in to lunch — the first in our series of lunches involving outside speakers. Helen Holdaway and Peter Knight sit in. A good-natured and highly informative occasion. We also hear that — with PMA — we have landed the environmental audit contract for Stanhope Properties. Later in the afternoon, three people come in from Southern Electric and ask us to prepare an audit proposal for them. They have apparently cross-checked with Manweb — and had excellent reports on our capabilities. Gordon Jackson, who is running BT's recycled paper programme from Edinburgh, comes in at 18.30.

The big news story today is the resignation of the Government of East Germany, throwing the country into turmoil and further accelerating the flow of dissidents to the West. 194,000 have gone West this year, 31,000 since last Friday. At times it seems as if the whole Eastern bloc is on the point of unravelling in front of our eyes.

In New York, Mrs Thatcher outlines a broad strategy for tackling the Greenhouse Effect to the UN General Assembly. She spoke of 'the prospect of irretrievable damage to the atmosphere, to the oceans, to Earth itself', arguing that it is now as dangerous as the threat of war. She calls for 'a vast, international co-operative effort' to save the global environment. 'Mr President,' she concludes, 'the environmental challenge which confronts the whole world demands an equivalent response from the whole world. Every country will be affected. No one can opt out.'

About 20 industrialised countries have agreed to freeze the levels of greenhouse gases 'as soon as possible'. The US, Japan and the Soviet Union had held back from signing a declaration, because a deadline of the year 2000 had been suggested for achieving the freeze. Britain managed to broker the compromise. Carbon dioxide emission are growing by 3.6% a year and the 20 countries are also now urging a further 20% cut in emissions by the year 2005.

Thursday 9 November
THATCHER UN CALL FOR GLOBAL GREEN CRUSADE, is *The Times*' front-page headline. MAGGIE NERVE CENTRE FOR WORLD WAR THREE, is *Today*'s. FoE and the Green Party attack the Prime Minister, arguing that her speech was 'long on rhetoric, but short on urgent action'.

My day starts at Euston Tower, where I see a senior figure in British Telecom. His office is on the 25th floor. Looking east, across St Paul's, you can see an ochre-coloured haze, presumably caused by traffic fumes. This BT man had recently commissioned an internal report on environmental issues — and desirable responses. The young woman who prepared the report subsequently said that she was continuing to wake up other people in the company to the environmental challenge. She was told to desist, that the idea was not to 'go green'. Her report ended up in the bin. I'm amazed I was even told.

Later in the morning, I make my way to the top of Ladbroke Grove, to visit a new Sainsbury's store alongside the Grand Union Canal. Taken around with three other Better Environmental Awards for Industry assessors, John Dickinson (Managing Director, Varta), Heather Forster (Body Shop) and Ivan Hattingh (WWF). Later, we go down to Streatham to see the company's greenest store yet, which has involved refurbishing a historic silk mill. It also has an 'ozone-friendlier' refrigeration system. Sainsbury's 'Greencare' range of household products is already outselling Ecover's products 2:1.

Body Shop director Stuart Rose attributes the company's continuing rapid growth to its green image. At the end of the half year to the 31 August, The Body Shop reported pre-tax profits up 30%. In August, it had 121 shops in the UK and 287 overseas — which by October had grown to 130 and 304 respectively. Green growth?

The Government shelves its plans to privatise the nuclear industry. Lord Marshall, chairman of the CEGB, is resigning in protest. National Power, which he would have chaired, will lose 20% of its generating capacity.

Extraordinary news on the radio as tap away at the diary. East Germany has opened up the frontier between East and West Berlin. East Germans have been walking back and forth across the once uncrossable line, in tears.

Friday 10 November

1989 once again proves itself to be a watershed year. THE IRON CURTAIN TORN OPEN runs the front page headline in *The Times*. The first East German couple to test the new ruling opening their country's borders did so at 21.52 last night. They were simply waved through by the guards. The TV news this evening shows the bulldozers beginning to tear down parts of the Berlin Wall, long described in East Germany as the 'anti-fascist protection barrier'. Extraordinary to see History happen in this way.

The press is also full of articles on what many of the papers see as the nuclear power industry's impending demise. 'This is a huge victory for the environmentalists for political campaigners and for common sense,' says Humphrey Temperley, a Somerset county councillor and a leading figure in the campaign against the Hinkley C reactor.

Saturday 11 November

Bulgarian head of state Todor Zhivkov, the longest-serving leader in the Warsaw Pact has been toppled by the accelerating pace of change in Eastern Europe. Last week, *The Times* reports, 'crowds of up to 10,000 marched through Sofia using the pretext of an authorised ecology protest to call for democracy and *glasnost*. That political demonstration, which was without precedent both in its size and the nature of its demands, indicated that Mr Zhivkov's days as leader were numbered'.

His voice shaking, Cuba's President Fidel Castro said on Wednesday: 'We are witnessing sad things in other socialist countries, very sad things.' He seems to be in something of a minority at the moment.

A company which may soon be feeling similarly beleaguered is British Nuclear Fuels. It publishes a full-page colour ad in *The Independent* today — 'Just how green are you about nuclear power?' The main feature of the ad is a palette of greens, from Bamboo Green through to near-brown Fern Green. 'Once upon a time,' the copy runs, 'green was just a colour. Now it's a universal movement. And what shade of green you are says more about you than even class or status.'

The ad argues that you can be green *and* believe in nuclear power. Whatever happens, it is harder to imagine environmentalists clambering all over Britain's nuclear power stations, as East Berliners are over the

Berlin Wall, and trying to dismantle them with hammers they had brought in their pockets.

The *Financial Times* today profiles David Bellamy. He apparently believes that conservationists lost 'an immense amount of potential clout by not all holding hands together and saying "we are the experts, come to us for advice. We are not going to give it to you. We'll sell it to you"'. He explains: 'The growth industry is re . . ha . . bilitation. We smashed it all up. We can't afford to put it back. So therefore we have got to make the money to put it back.'

The smashing up continues. The mother ship of Japan's four-vessel whaling fleet has sailed for the Antarctic, where it is intending to kill 300 whales in the third year of a controversial 'research' programme.

David Cadman calls to say we have landed yet another contract with Stanhope, looking at the potential for an Eco-Park in Ealing.

Monday 13 November
Fog wreathes the city. Almost impossible to see where the fog ends and Barnes Pond begins — except for a scattering of black coots, seeming to float in the lower layers of the sky.

It is hard to imagine a time when the environmental revolution sweeps across the world and top industrialists and politicians feel they have to end it all because they cannot adjust to the new order. But it may be on the cards if events in East Germany are anything to go by. Over one million West and East Germans may have partied the weekend away around the perforated Berlin Wall, but others were less happy. The Communist party bosses in the towns of Bautzen, Kothen and Perleburg committed suicide.

On a smaller scale, freedom still seems some way away for two sick dolphins, Nemo and Lemo, rescued from a hotel swimming pool in Cairo. Flown to the Antibes Marineland Dolphinarium a year ago, they are in poor condition — too ill, according to a vet, to be flown to the USA to prepare for a return to the wild. Nemo was once part of a nightclub act at the Moulin Rouge in Paris, where he appeared in a 12 sq ft tank. His task: to strip a bikini from a female swimmer.

Stephen Ronaldson comes in at 08.00 to talk through contracts and other legal matters. Later, I work on a presentation for the London Business School tomorrow. Rebecca and I go across to British Telecom for lunch with Mike Bowtell, and meetings with Guy Dauncey and a couple of BT people — one of whom is responsible for spending the company's £3 billion procurement budget. Imagine the leverage if we could green even a proportion of that expenditure!

The Times reports today that IBM plans to raise millions of pounds to found the Cambridge Interdisciplinary Environment Centre — combining the resources of such institutions as the World Conservation Monitoring Centre, the International Council for Bird Preservation, the Institute for Terrestrial Ecology and the British Antarctic Survey, whose scientists first uncovered the Antarctic ozone hole. If the plan goes ahead, the expectation is that it could help Britain's chances of hosting the proposed European Environmental Agency.

The Association for the Conservation of Energy (ACE) reports that sales of energy conservation products actually fell by 12% in the past year. Given that the average British household produces 45 tonnes of carbon dioxide every year, a figure which ACE believes could be cut by 30% by energy efficiency measures, this is bad news indeed.

Sad news from the South Atlantic. The yacht *Creightons Naturally*, on the second leg (from Punta del Este, Uruguay, to Fremantle, Australia) of the Whitbread Round the World race, lost a couple of men overboard yesterday. One, Anthony Phillips, drowned. Many of the yachts are only a few hundred miles north of the Antarctic ice-cap, with sea temperatures of between 0°C and 2°C.

Wednesday 15 November
Start out with Stanhope meeting, then on to the CBI's headquarters at Centre Point, for a conference on waste minimisation organised by the DTI. Talk seems to go well: inundated with people afterwards. Julia and Rebecca go to the Greening the Boardroom conference. In his speech, Tom Burke apparently predicted that I would become the first environmentalist millionaire! It's amazing how far perceptions can part company with reality.

In the evening, call back Clive Wicks of WWF. Turns out that a number of people at WWF are spitting teeth about the way in which we have pressured them to publish our audits report. They protest that they are busy, too. How easy it is to fall out with people when you are all pressed to the limit. Clive has now been asked to get the report out. Hallelujah!

Sign of the times: *The Times* carries an ad for an Environmental Law Group Head, salary c. £60,000.

Friday 17 November
Morning post brings first issue of English edition of *China Environmental News*, the newspaper which was appointed to the UNEP Global 500 Roll of Honour this year.

It mentions that the giant panda, already threatened by the flowering and withering of the arrow bamboo on which it feeds, now faces an even more serious threat. As its habitat is destroyed, groups of pandas are losing contact with each other — and becoming increasingly inbred.

Professor Pan Wenshi of Beijing University says that in 80 years one such group will be so inbred that it will no longer be able to reproduce.

Richard Branson, waiting on the island of Kyushu, southern Japan, to launch his attempt to cross the Pacific by hot air balloon, may have to wait for a couple of weeks for the right weather conditions. The balloon got a Shinto blessing yesterday, *The Times* reports. 'Letting out wails like sirens and beating a 9ft drum, the white-robed priests waved holy branches over sacred offerings of food and a dozen slightly less sacred cans of Pocari Sweat.' The makers of this 'sports drink' are among the project's sponsors.

Back in Britain, the focus is on the hot air and carbon dioxide we all emit. The country's carbon dioxide emissions, which promote global warming, will increase 37% by the year 2005, according to the latest forecasts from the Department of Energy — even though we are committed to cutting them by 20%. By 2020, our emissions will have risen by 73%. Without nuclear power, it is hard to see how Mrs Thatcher expects to tackle the problem — except by emitting more hot air.

'These estimates assume a continuation of business-as-usual, just as if the Greenhouse Effect did not exist,' commented Andrew Warren, Director of ACE. 'They simply cannot be allowed to come true.' The logical step would be to increase the funding of the Government's own Energy Efficiency Office, whose budget has been frozen for three years.

Meanwhile, a small states conference in the Maldive Islands yesterday sent out an SOS to the industrial nations — pointing out that predicted sea-level rises produced by global warming would increase the intensity of hurricanes in the Indian Ocean and swamp them. 'Developing countries increasingly find themselves put in a position where they are made responsible for global environmental problems they did little to create,' said Sir Shridath Ramphal, Commonwealth Secretary-General.

In the back of my mind as I wait for the bus around 21.00, a few lines that popped unprompted into my brain in the middle of Sloane Street in 1971 or 1972:

The harder you work,
the closer you are
to buying yourself out of
the system you
are in the process of creating.

From today's perspective, the hard work in the environmental business never stops!

On the Eastern front, Erich Honecker was forced to resign from the East German parliament last night, signalling the end of the old regime. Also in the news this week, Deng Xiaoping, largely responsible for the Tiananmen

Square massacre, says he is retiring. Paradoxically, however, the collapse of the Iron Curtain is now causing concern among German environmentalists. The no-man's-land that formed the border between the two Germanies has become the haunt of many forms of wildlife, including sea eagles, black storks and bluethroats. Now, *The Times* notes, the German Federation for the Protection of Birds is calling for this 'paradise' to be declared a national park!

Saturday 18 November
The news breaks that Erich Honecker, the ousted East German leader, ordered troops to use 'all means available, including an order to shoot' to crush the first major Leipzig demonstration. The order was ignored, but shows how close the country came to repeating the Tiananmen Square outrage. The long-feared Ministry of State Security has now been disbanded. Meanwhile, in Prague, baton-wielding riot police have beaten demonstrators taking part in the biggest protest since 1969 — when the Dubcek Government was overthrown by the Russians.

Tomorrow I fly to Oslo for the Nordic Council of Ministers conference.

Monday 20 November
Conference goes well. One of the organisers turns out to be Sylvi Ofstad, a Norwegian who many years ago gave me a Hundertwasser poster headlined 'Save the Rain' — and which still hangs on my study wall. What seems to be freezing rain falls while the first speech of the day is under way. Great deal of interest in how we managed to get green consumerism off the ground in Britain.

As I come back through Heathrow, catch sight of the front cover of *The Listener*: 'Green Alert. Time Bomb or Global Panic?' The eight-page survey of greenery instances the 300,000-odd sales of *The Green Consumer Guide* as proof positive of the green wave sweeping through Britain.

The Nineties will be the decade of the environment, predicts Tom Burke. 'If we do not put ourselves on to the trajectory for sustainable development within that period, it will become ever more likely that we never will. Two traditions will compete for attention, the millenarian and the pragmatic. If the pragmatists fail to deliver a green orthodoxy for the public to choose, the public will choose the millenarians with all their ominous historical precedents.' I totally agree — and believe that as we approach the year 2000 the millenarians will come back with a vengeance, exploiting environmental issues to the hilt.

On the pragmatic front, Christopher Patten called for every company to prepare an environmental audit in his speech to the CBI's annual conference at Harrogate today. The CBI is also launching a survey of the environmental attitudes, practices and needs of British companies. PA will be doing the work.

In the evening, watch a video of 'The Flooded Forest', a Partridge film showing the annual flooding of large areas of the Amazonian rainforest for months on end. Extraordinary footage of fruit-eating fish swimming through the canopies of giant trees, a sloth doing a passable crawl and a strange breed of white dolphins which are protected by local fishermen, even though they 'steal' fish from the nets.

Tuesday 21 November
The Queen's Speech to Parliament highlights the Government's Green Bill, to be published before Christmas. From waste disposal to genetic engineering, the evidence suggests that the pressures on industry are likely to intensify.

President Ceausescu of Romania, now 71, up to his old tricks again yesterday. He opened a Communist Party congress with a speech lasting more than six hours — punctuated with 67 carefully orchestrated standing ovations. *The Times* notes that all typewriters have to be registered in the country, to enable the tracing of all letters and pamphlets. Romanian newspapers and TV have not yet reported the fall of the Berlin Wall. There is a sense that the Ceausescus are sitting on a chair which has had all its legs sawn off — but no one has noticed yet.

China's birth control programmes have apparently been disrupted by the recent turmoil. Some contraceptive factories are working only three days a week because they cannot get raw materials.

This evening on to the Museum of Mankind for an event organised by the Gaia Foundation — and built around Dr Martin Hildebrand. He is Colombia's Head of Indigenous Affairs and personal adviser to President Barco. The Colombian Government has handed over a total of 18 million hectares of Amazon rainforest to the Indians — half of Colombia's Amazon, an area almost the size of the United Kingdom.

Actor Jeremy Irons introduces Hildebrand with a powerful speech. He notes that the collapse of the Peruvian fisheries, the opening up of the ozone hole and even the collapse of the Iron Curtain have been examples of the 'flipover effect' — in which systems change from one state to another in an unbelievably short space of time. He — and Jose Lutzenberger — believe that the same could happen soon with the Amazonian rainforest, with dire implications.

Hildebrand talks for perhaps 45 minutes as a spokesman for his Government. Then he removes his coat and tie and speaks in a personal capacity. He describes the way the Indians in the area where he worked initially fought off the rubber traders and then were faced, in turn, with the coca traders.

He paints a reasonably optimistic picture, but the growing power of the drug-traffickers is illustrated by a news story that appears on the front page of *The Times* today. The professional football season has been cancelled in Colombia after drug-traffickers had a referee murdered last week, because of his role in a match which ended in a disputed result that hit the traffickers — who invest in football clubs and bet heavily on the results.

Later, find myself discussing the future of rainforests with a group of people, just in front of a massive, eerie statue from Easter Island brought back to this country in 1868.

Wednesday 22 November
The Green Party has responded to the Queen's Speech with its own version. 'A few bolted-on environmental policies are not going to save the world,' spokesperson Liz Crosbie said. 'They can sugar coat the cyanide pill, but in the end the result is the same.' The *Daily Mail* makes much of the fact that the Queen 'would be stripped of Sandringham and Balmoral if the Greens came to power,' Sean Ryan writes. 'Her historic holiday retreats could be turned into flats.'

Spend the day at Britannic House West, with BP. The company had decided to open up its rainforest audit to a selected group of environmentalists and environmental specialists. They included representatives of FoE, IUCN, WWF and the Living Earth Foundation. Koy Thompson of FoE noted that he and other campaigners have been blacklisted in certain countries because of their efforts to slow the pace of rainforest destruction.

BP had already been working on its rainforest audit when *The Sunday Times* published its story on the company's Amazonian tin-mining operations. 'We planned to have an orderly procession of events,' Bill Syratt said, with a final report out in January 1990. But, 'when the shit hit the fan,' the process was accelerated sharply — with the final report being completed by October.

The seminar works well, with a succession of presentations by BP people and others. It falls to me to sum up at the end of the day — a difficult task, given the range of presentations. Clive Wicks of WWF, for example, reported on the latest progress on the Korup project in Cameroun, the test-bed for sustainable use of rainforest resources. New attempts are being made to value the uncosted services such forests provide. Clive noted that a new study of Korup suggests that it is worth $70 million simply as a carbon store alone, while the forests in the region also help keep offshore fisheries worth more than $10 million a year healthy.

Mark Collins of IUCN pointed out that by the middle years of the 21st century, four out of five humans will live in tropical forest countries. The oil industry may produce some fairly substantial impacts on the world's rainforests, but it is clear that those impacts will be dwarfed by those caused by these exploding Third World populations.

Roger Hammond of Living Earth reports that one group of Malaysians they trained recently seemed very confused about the Greenhouse Effect. They were shocked to see so many greenhouses in Britain — and apparently suggested that they should be demolished, to cut down global warming.

Isabelle went to the launch of a new study on global warming by the California-based International Project for Sustainable Energy Paths (IPSEP) today. Funded by the Dutch Ministry of Environment, the study warns that the pace of global warming is such that many forests could simply die — unable to adapt to the new climatic conditions. The rate of warming should not be allowed to exceed 0.1°C per decade, the study concludes.

Thursday 23 November
Arthur Kenny and I are visiting ICI Chemicals & Polymers, to see Richard Pocock, Director of Safety, Health and Environment. ICI has made enormous progress, with new environmental reporting links and auditing activities being introduced. But they still have a very long way to go.

The front cover of C & P's environmental report for 1988 sports a picture of scores of carp. It turns out that these fish thrive in the warm effluents from an ICI outfall on the River Weaver. Some are as big as small pigs. Indeed, there was one public complaint that there had been a oil spill in the Weaver — which turned out to be simply the heaving black backs of the shoaling fish.

Later, we are driven across to see ICI's FM21 chlor-alkali cells, which dispense with mercury and asbestos — and produced chlorine and caustic soda much more energy efficiently than the traditional mercury and asbestos cells. ICI is a strange mix of the cutting edge in technology, and environmental perceptions firmly rooted in the 1970s.

In the heap of post, an invitation to the latest NCC advisory committee meeting. *The Times* reports today that the Government is now thinking of announcing plans for a new body to oversee nature conservation in England, Scotland and Wales. The Government is moving quickly, worried that the uproar over the NCC's future could sour the debate about the soon-to-be-announced Green Bill.

Also a letter from Richard Caines of the Marine Conservation Society suggesting a joint MCS/SustainAbility campaign on plastic pollution of the coastline and seas. After our experiences on the Aquitaine coastline, I am very keen that we take up the offer. But it remains to be seen whether we can find the time.

Sunday 26 November

We must get on with *The Green Holiday Guide*. Not only is the phrase used in the latest issue of *Green* or *Environment Now*, but the *Observer* is now planning a new 'Travel Watch' series, a campaign to raise awareness of the effects of tourism on the environment. Our guide will be different, whenever it appears, but there is a tide a-building.

Late morning, we drive across to Richmond Park, under an astonishing winter-blue sky. The lakes are covered in a fairly thick layer of ice. People are skipping shards of ice across the shining surface: they hiss and chirrup their way over an amazing distance. Am sure the water fowl on the islands are not amused.

What we call the Secret Pond, to which I have taken the children in all seasons for years, has all but disappeared in the drought. We wonder what has happened to all the animals we have seen there, including the newt that played for ages under the water with a sparkling bubble of air. The girls recall the oaks coming down in the hurricane — the next day we found a bat colony struggling out of the ruins of one great tree. I extracted one and released it into the twilight. Strange feeling.

David Bellamy launched Plantlife this week, a new conservation group dedicated to plants. Professor Ghillean Prance, director of the Royal Botanic Gardens at Kew, explained: 'Plants are not cuddly like a panda or big bear, and they have been neglected in conservation. But they are vital for the future of life on earth.'

Interesting profile on David Puttnam in *The Sunday Times* today. It focuses on his role as President of the CPRE, whose membership has soared. In the past 18 months it has gone from 30,000 to 44,000. Puttnam takes none of the credit. 'Nicholas Ridley was the best membership secretary we ever had,' he says. 'They absolutely flooded to us.'

A petition was delivered today to No. 10 Downing Street, signed with muddy paw-prints. It is part of the protests against the official visit to Britain this coming week of South Korean President Roh Tae Woo. The protests are against the shameful treatment of dogs in his country. Some two million are eaten every year. What particularly angers the activists, however, is the way the dogs are killed. They are hanged from beams, with their back paws just touching the ground. Then they are beaten to death as they slowly asphyxiate. The Koreans apparently believe that their agonies tenderise the meat.

And in Holland an animal feed maker is to claim £3.2 million in damages from a West German grain trader over lead-poisoned cattle feed which has affected some 1700 cows in The Netherlands and Britain. Over 100 cows have already died and the vulnerability of the food chain has been horribly exposed.

Richard Branson has postponed his hot-air balloon crossing of the Pacific until next year, following overnight frost damage to his craft.

Monday 27 November
Spend day at IBC 'Green Strategies for Business', where I am in the chair. Speakers like Mike Cohen of the DTI's Business and Environment Unit, Tom Burke, Brian Clarke (who has pioneered in the field of environmental impact assessment for around 20 years) and people from companies like Volvo, IBM, Shell. The audience turns out to be very stodgy and have to work very hard to stimulate questions. Confirms opinion that we should throttle back on the number of conference invitations we accept, although the diary for next year is already filling up at the most amazing rate.

No one needs convincing, however, that the green pressures on business will persist, even if there is a recession. Item: a green tax may be imposed on fossil fuels to pay for the pollution they cause, Chris Patten said yesterday. He admits that the whole question of energy costs and fuel costs is inevitably going to be a central part of any market-based approach to the environment. He is also considering road pricing as a way of controlling traffic congestion — and possibly even a new policy on out-of-town hypermarkets, which promote unnecessary motoring. But there is many a slip 'twixt cup and lip.

Less positively, *The Times* reports that the Government's Pollution Inspectorate has failed to prosecute a single water authority during the more than two years it has monitored water pollution. An official attributed this weak-kneed performance to fears of jeopardising water privatisation. In contrast, the new National Rivers Authority has already announced prosecutions against Shell and Yorkshire Water, with more cases in the pipeline.

Today announces that British Airways have appointed 50-year-old Dr Hugh Somerville, previously with oil companies Occidental and Shell (where I came across him), as its Mr Green — at £60,000 a year.

Julia reports that *The Australian Green Consumer Guide* has already sold 63,000 copies and is in the bestseller lists there. She also has advance proofs of *The Young Green Consumer's Guide*, together with some of the watercolour illustrations. They are fantastic.

Annie has a successful meeting with Air Call and Richard Speir of The Gaia Quest Trust, the marine conservation group who could be in line to receive funds raised by the Air Call 'Greenline' telephone service. 70% of ocean life lives in only 6% of the ocean's area — the shallow inshore waters. Speir plans to build one of the world's largest catamarans, the *Gaia Quest 2*, to provide a platform for ecological research in the Indian Ocean. Part of the funding would come from two annual 17-day natural history tours or diving charters. Our own Gaia is already keen to go! A good case study for our green holiday book.

Wednesday 29 November
Stand in the bus queue, with breath steaming out for yards around. A heron stalks in slow motion across the ice on the pond. On reflection, the second day of the IBC conference was dramatically better.

Several of the papers carry the news that green campaigners are suffering from severe stress. 'Worried activists are becoming so depressed by the world's plight that they are suffering from burn-out,' says *Today*. A new course designed to help people suffering from green burn-out has been launched at the Health Hydro in Swindon. Considerable comment in the office. Interestingly, David Pearce's new book *Blueprint for a Green Planet* includes a definition of 'sustainability' as the 'ability to maintain some activity in the face of stress'.

In a new report on the Greenhouse Effect by the House of Lords Select Committee on Science and Technology, the peers predict that one result of atmospheric change could be an increase in anticyclones over Western Europe. 'It is therefore conceivable that the British Isles could become colder in winter, with a larger number of heavy snowfalls, and drier in summer with an increased frequency of droughts.'

Begin day at the RSA, judging the final shortlist of entrants for the Better Environment Awards for Industry. Hadn't had time to write my reports, so had to scribble frantically and give verbal reports on ICI and Sainsbury's. Recommended that Sainsbury receive an award — and it is among the six winners. Unfortunately, it looks as though I shall be in Canada when the awards are announced next March.

Ted Turner, the US media magnate, has launched a new award scheme in the States for writers addressing the theme of how we can combine survival and prosperity. 'We're floundering around as a species right now,' he told *Time* magazine. The winner will receive $500,000, the largest-ever prize for a work of fiction.

Meanwhile, in Colorado, three of America's super-wealthy families are at each others' throats. The Bass family of Fort Worth, Texas, are investing at least $50 million in what they hope will be the world's most modern intensive pig farm, National Hog Farms. They are being opposed by the Coors and Anschutz families.

Joseph Coors and Philip Anschutz, the *Guardian* reports, are billionaires too, and are suing National Hog Farms — on the basis that the prospect of 300,000 pigs pumping 2 million gallons of pungent porcine effluent into the scenic South Platte river every day will be environmentally devastating. National Hog Farms counter-claims that the proposed 25,000-acre plant will be the most eco-friendly hog-raising facility on the planet.

In Britain, Agriculture Minister John Gummer announces that straw burning will be banned from the 1992 harvest. Some five million tonnes of straw were burned this year, according to the National Society for Clean Air. The filth that floats over the countryside is indescribable, while the damage caused to hedgerows and trees has to be seen to be believed. It's amazing how farmers still have something of the Farmer Giles image, at a time when their operations are more like those of chemical-spraying robots.

European Community environment ministers have endorsed plans to create a European environmental agency — and have said they would be prepared to include countries from Eastern Europe. Although Britain wants the centre for Cambridge, Berlin would perhaps be a more potent symbolic location. And a new report from the Panos Institute, *Banking the Unbankable*, argues that the environmental clean-up of the Eastern bloc countries will be funded at the expense of aid to Africa and the rest of the Third World.

This is a very real problem, given that the distribution of aid is essentially a political process. Will we see parts of Africa drop off the aid map in the 1990s?

Thursday 30 November
Heavy frost. As I walk to the station, spot magpie sitting on a chimney-pot, warming its bottom.

Talk about stress! Annie's sheet of instruction sends me by train to Reed at Quadrant House, Sutton, when I should have been at The Quadrant, Richmond. Arrive over an hour late for the meeting, which I had been meant to kick off. A number of senior people from Reed in the USA and Canada have come over to pick up on emerging trends in Europe. Today's theme is the environment. I am so full of adrenalin by the time I get to Richmond that I give them both barrels — a future vision woven of a Greater Europe, the Greenhouse Effect and (an almost inevitable trend) eco-terrorism. By the end, their eyes are out on stalks. But they seem to take the key messages on board.

Because of the Reed meeting, fail to make the launch of the £35 million Merlin International Green Investment Trust (MIGIT), managed by Jupiter Tarbutt Merlin. Tessa Tennant, meanwhile, is having major problems with Jupiter Tarbutt — who have apparently sat on the report on the environmental implications of water privatisation which was to have gone out under Merlin's name. The firm's Managing Director, Michael Heathcoat-Amory, may be nervous about upsetting the Tories. His brother is David Heathcoat-Amory, appointed junior Environment Minister on 27 October. Instead, the report — commissioned by WWF — had to be published by Media Natura. WWF, not surprisingly, are incensed.

DECEMBER

Friday 1 December
The news breaks that West Germany's Red Army Faction (Rote Armee Fraktion, or RAF), whose roots go back to the Baader-Meinhof Group, have assassinated Alfred Herrhausen — one of the country's leading business figures. A remote-controlled bomb attached to a bicycle tore apart his bullet-proof Mercedes. Herrhausen, who headed the Deutsche Bank, had been involved with the Bank's £950 million bid for Morgan Grenfell, launched four days ago.

We discuss the cycles of history and the prospects for the re-emergence of RAF/Red Brigade-style terrorism in Europe. I see a strong likelihood that some terrorists will try to 'green-badge' their activities in the 1990s, claiming to be fighting for the environment when, in fact, they have other priorities.

In the Philippines, Mrs Corazon Aquino appears to have fought a sixth attempted coup to a standstill, with help from American warplanes.

The Czechs announce they will open their barrier with Austria, opening a new hole in the Iron Curtain. Mikhail Gorbachev has denounced the Soviet role in the 1968 crushing of Czechoslovakia's 'Prague Spring'. East Germany, too, has apologised to the Czechs.

Speaking in the Campidoglio in Rome, where he has been talking with the Pope, Gorbachev said yesterday: 'In the final analysis, we envision Europe as a commonwealth of sovereign democratic states with a high level of equitable interdependence and easily accessible borders, open to the exchange of products, technologies and ideas, and wide-ranging contacts among peoples.'

Once that would have been a significant statement from a Soviet President. Today, it sounds like little more than an acceptance of the facts. Europe is changing rapidly — and will probably emerge as a dominant influence in the 21st century.

A difficult year, though, for the UK nuclear industry. John Collier, chairman of Nuclear Electric — the new company set up to manage Britain's nuclear power industry once the electricity industry is privatised — says he plans to build more nuclear stations once the Government's five-year nuclear freeze ends. He sees the threat of global warming, with coal-burning power stations responsible for perhaps 30% of Britain's annual carbon emissions, as a strong argument for further nuclear investment.

Saturday 2 December
Following the defeat of Rajiv Gandhi's Congress Party, Vishwanath Pratap Singh has been named as India's new Prime Minister. Meanwhile, exactly five years after the Bhopal disaster, Indian official estimates put the death toll at 3,150. The leak of deadly methyl isocyanate gas from Union Carbide's chemical plant occurred on the night of 2 December 1984. The official estimates say 30,000 people were left with permanent total or partial disability, and there were another 20,000 temporary cases. Another 50,000 people, it is claimed, suffered minor injuries. But new estimates reported in the *Guardian* suggest that as many as 500,000 people could be injured, disabled or disturbed.

The MIGIT prospectus appears in the *Financial Times*. Who, even a couple of years back, would have expected to see the launch of a £35 million investment trust whose prospectus included such headings as 'The Greening of Industry'? The Bhopal disaster — and the subsequent difficulties experienced by many companies in getting environmental impairment liability insurance — is given as an example of the way in which environmental pressures on business are intensifying.

Tessa Tennant rings during the morning. Apparently the *Observer* is sniffing around the Merlin/water privatisation story. Suggest that the Environmental Advisory Committee should meet quickly to review our position. Later in the day, talk to Nigel Haigh and Robin Grove-White. Given that the privatisations of water and power are the most environmentally significant investment issues of the day, we cannot afford to be deflected by City peer pressure from highlighting these issues.

All media eyes are currently on Malta, where the Saltwater Summit between Presidents Bush and Gorbachev is now under way. With the weather deteriorating rapidly, the water had a nasty chop even in Grand Harbour. The security is intense. The *Guardian* reports that there are 'so many electronic beams and sensors pumping microwaves through the waters of Marsaxlokk Bay that the locals tell you the fish are cooked before you catch them'.

Sunday 3 December
Ferocious winds and pounding seas conspired to keep Presidents Bush and Gorbachev ship-bound yesterday afternoon, Bush aboard the *USS Belknap* and Gorbachev aboard the *Maxim Gorky*.

And the *Observer* tries to make waves with its piece on Merlin's water privatisation report. The Heathcoat-Amory axis pour cold water on the conspiracy theorists. 'I have no idea what my brother does,' says the

DoE's David, of Jupiter Tarbutt Merlin's Michael. 'I have never heard of this report,' is Michael Heathcoat-Amory's line, 'and if I had I would certainly have been very careful not to interfere in any way.'

Nigel Haigh rings during the morning to say that he is writing both to Michael Heathcoat-Amory and Tessa to establish the facts of the matter. Both Robin and I support the move and feel that we really must ensure that Tessa is given greater freedom of manoeuvre.

Monday 4 December
The Cold War is over, Bush and Gorbachev announce. 'Tonight,' said President Bush yesterday, 'we stand at the crossroads of history, on the way to a Europe whole and free.' The signs are certainly hopeful, but wonder whether Bush won't be seen as the late 20th century version of Neville Chamberlain at some future date?

The world is changing, however. A lump of masonry now sits on Rebecca's desk — a piece of the Berlin Wall brought back this morning by Paul Scott, a colleague at Brand New. He reports that people are attacking the Wall from all sides, with everything from hammers to pneumatic drills.

In East Germany, the Politburo and Central Committee have resigned. Despite the breaching of the Berlin Wall, Egon Krenz does not appear to have won the country's confidence. A senior member explained that the Politburo accepted that it was not capable of laying open the full extent of the errors committed by the previous leadership, nor of drawing the correct conclusions from this. 'We accept this criticism and resign unanimously.' In Czechoslovakia, the Civil Forum has rejected the new Government just announced there as totally unacceptable.

Julia spends the morning at the Business and Industry Panel for the Environment awards, where Chris Patten makes a speech touching on, among other things, green consumerism and environmental auditing.

We are seeing a tremendously important shift in attitudes taking place, driven in large part by a generational shift. Younger people are coming up at every level of society, bringing with them a new green awareness. This trend is particularly noticeable in business, where a younger generation of managers is opening up to the outside world, just like the Eastern bloc countries.

According to a new study from the Henley Centre of Forecasting, the 'intoxication of hedonism' which marked the 1980s, when greed was good, will give way to a 'hangover of guilt' in the 1990s. Consumers will be 'anxious, guilty, lost souls', appeasing their consciences by spending their money on ecologically-sound products and charitable causes.

A new report on the Greenhouse Effect is published by the Royal Institute of International Affairs, based at Chatham House. It suggests that every country should be given a permit for carbon dioxide emissions, which it could trade internationally. Developed countries would have to buy permits to emit carbon dioxide from the developing countries. The currency of exchange would be limited to development and pollution abatement programmes, and related transfers of technology and expertise. A good idea — and relatively easy to implement technically. Politically, though, it sounds like quite a challange.

Victoria Cliff-Hodges of FoE — and Director of Arts for the Earth — comes in to lunch. It looks as though there will be a number of initiatives launching next spring which aim to green schools. We shall be talking to FoE's people in the coming weeks to ensure that any overlap is kept to the minimum. But it's great that young people will get strong encouragement to go green at the dawn of the 1990s.

Can people like Victoria, who says she often gets only two to three hours of sleep a night, expect to find things calming down a bit? The Henley Centre believes the 'hurry sickness' of the 1980s will give way to a much more relaxed lifestyle. Victoria, in fact, leaves FoE next summer — and is thinking of launching a new arts and environment centre in London. Doesn't sound too restful.

Tuesday 5 December
GREEN CHIEF SUICIDE blares a headline which takes up about a third of the front page of *Today* this morning. Brian Ponsford, Director of Her Majesty's Pollution Inspectorate and reporting directly to Chris Patten, killed himself with his car's exhaust fumes. His job, which might once have seemed fairly uncontentious, became a searing hot-seat once the green wave stared to build.

Ponsford and his staff have been caught between rising expectations and the Government's long-standing unwillingness to put the necessary resources behind environmental protection. That position may be on the verge of changing, but the disarray of HMIP is an indictment of Mrs Thatcher's management of this area to date. Three of Ponsford's senior staff had already left for jobs in industry — and Ponsford, who I last met three years ago, was criticised in the press.

Early meeting with the Commercial Union, at which we agree to submit a proposal. They want help in screening companies which they are thinking of investing in. They are looking for a long-term relationship, with regular briefings for their senior staff on environmental trends and opportunities. [ERL ultimately won this contract.]

Julia goes across to the DoE/DTI meeting on green labelling, attended by Ministers David Heathcoat-Amory and Eric Forth. It looks as though an announcement will be made shortly that the Government will back a cradle-to-grave labelling scheme — which is what most environmental groups have been calling for.

In the evening, Isabelle and Rebecca go to listen to Davi Kopenawa Yanomami, who has become the leading spokesman for Brazil's 10,000 Yanomami Indians. He has met the President of Brazil three times over the last five years, in an attempt to get the Yanomami area recognised as a protected 'Indian park'. It has been invaded by 50,000 illegal gold miners — and the Indians are being killed in armed confrontations and dying of imported diseases. Davi Yanomami has left Brazil for the first time to accept the Right Livelihood Award, dubbed the 'Alternative Nobel Prize' on behalf of the winners, Survival International.

Wednesday 6 December
And now the Pope. 'The increasing devastation of the world of nature is apparent to all,' he says in a new publication, *Peace with God the Creator, Peace with all of Creation*. 'It is the result of a callous disregard for the hidden and perceivable requirements of the harmony which governs nature itself.' Attacking 'selfishness, greed and disregard for nature in industrialised countries', he argued that modern society will find no solution to the ecological problems unless it takes a serious look at its lifestyle. He is calling for a right to a safe, clean environment to be part of a new Charter of Human Rights.

Welcome, as far as it goes. But with population pressures now proving the most important driving force behind the wave of environmental destruction, the real test of the Vatican's commitment lies in the area of birth control — which Pope John Paul has repeatedly said he is totally against. As long as Catholicism stands against birth control, it must be seen as a major part of the problem.

Egon Krentz has stepped down as East Germany's head of state. The Government is appealing for calm. Palpable sense of unease in the West as something of a power vacuum begins to open up in this critical part of Eastern Europe.

Commercial Union announces launch of its Environmental Screening Service and its Environmental Exempt Pension Fund. Julia speaks to a Marketing Society conference. At lunch, a man from Citroën tells her that three years ago the company decided to turn its back on the environment, as the preserve of long-haired, leather-sandaled hippies. It is now stunned by developments in Britain and elsewhere — and is urgently considering what to do next.

Midland Bank ring during the day to see whether we would be able to carry out an environmental audit of their operations!

Thursday 7 December

Crashing space-classical music echoes around the Queen Elizabeth II conference centre in Westminster as the Russians launch their 'Earth Mission 2000', billed as 'A Soviet Commercial Blueprint for Planet Management'. As I ride up in a lift along with a number of voluble Russians, it is clear that *glasnost* and *perestroika* are now affecting our world, too. Shivers run down my spine as slides of spiral galaxies and of the Earth rising are flashed up on a massive screen, to the strains of Richard Strauss's *Also Sprach Zarathustra* and Johann Strauss the Younger's *An der schonen blauen Donau (The Blue Danube)*.

Thick Russian accents pumping out endless technical achievements make for difficult listening, but it is clear that Glavkosmos, the Soviet space agency, is waking up to the export potential of the new concept of 'planet management', a concept which Norman Myers, myself and others at Gaia Books, outlined in the *Gaia Atlas of Planet Management*, published in 1986. The Russian faces are deeply, deeply serious, almost Brezhnev-like, but every so often a startling flash of humour breaks through. It's strange how much less ominous the hammer and sickle seems these days.

Julia sits on the jury for the FoE's 'Green Con of the Year' awards. Perhaps not surprisingly, British Nuclear Fuels wins for its 'Shades of Green' ad. (see page 236).

In the news: Ladislav Adamec, Czechoslovakia's Prime Minister, resigns. And in Britain, Cabinet Committee Misc. 141, chaired by Mrs Thatcher, met today for the first time — the beginning of the process which will produce the White Paper on the environment next year and, if Christopher Patten gets his way, the greening of Whitehall.

Saturday 9 December

Norman Tebbitt warned yesterday of a possible 'witch-hunt' of companies by managers of ecological funds! Speaking at a seminar on ethical investment organised by Abbey Life, he said that undue pressure would do little to encourage companies to change their stance on the environment.

'There is a nasty touch of McCarthyism developing in some of the enquiries being made to companies,' he said, according to *The Times*. 'Some of these enquiries go right over the top and lose touch with the basic business with which managers of the funds should be concerned.'

Clearly, ethical investment is beginning to rattle the City. Indeed, the *Financial Times* reports today that Shell (the name isn't used, but the clues are clear) has rung up Tessa Tennant at Merlin and demanded 'to know why its shares are not included in (Merlin's) portfolio'. The article also reports, as Tessa told me last night, that MIGIT has already attracted applications from institutions of £22.75 million, with another £12.75 million on offer to private investors. Ethical investment — or the growth of genuinely green funds — represents one of the most hopeful areas in the greening of the market. If, and it is an enormous if, we can ever green the world of money, most other things would fall into place.

The Land and Food Company has apparently just signed its first lease on a site for a green supermarket, due to open in the late spring or early summer of 1990. It says it hopes to open another ten sites.

Interesting profile of Davi Yanomami in *The Independent*. His mother died of measles when he was about ten. 'Among the Yanomami,' he tells Ray Connolly, 'when someone dies the family do everything they can to cancel out his or her memory. You cannot speak about that person, you cannot even pronounce his or her name any more.' How will we act if the Yanomami people are wiped from the face of the Earth by our diseases, illegal gold miners and other development pressures?

And an interesting fact in yesterday's *Guardian*. The junk mail Americans receive in one day would produce enough energy to heat 250,000 homes. And 44% of the mail is thrown in the bin unopened. I know, I know.

Sunday 10 December
As I work on the proofs of *The Young Green Consumer's Guide*, the radio broadcasts the sound of the Czech crowds in Prague's Wenceslas Square as the new, pro-democracy government is announced. Enough to make one's hair stand on end.

Michael Heseltine points out in *The Mail on Sunday* that, while euphoria surrounds the dash for freedom by all those who have lived so long under the yoke of Communism, the freedom of choice is 'only half a freedom'. The individual citizen, he says, cannot buy clean streets or rivers. 'It is the job of Government to ensure that freedom of choice is not won at the expense of the quality of life.'

Sir Richard St Barbe Baker, forester, author and conservationist, wrote over 30 books, but is best remembered for founding Men of the Trees. 'Man in his dire folly has removed vast areas of virgin forest,' the *Observer* quotes him as saying. 'There is no time to be lost if man is to be saved from bringing disaster on this planet and himself.' Strange to think that he wrote these words in 1949, the year I was born.

Posted to Kenya as a forester in the British colonial service, he was appalled by the destruction of the Empire's trees. He introduced a Dance of the Trees to complement the ritual planting of ten trees a year by each member of Men of the Trees. Today, the society has 20,000 members worldwide, dedicated to tree-planting. His views were anathema to the British establishment. A tree nursery he set up in Kenya was paved over to provide tennis courts. And he was finally dismissed from the colonial service after parrying a blow aimed by another Briton at one of Baker's African workers.

Polly Ghazi, who wrote the article, notes that this dismissal was a blessing in disguise — and that Baker went on to preach forest revival and desert reclamation around the world. At 88, he helped to inspire the Himalayan Chipko (tree-hugging) movement, whose members save trees earmarked for felling by hugging them, even at the risk of their own lives.

Some much less salubrious stories in the news. Massive, deeply-embedded corruption in the Communist Party is being uncovered in East Germany. The people's anger is explosive. 'Already,' one East European diplomat told *The Sunday Times*, 'many in the provinces want to hang the district (Party) secretary from the nearest sour apple tree.' It is confirmed that hardliners were only inches away on 8 November from repeating the Tiananmen Square outrages, but no one trusted the conscripts to fire on the pro-democracy protestors — and then, the very next day, the Berlin Wall was opened.

Monday 11 December

As the bus crosses Hammersmith Bridge every morning, I often watch boats picking their way through what the *Daily Mail* this morning calls 'a filthy tide of flotsam and jetsam'. Typical rubbish includes hamburger boxes, cans, bottles, pieces of timber, chunks of polystyrene foam and even dead rats. 'The amount of rubbish is disgusting,' Lisa Ross-Magenty, who could be the cox for the Cambridge boat crew next March, says in the article. 'I saw all sorts of horrible things, like bloated rats. When you're sitting very low in the water, it feels as though you are almost eye to eye with them. It's revolting.'

And the National Rivers Authority is saying that, short of an extremely wet couple of months, 1990 will be a drought year like 1976. The worst affected areas of Kent and Sussex are reporting the lowest water levels ever recorded.

On to Portland Close for launch of the NCC's 'Second Nature' film, sponsored by Shell. David Trippier, Environment and Countryside Minister, points out that the film is aimed at medium- and small-sized firms, which together account for 96% of the economy. It turns out that

Patrick Veale of IBTV has done an excellent job in dramatising environmental issues. Bit of a shock to see my face ten feet high on the screen, but the reaction to the film — and to my role as myself — seems very positive.

The problem is that the film, which is going to be widely shown around the country, could well bring in even more work for SustainAbility. United Biscuits ask me if we could do an audit for them at the launch today.

Spend the afternoon working on the BT report. Rebecca and Isabelle spend the day at conference on 'green building'. Julia, who also came to the launch, goes on to High Street Kensington, to do an interview on green shopping for *Today*. She is doing an endless string of interviews on the theme of the 'Green Christmas'. I coined the rather obvious phrase 'dreaming of a Green Christmas' in *The Green Consumer Guide* — and it has turned up in the newspapers dozens of time this year. Friends of the Earth blast Woolworth's and Ryman for selling CFC-containing aerosol products like 'Christmas Snow' and 'Silly String'. On the way to work I noticed some shop windows with fake snow sprayed on them. Ironic to think that the shopkeepers who use 'snow' aerosols with CFC propellants are almost certainly helping to ensure that global warming accelerates — and white Christmases become even rarer.

In the States, a report from the George C Marshall Institute, a Washington think tank, suggests that the real cause of the global warming trend is solar activity, which has been exceptionally violent this century. An article by Adrian Berry in the *Daily Telegraph* reports that the White House is delighted by this latest publication — which is behind the Bush administration's refusal to agree to cuts in carbon emissions. The Institute argues that evidence from tree-rings proves that the global warming trend will peter out in the next century and that we will then experience a mini ice-age 'that will offset any Greenhouse Effect'.

In the Soviet Union, Gorbachev apparently threatened to resign when a Siberian party chief accused him of currying favour with capitalists and the Vatican in recent months. Gorbachev was immediately supported and Aleksandr Melnikov ended up having to apologise. In East Germany, meanwhile, the Communist Party thinks it may have pulled a rabbit from what *The Times* describes as its 'seemingly empty hat'. He is Gregor Gysi, the Party's new leader. He talks of a 'third way beyond Stalinism and monopoly capitalism', apparently woven from threads like humanism, ecology and equal rights for women.

With their track record on all three of those, the Communists are going to have some credibility problems, but if they are going to survive politically they will have to drag themselves into the modern era.

A new EEC report, prepared by a team led by Gunter Schneider of West Germany, says that 1992 will bring increased development pressures and traffic in many parts of the Community — and further threats to the environment. Among other things, the report calls for more information to be made available to the public 'to permit consumers and members of the local community to evaluate environmental risks'. We'll see what we can do.

Late in the afternoon set off by cab for Heathrow. Catch flight to Charles de Gaulle. Sit next to an international lawyer, probably in his early fifties, who is a partner with White & Case. Wide-ranging conversation as the Air France plane fights its way through turbulence, inevitably touching on the environment. He initially says that, with 400 lawyers in the firm, there must be environmental work being done somewhere in the system. But as we continue to talk, it becomes clear that environmental issues cut across the firm's work in many ways. And, it turns out, one of his friends represented Greenpeace when they sued the French Government following the sinking of the *Rainbow Warrior* in Auckland Harbour.

Interestingly, though, he hadn't heard of the Greenhouse Effect. Explain — and the penny drops. He says he has been going to Austria for the last 25 years, as a serious, off-piste skier. But each year the snow has been harder to find, with one major resort where he used to ski every Christmas now routinely snowless.

Picked up by a taxi and driven through the night — and dense fog — to Fontainebleau.

Wednesday 13 December
Walk past the palace of Fontainebleau in light drizzle, to INSEAD — Europe's leading business school. A great deal of building work under way on the impressive campus, on the fringes of a large forest. Met by Professor Landis Gabel, who is in charge of the new environmental resources course. This has been largely put together by the MBA students — and Landis says he has got three times as much work out of the students as he would on a normal course — and 36 students, instead of the normal 20.

Speak for an hour — and then take questions for an hour. One Swiss student describes waking up at three in the morning a few years back with the air-raid sirens howling. Everyone switched on the radios, as they had been told to do, but there was no news. Eventually a local radio station announced that the Sandoz plant had suffered a major chemical disaster. Everyone locked themselves in their homes, remembering Bhopal. Even when they went out the next day, their eyes streamed with tears because of the fumes and the Rhine had turned red.

In the news: Industrial Society Director Alastair Graham says young people will increasingly refuse to work for companies with a bad environmental record. Separately, IBM confirms that it is pressing ahead with plans to raise millions of pounds for a centre for the environment in Cambridge, described as a 'green London School of Economics', even though the British Government has not yet said whether it will provide funding too.

Banshee police sirens echo through Barnes High Street and blue lights ricochet off shop windows as I walk past Barnes Pond on my way back from Heathrow.

Thursday 14 December
The Ministry of Agriculture has accepted a report by the independent Advisory Committee on Pesticides which concludes that Alar, the chemical used as a growth regulator on apples and pears, poses 'no risk to consumers'. It seems unlikely that Alar will fight its way back on to the market, however. I can't see the supermarkets wanting to antagonise Parents for Safe Food yet awhile.

A key part of the problem is that the chemical industry simply does not have the confidence of the consumer. ICI is being pilloried at the moment, because of its poor environmental performance. 'We are convinced we need to raise our environmental performance,' the company says in today's *Financial Times*. 'We aim to reach 100% compliance with legal limits related to waste emissions, but we have no date as to when we will achieve this.'

Part of the blame is now being laid at the door of ICI chairman Sir Denys Henderson. 'He would much rather be talking about how ICI can improve its image among shareholders and customers than engage in dialogue with environmental groups,' one of his managers explained.

A charity I have never heard of, Worldwatch, has announced that it plans to launch a GreenPoints labelling scheme, with firms invited to apply for the right to use a new logo — and charged £10,000 apiece to fund an initial £400,000 campaign to publicise the scheme. The claim is that it will be the UK version of the Blue Angel, although they will apparently start by focusing on household cleaning products and washing powders. The potential for confusion in this area is growing rapidly.

Friday 15 December
Andrei Sakharov died last night, too late to get into today's papers. Soon, people were standing outside the mansion block where the Sakharovs

lived on the Moscow ring road, in 10° of frost, mourning the man described as the Soviet Union's 'conscience'.

Unbelievable. The Communist Party in Bosnia, one of Yugoslavia's six republics, is now trying to go green. In an attempt to halt or slow the haemorrhaging away of its members, it has hired a marketing agency, downgraded its traditional emblem — a giant red star — and instead adopted an exclamation mark alongside a green question mark.

Not surprisingly, the public is sceptical, to put it mildly. When the party moored a hot-air balloon in nearby Croatia earlier in the week and offered rides to passers-by, the *Daily Telegraph*'s correspondent overheard one say: 'You must be joking. They've been taking us for a ride for years.' It's wonderful that they can still laugh about such things.

And, speaking of hot air, scientists from the Institute of Terrestrial Ecology are saying that last winter was the mildest since 1659, when records began. As a result, there was in increase in plant pests, weed populations, farm animal illnesses and many insect species — an indication of what could happen if the Greenhouse Effect really takes hold.

Meanwhile, in a new report from FoE, Norman Myers says that the rate of tropical forest destruction has nearly doubled during the 1980s. The equivalent of seven Hyde Parks an hour are being burned or logged so extensively that 'the remaining forest is a travesty of natural forest'.

Bulk of day spent in meeting with Procter & Gamble and WWF, evaluating some new green product ideas from P & G.

Saturday 16 December
Papers full of the death of Sakharov. A symbolic passing. A key figure in the development of the Russian H-bomb, he died in the year that the Cold War 'ended' — and as a long-time opponent of nuclear warfare, the Soviet invasion of Afghanistan and the iron rule of the Communist Party, he also died at the end of the year that saw the Berlin Wall and many Communist regimes fall.

The man who won the 1975 Nobel Peace Prize died an exhausted man, aged 68 but looking ten years older, his health broken by KGB harassment and six years in exile in the 'closed' provincial city of Gorky. Ironically, in the three years since Gorbachev brought him back from exile, he had been more hounded by the media than the KGB.

Most memorably, in the closing moments of the first session of the Congress of Deputies, he defied Gorbachev and everyone else, broadcasting live to the nation, and read his Decree on Power. It called for an end to the monopoly rule of the Communist Party and for the KGB to be made answerable to the deputies. He has been a forceful supporter of *perestroika*, arguing that its failure 'would mean a loss of stability throughout the world'. Gorbachev may have found him a difficult ally, but he will miss him badly.

Meanwhile, the superpower thaw has brought a new crop of announcements from Washington. The US is to cut back on the flights of its nuclear war command planes, known as 'Looking Glass' — designed to take charge if the President and other leaders were killed in the early stages of a nuclear war. And US drug police are to train KGB agents to trap drug traffickers.

The Colombian Government has scored a success against the drug cartel, with the shooting of Gonzalo Rodriguez Gacha, his son and 15 henchmen. Gacha — known as *El Mexicano* — has been regarded as second only to Pablo Escobar Gaviria, still at large, among Colombian drug traffickers. Among other outrages, he is held responsible for the mid-air explosion of an Avianca jet last month, which killed 111 people, and the truck bomb which killed 65 outside Colombia's security police headquarters. Rumours are spreading that there will be a new wave of 'narco-terrorism' as a result.

Meanwhile, 'Adopt a Plant and You May Save a Child' is the message being beamed from the Royal Botanic Gardens at Kew. The Queen's physician, Dr Ronald Davey, has warned: 'We are a planet in danger from the burning of our rainforests, and we need new medicines. The case for plant conservation is compelling. 80% of the world's population looks to natural sources for remedies despite the amazing advances of technological medicine. Many drugs come from plants and fungi, and many, even today's designer drugs, get their inspiration from plants.'

Ramblers are celebrating the 40th anniversary of the National Parks and Access to the Countryside Act. They are still pushing against 'the landowning mafia', claiming to represent the estimated 8.5 million British adults who take a two-mile walk in the country at least once a month.

Monday 18 December
Wild weather; high winds brought havoc to the South West over the weekend.

Now it's the fascists. The latest edition of *National Front News* sports a picture of ravaged rainforest on its front cover — and combines 'respect for nature' as a slogan alongside 'racial separation'. Bizarre — and vile. Also, according to the *Sunday Correspondent*, wildlife-loving National Front members can now join their own Greenwave, described as 'non-profit ecological movement'. Greenwave election literature used for a council by-election in Havering did not mention that the Greenwave candidate was a National Front member.

Massive banner headline in the *Daily Mail*: UNFRIENDLY! Based on news that FoE is to launch a campaign against 111-trichloroethane, a chemical found in such products as Tipp-Ex correction fluid, UHU spray glue and Dabitoff stain remover. The chemical is another ozone-destroyer. One leading manufacturer is ICI. Dow are among the second-rank producers. The consumer must be starting to wonder whether anything is safe?

And British Gas — which has spent millions of pounds promoting gas as a green fuel — is likely to be embarrassed by research, published in *Nature*, which shows that between 3% and 10% of the gas produced by British Gas leaks into the atmosphere. This is worrying, given that methane, a key component of natural gas, is — molecule for molecule — about 25 times more powerful as a greenhouse gas than carbon dioxide. The research, carried out by the University of Wales in Cardiff, suggests that the methane equivalent of 125 billion cubic metres of carbon dioxide — as much as is produced by Britain's power stations — may be leaking from the British Gas network.

Tuesday 19 December

Spot what I at first take to be enormous squirrel dreys in a tree in Holland Park. Turn out to be half a dozen peacocks, roosting in the branches.

A stark contrast from the news coming in that hundreds have been killed in Romania as police opened fire on demonstrators in the city of Timisoara. President Ceausescu — who runs one of the most notorious regimes in terms of human rights — had left yesterday for a visit to Iran. Ironically, given its long-standing campaign to stamp out its own Communists, the Iranian regime has seemed uneasy about the collapse of Marxism in Eastern Europe. President Rafsanjani has said that no one should believe that the authority of Islam would collapse in the same way. But maybe some of the regimes that have wrapped themselves in the cloak of Islam will!

Also in the news: The Government is to publish air pollution bulletins for urban areas, aimed at joggers, cyclists, asthmatics and other particularly exposed groups. I wonder how many Labour politicians jog or cycle. 'Peace on Earth may now be within our sights,' said Labour environment spokesman Bryan Gould, launching a new Labour Planning Group, 'but unless we give new impetus to our thinking on the environment it will be "peace without Earth".'

And in Colorado, glitzy ski-resort Aspen is trying to position itself for the 'greener, more caring 1990s'. The town council has decided to hold a referendum on whether it should become the first 'fur-free zone' in the world. Over in New York, *The Times* reports, a group called Friends of

Animals has been putting up thousands of posters showing an animal's paw caught in a trap. 'Get the feel of fur,' the poster encourages. 'Slam your hand in a car door.'

Grab a copy of *BBC Wildlife* as I streak through Paddington. Interested to find a review of *The Green Capitalists* by Chris Baines. 'Three cheers for bandwagons,' he writes. 'While most people simply struggle aboard them and cling on with their eyes tightly shut, bandwagons do have drivers, and people to oil the wheels. In the phenomenal case of the green bandwagon, John Elkington is undoubtedly one of the drivers, with a very clear sense of direction and unerring navigation skills.' Makes me wonder whether we are going to end up in the ditch with our wheels spinning?

Wednesday 20 December
News comes through that thousands of Romanians may have been killed and wounded, in a virtual re-run of Tiananmen Square. Even if it is true, there will be many who feel it is a price worth paying for an end to the Ceausescus and all that they represent.

Extraordinary development as — only hours before the next Shuttle launch — the Soviets accuse the Americans and NASA of causing massive destruction to the ozone layer with every Shuttle flight. The Soviet Union is aiming to promote its shuttle, *Energia*, as more ozone-friendly than *Columbia*!

Although NASA will apparently present research results to Congress in January to show that its shuttle programme is environment-friendly, the Russians argue that the *Columbia* destroys up to ten million tonnes of the three billion tonnes of atmospheric ozone with every flight. 'Three hundred launches is enough to do away with the thin ozone layer, which is already holed,' they are quoted as saying in *The Times*. The United States uses a solid fuel, made from aluminium chips and ammonium perchlorate, whereas the Russians use oxygen and hydrogen. The *Energia*, it is claimed, destroys less than 1,500 tonnes of ozone with each flight, 7,000 times less than the US shuttle.

Not that the Russians are perfect. The *Guardian* carries a terse report saying that toxic chemicals seeping from a Soviet defence plant have killed three miners, with 26 miners and 123 rescuers in hospital suffering from various degrees of poisoning.

The OECD in Paris calls to say that next April marks the 20th anniversary of its Environment Committee. Invited to give plenary speech on green consumerism to kick off their birthday conference.

BT report finished and biked. Julia drives me home through the rain-washed streets.

Thursday 21 December

More than 100 people have been killed as American troops invade Panama, determined to overthrow the man recently described as a 'pock-marked Caligula', General Noriega. No one wants a world in which every superpower enters the 'topple your local despot' stakes, but, once again, Noriega would not be sorely missed.

Successful five-hour meeting with Dow, at which we agree a pro-gramme of interviews across Europe and undertake to organise a workshop on the role of plastics in transport systems in the greenhouse, probably in Bonn in June. It could be a fascinating exercise, pulling together environmentalists and industrialists from around Europe.

Friday 22 December

Slack tide as the bus thrums across the Thames. Four iridescent peacocks stalk among the trees in Holland Park.

The papers are full of events in Romania, where another wave of killings has failed to halt the protests. Police have been firing into the crowds from armoured cars, tanks, helicopters. The bravery of ordinary people is incredible, the brute cynicism of the regime utterly transparent.

Watch the 9 o'clock news on TV. Unbelievable emotion stirred up by the pictures of the Romanians fighting the security forces. The Ceausescus are reported to have fled the country, but their son Nicu has been captured and is paraded on Romanian TV. Meanwhile, between the Germanies, the Berlin Wall is opened up in front of the Brandenburg Gate. A new Europe, deeply rooted in an older Europe, is taking shape before our eyes.

FoE warn that 'couch potatoes' who use their remote controls to leave their TVs 'on hold' are adding almost 200,000 tonnes of carbon dioxide to the atmosphere each year. This figure assumes that half of Britain's remote controlled TVs are not properly switched off at night. The wasted energy would be enough to light and heat towns of the size of Basingstoke or Burnley.

Saturday 23 December

The bloodbath continues in Bucharest. Last night the Securitate launched an abortive counter-attack, machine-gunning unarmed demonstrators. According to *The Times*, these attacks are the work of 'black shirt' units, who are believed to have orders to fight to the last to protect the President — a.k.a. the Shining Light of the World, the Hero of Heroes, the Genius of the Carpathians. They are rumoured to commit suicide by biting into a cyanide capsule in their collars.

The bodies of 4,600 people were found yesterday in a mass grave outside Timisoara. The reports are now coming in that as many as 12,000 people may have been killed. Ceausescu, like Noriega, seems to have disappeared off the face of the map. Noriega, it now appears, had a double, pock-marked just like the general. During his rule, or misrule, Noriega is said to have moved house as many as four times a night.

At times, 1989 has been like something from the most outrageously far-fetched novel. Take Elena Ceausescu, deposed first lady of Romania. Wishing to boost the country's population from 23 million to 30 million, she outlawed birth control. She set up 'demographic command units' which, as *The Independent* reports, 'performed monthly gynaecological tests on all women of child-bearing age to test for illegal contraceptives'.

Lightning crashes across the sky and the heavens open. Think of the Securitate secret policemen who are using the extraordinary rabbit warren of tunnels under Bucharest to wage a continuing hit-and-run war on the Romanian army. The tunnels were apparently dug by political prisoners, subsequently shot to keep them secret.

Sunday 24 December

News breaks that the Romanian army has captured the Ceausescus. As we drive down to Gloucestershire, the motorway is lined with dead witnesses — and victims of — our mobility, mainly foxes.

Monday 25 December

A family Christmas. The church bells are ringing in Romania for the first time in decades. At 16.00 on Christmas Day they execute the Ceausescus, with the erstwhile President now described by some Romanians as the anti-Christ. As her execution was prepared, Elena Ceausescu asked a soldier: 'Why are you doing this to us? I was a mother to you.' The soldier replied: 'What kind of mother were you who killed *our* mothers?'

In her Christmas Day broadcast, the Queen speaks directly to children around Britain and the Commonwealth, many of whom have written to her saying how worried they are about the future of the planet. 'Many of you will have heard of the Greenhouse Effect,' she noted, 'and perhaps you've heard, too, about even more urgent problems caused by the pollution of our rivers and seas and the cutting down of the great forests.'

Stressing that such problems could affect regions well beyond the borders of any given country where the fossil fuels are burned or forests felled, she continued: 'With all your lives before you, I am sure that you take an optimistic view of the future. But it is already too late to prevent all forms of damage to the natural world. Some species of wild plants and animals are, sadly, bound to become extinct. But the great thing to remember is that it is not too late to reduce the damage if we change our attitudes and behaviour.'

Tuesday 26 December

Is the world facing a greenhouse cataclysm or not? *The Times* reports that researchers at the Meteorological Office at Bracknell, Berkshire, have taken delivery of a new Cray supercomputer, which should help them untangle the interactions between pollution and climate.

'Everyone is expecting (the Greenhouse Effect) to happen quickly,' says Dr Michael Cullen, who heads the project. 'We have a hot summer in Britain and everyone says it must be due to the Greenhouse Effect. This is not what scientists are talking about at all. What we need to know is what is going to happen over the long term.' He adds: 'We are not talking about the Earth turning into Venus. But on a regional level these changes are quite significant in terms of what will grow and how we feed the planet's population.'

Wednesday 27 December

The dead eyes of President Ceausescu stare out from the front page of *The Times*. The papers are full of 'these were the 1980s' features. The storms have damaged one of the tall Cotswold stone chimneys, blowing one massive stone around on its axis, like a secret panel. Either that, or Santa Claus and his reindeer clipped it on their way back to Icicleland.

The thickness of the Greenland ice-sheet is increasing by 0.23mm a year, according to data collected by satellite sensors and reported in the latest issue of *Science*. At the same time, the satellites found that more of the Greenland ice has been melting during the summer — supporting earlier research suggesting that the melting of the polar ice-caps has caused sea levels to rise by around a third of an inch a year.

Thursday 28 December

Australia hit by its first fatal earthquake, with dozens feared dead.

And Ethiopia again. Peasants in eastern Tigre, one of the areas worst affected by the drought and war, are already eating the seed grain which should have been used for next year's crops. A UN worker says that 1,500 children are dying every day from causes related to hunger. The country looks set to suffer what the UN already fears could be 'the worst famine of the decade'.

But elements of the message are getting through. Pick up the January issue of *Hello!* magazine and find it is stiff with celebrities talking about the environment and Third World issues. 'We have to do something for our children,' says Britt Ekland, to pick an example almost at random. 'Ecology has to be a universal commitment during the next decade.'

And this evening a neighbour's son calls. He's studying for an advertising exam and wants help with a couple of questions, the first of which runs as follows:

> 'Green' is an issue that's here to stay. Soon people will buy products not on performance but on their impressions of the company that made them. Some say this is an opportunity for advertisers — others a minefield. What do you think?

Friday 29 December
The Gaia hypothesis gets a friendly airing by Michael McCarthy in *The Times*. In the spotlight, Professor James Lovelock, one of two people I have just recommended for the Volvo Environmental Prize. As McCarthy puts it: 'The 1980s began with a Big Idea — the revival of laissez-faire capitalism — that allowed no room for the daring hypothesis of the wiry-haired, bespectacled independent scientist: *that the Earth is alive.*' This hypothesis, McCarthy says, has gradually become the new Big Idea.

Meanwhile, the bad news continues to pour in. Drums of dangerous chemicals are washing ashore along the south coast, following the sinking of a Pakistani freighter off Devon on 28 October. The public has been warned to keep away, since five contain sodium cyanide — and others contain liquid oxygen or acids.

Better news, though, from Sheffield. The first successful prosecution of a water authority by the National Rivers Authority is reported. Yorkshire Water Authority has been fined £1,000 and ordered to pay £215 in costs by Sheffield magistrates, following a pollution incident that killed hundreds of fish. 100 gallons of a spilled chemical, polyelectrolyte, had been flushed into a trout stream. 'Someone made the decision,' noted Catherine Carter, prosecuting for the NRA, 'that, as it was a water treatment chemical and therefore safe in water, they could get rid of it down the beck.'

In Scotland up to 50 people on the island of Islay will be paid to spend the next few months charging around fields, screaming their heads off. The idea behind the Government-backed Goose Scaring Scheme is to frighten off wintering Greenland geese which would otherwise strip farmers' fields — and run the risk of being shot. 741 barnacle geese and six white-fronts were shot last year under Government licence. The Department of Agriculture and Fisheries, Scotland, is giving up to 54 farmers £50,000 to employ human scarecrows.

Saturday 30 December
The first greenhouse gong? James Lovelock is awarded the CBE in the New Year Honours, 'for services to the study of the atmosphere'.

Also coming in from the cold, Vaclav Havel. 'I am constantly conscious of the ridiculousness and absurdity of my situation,' *The Independent* quotes Czechoslovakia's new President as saying. A great friend of the late playwright Samuel Beckett's, Havel luckily has a finely developed sense of the absurd. With a friend now acting as his bodyguard, he says, 'we used to have moments when we were out of sight late in the night, when we laughed hysterically. It was a way of getting rid of that nervous tension we had been under the whole day'. How many people experience the Cinderella-style shock of going from prisoner — Havel has spent five years in prison as the country's leading dissident — to President in such a short time?

A strong green strand in Romania's new constitution. Among its central principles is the following:

'The reorganisation of ecological balances which will eliminate subsidies to any goods or process bad for the earth and the environment.'

The dire state of the Romanian economy under Ceausescu is indicated by the pace of deforestation in the country. 'Maybe you noticed how few trees are left in this part of Arges province?' an agricultural student asked a correspondent from *The Times*. 'The peasants are desperate for firewood, but they have had to move further and further away to find any.'

In the States, meanwhile, John Giedraitis, city forester in Austin, Texas, is calling for all America's 35 million Christmas trees to be recycled, rather than buried in landfill sites. The trees can be put through a chipper to make mulch, fuel or materials to stabilise eroding sand dunes.

Sunday 31 December
It's official: 1989 was the warmest year since records began 330 years ago, in 1659. Hedgehogs have come out of hibernation and heather which normally stops blooming in October is still in flower. 'We believe global warming is already happening in Britain,' Met Office Director-General Dr John Houghton tells *The Sunday Times*. 'We cannot prove it at present, but we believe there is strong evidence.'

The chlorination of water, which kills potentially dangerous bacteria, may increase the risk of childhood leukaemia, according to the *Observer*. Research at Newcastle University's Department of Child Health suggests that chlorine reacts with peat and other materials in water taken from moorland reservoirs and lowlands rivers to form chemicals called trihalomethanes. One of these, chloroform, is thought to help cause some cancers, including cancer of the bladder, colon and rectum. The Water Services Association retorts that chlorination poses 'absolutely no health hazard whatsoever'.

Observer also reports that the Japanese, forced to bow to international pressure and impose a ban on the import of all ivory, is now looking to the Soviet Union for an alternative. Japan uses ivory for fancy chopsticks, the plectrum of the *shamisen* (traditional lute), piano keys and, above all, *hanko* — the name seals used in place of signatures. The new idea: to dig up some of the estimated ten million mammoths preserved under the Siberian permafrost. It is estimated that each adult tusk weighed around 200lb, the total value could be well over £800 billion.

We see in the New Year at a party hosted by Roger and Rebecca Poulet. Gaia is still dancing at 04.00 in the morning.

EPILOGUE

In retrospect, the events recorded in *A Year in the Greenhouse* pulse with mixed omens. Many of the events of 1989 provided ample grounds for pessimism. The unbelievable stupidity of the *Exxon Valdez* grounding; the long-term radioactive pollution caused by at least one more Soviet nuclear submarine foundering off Norway; the Adriatic, paradoxically, turning green with algal slime.

Overall, though, I emerged into the 1990s in a much more optimistic frame of mind than was possible in a world overshadowed by the Bomb, Star Wars and the Wall. Instead of the bleak pessimism of Samuel Beckett's *Waiting for Godot*, which had a profound impact on my teenage vision of the future, I sense that the 1990s will be an exciting, high-octane decade, very much like the 1960s. The message of the 1980s is clear, however. As human populations press ever harder on the planet's already over-burdened environment, we must increasingly try to master the complex art of planet management.

One thing seems certain: as the pressures continue to build, some people — and they may adopt green colours — will seek to break not only with tradition, but with history. It is not inconceivable that environmental pressures may push us towards our own version of Cambodia's horrendous 'Year Zero'. The real problem, they will say, is not just capitalism, but the entire industrial mentality.

The desire for radical solutions is almost certain to grow as we approach the third millennium. New groupings will emerge, some of which will successfully pioneer new approaches. But as environmentalists we should welcome a diversity of initiatives, given that no one really knows how to achieve a sustainable society starting from where we find ourselves today. Deep Greens may dismiss green consumerism as peripheral, but it has been a profoundly important step in waking up ordinary consumers to the impact of what they do day-to-day. It has helped to prepare many consumers and some of the more perceptive people in business for some of the changes that must come.

1989, yet again, taught us that there is no such thing, ecologically speaking, as a 'free lunch'. The scramble to develop 'cold fusion', the new power source that was going to save the Earth and earn its inventors zillions, was a case in point. But new technologies — among them biotechnology, new materials, satellite remote sensing and artificial

270

intelligence — will provide new tools for those who work to make economic development more environmentally sustainable. We are entering a period of intense experimentation, which will throw up its own failures, even disasters, but they must be seen as part of the essential, painful learning process. We need a positive vision of the future to sustain us — and others — on the path to sustainability. It is still too easy for environmentalists to be typecast as 'professional attackers' or as the harbingers of a new form of Green McCarthyism. The next step, already under way with such ground-breaking publications as the World Conservation Strategy and the Brundtland Commission report, *Our Common Future*, is to develop a vision, or visions, of the greener world we want to move towards.

Indeed, the prospects for the global environmental movement have never been better. As the old order, including the world's largest country, the Soviet Union, threatens to break up in front of our eyes, the old answers simply will not work in the new realities now taking shape around us. The 'ending' of the Cold War provides an unparalleled opportunity to begin switching military spending towards broader social and environmental priorities based on the emerging concept of *environmental* security.

Genetically, we are still — and always will be — territorial animals, programmed to behave in exactly the same ways that we did through all the bloodstained millennia of our 'civilised' history. The real question of the 1990s is whether we can begin to switch our allegiances from narrow definitions of ethnic or nationalistic interests to new, more global allegiances and alliances.

Ironically, one of the most serious threats now is that the environmental movement will be throttled by its own green growth. If environmentalists are to maintain their current momentum, they will need to switch from defensive to offensive strategies. The battle needs to be moved on to new ground and fought in new ways.

At no stage will environmentalists be able to pack up their bags, declare the war won and cycle home. Indeed, the challenge facing us grows day by day. For as far as one can foresee, we will be fighting a losing battle, in the sense that we will continue to lose habitats and species, with the result that we will find our own headroom reduced in this global habitat. But, however many battles we may lose, we have no future unless we genuinely believe that the war can be won.

Index

The following index mainly focuses on some of the people and environmental organisations covered in *A Year in the Greenhouse*.

National Centre for Organic Gardening, 160, 205
National Front, 261
National Power, 41, 94, 170, 217, 220
National Rivers Authority, 149, 186, 256, 267
National Trust, 87
National Wildlife Federation, 163, 169
Nature Conservancy Council (NCC), 18, 39, 129, 137, 153, 159, 160, 194, 212, 256
Nelson, Dr Elizabeth, 217
New Consumer, 39
Nicholson, Max, 131–132, 186
Nicholson-Lord, David, 80
Nixon, President Richard, 89
Noriega, Manuel, 264, 265
Norman, Sir Arthur, 131
North, Richard, 46, 199
North-South Productions, 29, 49, 216

O'Keeffe, John, 212
O'Riordan, Professor Tim, 52
Ocean Earth, 204
Onassis, Aristotle, 206
One World Week, 219, 222
Ono, Yoko, 206
Ozone Help, 95
ozone layer, 44, 45, 56, 263

Panos, 39
Parents for Safe Food, 115, 154, 205, 259
Parkin, Sara, 128, 140, 201, 225
Parkinson, Cecil, 101, 141, 147, 156, 163, 197
Patten, Christopher, 55, 93, 147, 153, 157, 168, 173, 178, 179, 194, 197, 200, 201, 209, 212, 213, 219, 251, 254
Paul, Robin, 52, 199
Pearce, Professor David, 135, 179, 192, 200
Peccei, Dr Aurelio, 184
Perriman, Rod, 76
Phillips, Cassandra, 219
Pilger, John, 223
Planet Protection Fund, 219
Pons, Professor Stan, 71, 84, 91, 93, 107
Ponsford, Brian, 252
Pope, The, 249, 253
Porritt, Jonathon, 14, 34, 35, 46, 54, 74,

77, 78, 137, 140, 148, 154, 158, 162, 198, 203, 213, 214
PowerGen, 41
Prince Charles, 11, 18, 33, 43, 47, 48, 52, 100, 114, 127, 133, 161, 189, 219
Prince Philip, 42, 43, 44, 76, 145, 186, 192
Princess Anne, 43
Procter & Gamble, 17, 25, 28, 38, 142, 193, 197, 205, 208, 212, 260
Produtos da Amazonia, 157
Pryor, William, 82
Pugh, Dr Richard, 21
Puttnam, David, 67

QE2, 152, 182, 183
Queen, Her Majesty the, 265

Radford, Tim, 17, 80
Rain Forest Foundation, 98
Rainbow Warrior, 23, 258
Ramblers, 261
Ratcliffe, Dr Derek, 155
Rawl, Lawrence, 80, 116, 117
Reagan, President Ronald, 30
Rechem International, 35, 177, 178, 209–210, 224
Redford, Robert, 118, 133
Reid, Sir Bob, 33
Reilly, Dr William, 155
Richard, Cliff, 54, 120
Ride, Dr Sally, 127
Ridley, Nicholas, 54, 57, 58, 59, 61, 68, 75, 95, 104, 111, 134, 149, 151, 155, 158, 159, 160, 165, 166, 168, 194, 200, 213
Rifkind, Malcolm, 223
Right Livelihood Foundation, 38, 225, 253
Ripa di Meana, Carlo, 106, 108, 134, 142
Robertson, Tessa, 78
Robinson, Steve, 78
Rocard, President Michel, 82
Rocky Mountain Institute, 99
Roddick, Anita, 49, 193, 198
Ronaldson, Stephen, 91, 168
Rose, Chris, 203
Rossi, Sir Hugh, 178
Rothschild, Miriam, 23
Rowland, Dr Sherwood, 60
Royal Commission on Environmental Pollution, 155